EDUCATIONAL STUDIES IN EUROPE

International Educational Studies
General Editor: Dieter Lenzen

Volume 1
Educational Studies in Europe. Amsterdam and Berlin Compared
Edited by G.F. Heyting, J.K. Koppen, D. Lenzen and F. Thiel

EDUCATIONAL STUDIES IN EUROPE

Amsterdam and Berlin Compared

Edited by

G.F. Heyting, J.K. Koppen, D. Lenzen and F. Thiel

Berghahn Books
Providence • Oxford

First published in 1997 by

Berghahn Books

Library of Congress Cataloging-in-Publication Data

Educational studies in Europe : Berlin and Amsterdam compared / edited by G.F. Heyting ... [et al.].
p. cm.
Papers from a conference organized by the Free University of Berlin and the University of Amsterdam.
Includes bibliographical references.
ISBN 1-57181-938-X (alk. paper)
1. Education--Germany--Berlin--Cross-cultural studies--Congresses. 2. Education--Netherlands--Amsterdam--Cross-cultural studies--Congresses. 3. Education--Social aspects--Germany--Berlin--Cross-cultural studies--Congresses. 4. Education--Social aspects--Netherlands--Amsterdam--Cross-cultural studies--Congresses.
I. Heyting, G. F.
LA775.B5E38 1997
370'.943'155--dc21 96-53054
CIP

British Library Cataloguing in Publication Data

A catalogue record for this book is available from the British Library.

Printed in the United States on acid-free paper.

CONTENTS

LIST OF TABLES

LIST OF FIGURES

Preface

EDUCATIONAL DISCOURSE

A Contribution to Science or Practice

Peter Mortimore

Whilst attendance at international conferences is a standard activity for academics throughout the world, joint conferences held by leading universities from different European countries are somewhat rarer. This book is the result of such a conference, which was organised by the Free University of Berlin and the University of Amsterdam in order to promote cooperation in educational research between European universities. Through the comparison of methods, philosophies and examples of empirical study considerable understandings of the way the educational science is interpreted in different cultures can be appreciated. The Amsterdam/Berlin similarities and contrasts are interesting and informative. The University of London will be next to join the cooperation project. On the basis of this volume, its representatives have the opportunity to prepare their contributions. The contents of this volume, however, reflect the state of the art of research activity on the continent. As such, it will certainly inspire British scholars in the field.

From my reading of the published papers, I wish to make a number of comments.

What is the Relationship Between the Scholarly Activities Represented by these Papers and *Real World* Educational Issues?

Research can never match the *real world* in its complexity. Indeed, one of its main purposes is to focus on the mass of information and interactions that make up so much of our social contact, in order to home in on particular aspects so as to distinguish patterns of correlation and causation. This approach means that the social-scientist has to be selective. Populations are sampled, questions are chosen, responses are pared down. The skill of the social-scientist lies in how best she or he makes such choices. Many of the steps towards successful social science depend not only on a scientific approach but also on the art of choosing.

Another difference between research and the real world is that, inevitably, research follows events. Accounts are retrospective; analyses of calibration and causation follow the events. In some cases, of course, it is possible to design *prospective* studies but these are rare and there is always the risk that promises may not be fulfilled and the costs of the research wasted.

In the case of the Berlin Conference, in a number of papers – notably that of Lenzen but also in the work of Heyting, Merkens, Gehrmann, Van Der Wolf, Tietze and Drinck – real world issues are addressed and solutions to problems are formulated.

How Much Variety is There Between the Papers?

My second comment concerns the variety between these papers in terms of the range of topics: the subject matter ranges from young children to higher education. Both theory and policy matters are addressed, as well as inter-cultural education dealing with class, race, gender and special educational needs. Interestingly, the largest section deals with the organisation of education and its policy implications. Three papers from Amsterdam and three from Berlin deal with a range of topics including vocational education, streaming in schools, devolution from central government, and gender differences in principals' behaviour. The reunification of Germany and its implication for the quality of schooling is the subject of the paper by Gehrmann.

The diversity of the papers helps us to explore what researchers from the two universities are doing and to lay out territory. The resulting collection allows a view on the academic context in which the various specific research projects have developed, thus giving a better understanding of the chosen subjects and approaches. At the same time, this overview allows for more specific cooperation projects, in which researchers from different universities and countries can explore the *same* theme, whether theoretical or empirical. In particular, the comparative nature of the joint collaboration could be developed and be enriched by a British input. The question of school tracking, for instance, would benefit considerably from exploration within the different cultures of Berlin and Amsterdam. Similarly, vocational preparation would present a very interesting analysis.

Who Benefits?

My next question is about who benefits from the joint publication of this work. The answer, in my judgement, is that there could well be benefits for a number of different agencies. First, it is only fair to comment that initially, the researchers themselves are likely to be the greatest beneficiaries. The close involvement – both formally and informally at the conference – with colleagues working in a different tradition is always helpful. Insights are gained through the discussion of one's work with fellow researchers who do not share the same assumptions. There is the opportunity for discussion of methodological issues. Previously unthought-of solutions can be identified. If only the researchers benefit, though, the exercise can be seen as an excuse for self-indulgence.

In this case, I consider that a number of the papers are likely to provide tangible benefits for both practitioners and policy-makers. Practitioners should benefit from Krüger's careful discussion of how 'differences in leadership between men and women are determined by gender in combination with school culture'. Singer has pointed out that 'governments and experts (…) have to take the reality of parents, children and care givers as a starting point of their policy making and theoretical thinking. (…) Special attention has to be given to the position of poor families in a commercialised day-care system'. Finally, Drinck alerts us to the fact that 'educational certificates are becoming increasingly important … the market value of state-recognized leaving certificates is constantly on the increase, forcing individuals to compete for socially recognised posts'. In each case, the practitioners involved with particular services can benefit from new information and better analysis of what their clients need, think and feel about the services offered.

Policy makers, and here we are talking of a wide range of central and local government politicians and civil servants, stand to gain from the use of educational science. Empirical data and conceptual analyses can illuminate difficult choices. Clearly the politicians need to pay close attention to the views of their voters but, at the same time, they need authoritative knowledge about the services for which they are responsible. This is the strength of evaluation. It enables those responsible for policies to assess the consequences, both planned and unplanned, of their policy choices. In the case of this collection, for example, the work of Heyting makes clear that the somewhat stereotypical views of some policy makers mask a much more complex reality. She alerts us to the fact that only a small proportion of the problems 'is explained by differences between the various ethnic groups, especially in the field of crime, and how poorly founded the definition of ethic minorities is'. As she points out, this has implications for the Amsterdam Youth Policy. Similarly, Boerman's paper discusses the degree of centralisation necessary within organisations. His view is that a multidimensional approach is likely to be better than one drawing only on single dimensions. The domains of teachers and of administrators need to be linked with those concerning the flow of information.

In the case of early childhood, Tietze points to the tension existing between the rather different systems for early childhood education in the formerly separate East Germany and West Germany. In his view, the Treaty of Maastricht may well provide a better framework for policies in pursuit of unification than any simple compromise between the two.

The tracking of students includes the provision of different kinds of schools and within the schools the provision of different streams or tracks. A very interesting study would consist of a description of existing practice in the three countries (regions/states/cities). It would also include an analysis of the advantages and disadvantages of the varying systems within a common framework incorporating both educational and cost-benefit perspectives. Of course considerable notice would have to be taken of the different cultural environments in which these systems are located. In the light of the outcome of this analysis researchers would be in a position to consider whether there were lessons that could be learned about best practice. Similarly, vocational preparation would present a very interesting analysis. Current systems of vocational preparation in the different countries (regions/states/cities) would need to be described and evaluated. Successful features would be identified and analysed. Researchers would be asking the question of whether this aspect of the educational system could work in a different culture or whether it was so enmeshed in national attributes and traditions that translation elsewhere was impossible. The ideas that have been discussed here, of course, are mostly theoretical. Given, however, a modern world, a unified Europe, excellent communication systems and it is not inconceivable that – at some stage – policy makers and practitioners may seek to test this theory in practice. The impact of such an event on the research community would be considerable: our work would be recognised not simply as a commentary on society but as a means of changing it. In this way the comparative nature of the joint collaboration could be better developed and, incidentally, the inclusion of researchers from London would provide yet another point of comparison.

Whose Judgement Counts?

Researchers, and those writing scholarly papers, need to guard against the opinion that theirs is the only worthwhile judgement to be made. It is heartening, therefore, that within this collection a number of authors are prepared to criticise their own work and to make explicit its limitations. Thus, Lenzen asks whether 'the empirical-analytical and hermeneutic approaches to the phenomena of educational reality, so characteristic of discussions (...) in Germany, is unnecessary' and from the University of Amsterdam, Mulder comments that there is 'no unifying idea, let alone a theory' in the field of educational sciences. As he puts it, 'educational scientists appear to hesitate between mourning the loss of values, and celebrating the victory of facts'. The balance between, on the one hand, honest breast-beating and, on the other, authoritative statements is difficult to find. From my own experience in the United Kingdom I know that an overdose of breast-beating leads mainly to a reduction in the confidence of practitioners and policy makers to take educational research findings seriously. Difficulties are also posed when researchers 'nit-pick' with each other over relatively trivial differences of interpretation. Whilst academic minds are sharpened by such activity, those outside of the university tend to lose interest and, depressingly, seek authoritative views from others possessing neither the capability nor the interest in drawing inferences from evidence. On the other hand, the so-called expert scientist who is proved wrong can easily become a figure of fun. Scientists know that progress is made when new discoveries overturn established views. In the social sciences, however, where the subject matter is ordinary life and the lay person sees him or herself as an expert, well-publicised disagreements are used to justify a disregard for research findings and, in extreme cases, a lack of investment in enquiry.

This is an interesting collection of papers. The subject matter is broad and the matters eclectic. I look forward to seeing a further volume encompassing papers from Amsterdam and Berlin with contributions from London.

Chapter 1

EDUCATIONAL SCIENCE IN GERMANY

Theories – Crises – Present Situation

Dieter Lenzen

In view of the highly individual development of the educational sciences not only in Germany but also in Austria and Switzerland, a report of this kind must needs be arranged along historical lines, for the specific relationship of, for example, the empirico-analytical approaches to those of the human sciences and, later on, to the social theory approaches and our present-day plurality of theories, all these developments can hardly be understood outside the historical viewpoint.

I must, therefore, go back quite some way.

I shall begin by recalling Wilhelm Dilthey (1959 and 1961): his theory of science as the science of the human mind (called 'Geisteswissenschaft'), published at the end of the nineteenth century, was characterised, among other things, by the following features

- The science of the human mind is distinct from the natural sciences.
- Man and his products are historical.
- The creations of the mind must be *understood*.
- The method of understanding is hermeneutics.
- If we understand, we are situated within a '*hermeneutic circle*'. This consists in an interaction between experience, expression and understanding. Experience finds its expression in objectivations of intellectual life. These are understood, re-experienced and, as such, have a modifying effect on intellectual life. Thus pre-under-

standing is constantly being modified. (See figure 1.1, Kunzmann et al. 1991:181)

Figure 1.1 Experiencing – Expression – Understanding.

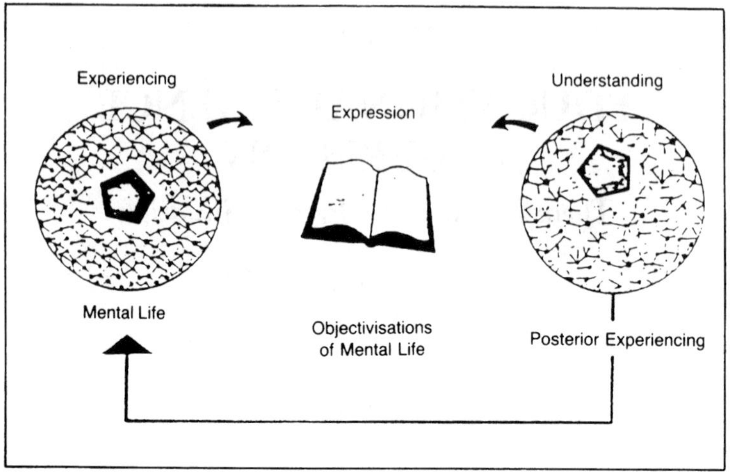

This conception was intended by Dilthey as a method aimed at text interpretation. Its assumption into educational science, particularly by Herman Nohl, Wilhelm Flitner, Eduard Spranger and Theodor Litt, resulted in one important change: it was now no longer a question of the interpretation of texts but of the explanation of educational *reality*. What arose here was given the name 'Geisteswissenschaftliche Pädagogik' (see figure 1.2). It first blossomed in the period of the Weimar Republic. It ended, partly abruptly, partly successively, with the rise of Fascism. The National Socialist 'State Pedagogues' Ernst Krieck and Alfred Bäumler are in no way descended in direct lineage from this school.

It was thus only natural that the 'Geisteswissenschaftliche Pädagogik' should experience a renaissance after the Second World War. This was partly due to the re-instatement of its great supporters to professorial chairs. They were joined by a first generation of pupils of whom Erich Weniger is probably the most prominent, closely followed by a second generation which then brought the 'Geisteswissenschaftliche Pädagogik' in its original sense to a conclusion. This generation includes Wolfgang Klafki, Klaus Mollenhauer and Herwig Blankertz. Even Wolfgang Klafki's dissertation was still entirely written within an understanding of the 'Geisteswissenschaftliche Pädagogik'. Herwig Blankertz had, in his dissertation, turned towards Neo-Kantianism. Klaus Mollenhauer (1972), on

Figure 1.2 'Erziehungswissenschaft': Crises – Development of Theories – Present State. An Overview.

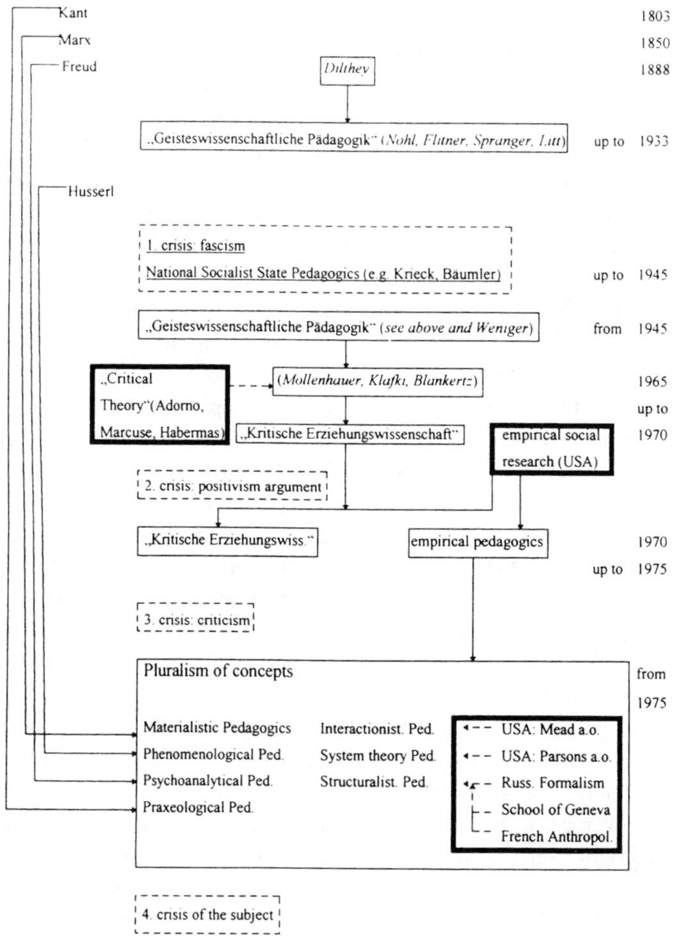

the other hand, was the first of this generation to embrace the influences of a neighbouring discipline: sociology. If one includes the crisis which the 'Geisteswissenschaftliche Pädagogik' underwent during the Fascist era, the concept of the human sciences may be said to have undergone its second and, at the same time, final crisis in the middle of the 1960s. For it was not just any old conception that was adapted from sociology, but that of the Frankfurt Critical Theory. How did this happen? In the 1960s the post-war generation began to come to terms with their fathers' generation and its involvement in Fascism. Theoretically, this meant, for educational science in particular, asking how Auschwitz had been possible and what could be done to prevent, as Adorno (1970:92) put it, 'Auschwitz from happening again'. In the memorial publication *(Gedenkschrift)* for Erich Weniger, which appeared in 1965, a generation of his pupils devoted themselves to the necessary task of working through the arrears. They thus came to the decision that the hermeneutic method, in particular, would have to be considered a reason why the pedagogics of the human sciences had had no weapons with which to prevent Fascism from overpowering it. The problem was seen to be in transferring the hermeneutic method, which was originally intended for the interpretation of texts, to the interpretation of educational reality. Just as texts can only be interpreted when they have been *written*, so the *reality* of education could, of necessity, only be interpreted insofar as it already existed. In other words: an analysis (and possible criticism) of Fascism using this conception was only possible after the worst had happened. It was thus only logical to demand that two things be changed: firstly, things should never stop at the mere *interpretation* of reality. A *criticism* of reality was required. Secondly, this ideological criticism had to be related to the intentions of education and not to the reality produced once education had taken place.

To this extent the adoption of the concept of ideological criticism as borrowed from the critical theory of the Frankfurt School was logical. The authors (see Dahmer and Klafki 1968) working on the commemorative publication for Erich Weniger in 1965 intended to preserve *interpretation* as the human-science core, merely enriching and improving it in the sense of ideological criticism.

What now developed within a very few years was the conception of 'Kritische Erziehungswissenschaft', which remained for ten to fifteen years the dominating educational-science model in Germany. It should not, however, be overlooked that 'Kritische Erziehungswissenschaft' was attacked right from the start from a completely different direction, not by the defenders of the old human sciences but from the bastion of empirical social research. There were several reasons for this: firstly, empirical social research, particularly in sociology, was 'imported' from the United States more intensively after the Second World War than had previously been possible. Secondly, empirical sociology (quite independently of educational science) contrasted violently with the critical theory of the Frankfurt School. This dispute has passed into the history of sociology as the 'positivism argument'. Which point in this dispute was the most important one for educational science? It was the problem of values. Put in simple terms, the position adopted by the empirico-analytically oriented theory of science was that of demanding that axiological questions be left outside the bounds of science. Questions about empirical truth should not be mixed up with questions about values. The aim is objective knowledge. If one allows subjective aspects it becomes impossible to discover truth via (educational) reality and one is only fooling oneself. However, if one spreads false truths about educational reality, science passes (educational) reality by, and can no longer contribute towards the improvement and formation of this reality. It is then 'ideological' in the negative sense. From the standpoint of Critical Theory this way of looking at things has been, to some extent, stood on its head: the positivists were criticised on the grounds that the call for freedom from values was in itself a value, so that it was impossible for freedom from values to assert itself. The objectivism of the search for truth, in the view of the Critical Theorists, neglected that science always pursued interests. This, it was said, was unavoidable. The main thing was, rather, to reveal the interests pursued by certain scientific research. Jürgen Habermas (1973), in his epoch-making book of the period *Erkenntnis und Interesse*, distinguished between three basic types:

- A technical interest in utilising nature.
- A practical interest in solving questions that are practical in the philosophical sense, i.e.,the question of what is to be done on the social plane.
- An emancipatory interest in liberating people from superfluous social domination.

The position of the Critical Theorists thus went as far so to demand that science must follow an emancipatory interest if it wished to be legitimate.

This theory was applied directly to educational science. Here the demand was now for educational science to help emancipate humankind from superfluous social domination. This demand was soon expanded: education, they said, also had to be emancipatory education. This corresponded to the traditional postulate of education towards an individual's maturity, or coming of age, and reference back to Schleiermacher was made. In summary form it was possible to reduce the concept of Critical Educational Science to the following formula: The aim of Critical Educational Science is to criticise social conditions considered to be an obstacle to education which, on its part, serves to emancipate the individual via education.

The conceptions of Critical Educational Science and Empirical Educational Science remained irreconcilable throughout the 1970s. There were a few attempts to incorporate the claim to certainty of empirico-analytical pedagogics, as in Oevermann's conception of objective hermeneutics. These attempts were, however, rather half-hearted, and one thing has to be seen with crystal clarity: the representatives of Critical Educational Science generally understood nothing of empirico-analytic research, just as reflections on the theory of education do not necessarily comprise part of the standard repertoire of positivist educationalists. During the 1970s the concept of Critical Educational Science soon reached its limitations. For if the idea of criticism was taken very seriously, educational science specialists were forced to limit themselves to ideological criticism of the 'ideological' conditions which confronted them. The conception of Jürgen Habermas was, in fact, intended to place all hope in the power of reason. In other words, Habermas assumed that reason itself had a capacity to assert itself. Put in concrete terms: if conditions of domination were 'unmasked' as subjectively superfluous, one could assume that reason would be striving to set activities in motion to abolish these conditions of domination. This purely academic critical conception was, however, confronted by the requirements of, in particular, practical educational policy. As the 1970s dawned on the Federal Republic of Germany, the Social Democratic Party came to power for the first time. The field of educational policy was one of its most important areas of activity. Education was to be reformed. The intention was to abolish the three-tier system of secondary education because, it was thought, it contributed towards social inequality within society. This system was to be replaced by the comprehensive school as the uniform system in which all pupils would receive their education together. The realisation of these ideas called for educationalists who were prepared to help build up the new schools and give scientific support to them as they developed. So it was that representatives of Critical Educational Science, who were generally sympathetic to the aims of the Social Democratic Party soon found themselves in an embarrassing position: they were asked by politicians to actively develop positive concepts for educational reform. Depending on their reactions to this request they got into varying degrees of difficulty.

Klafki and Blankertz allowed themselves to become involved with the political expectations, produced plans for reform and attempted to transform these into educational reality. The result was that they were forced to give up the purely analytical claim of the Critical Theory and leave the realms of this philosophy. Klafki (1976) attempted to make up for this step theoretically, by producing a concept of 'constructive-critical' educational science. Blankertz made no changes in the theoretical conception and involved himself as a result in serious contradictions between his theoretical approach and practical educational policy. This was not true of Mollenhauer. He stuck to his theoretical guns only to involve himself in a different kind of difficulty which also latched onto Critical Theory outside the bounds of educational science: by the mid 1970s a kind of saturation effect had arisen with regard to criticism as a principle, with regard to an understanding of science that was suspected of following the academic habit of niggling instead of providing development via hard facts. Thus the Critical Theory and, with it, Critical Educational Science, at least in its pure form, ran out of steam. It became a victim of the third theory crisis of German educational science, the crisis of criticism. This crisis emerged from the ineffectuality of Critical Educational Science.

At the end of the 1970s, following the disaster of the German Educational Council, which was dissolved in 1975, the search began for a new method that would have to be more competent in linking questions of facticity with questions of validity than was objective hermeneutics that is; relating questions of should-be desiderata to the as-is situation. What resulted was the concept of action research or, that of so-called *everyday orientation*. In 1980 some authors were already pompously referring to a turning point in the everyday situation. Some were even celebrating a change of paradigms which was at last to consist of a combination of the two great traditions, of the empirico-analytical with the normative-practical. Even today I am still pleased that in my book *Pädagogik und Alltag*, published in 1980, I expressed my doubts as to whether one would really be entitled to talk about a change of paradigms in this context. My scepticism was justified. The attention paid to the everyday aspect remained a theoretical postulate. As far as problem solving in the day-to-day reality of education was concerned, the term was, perhaps, a success. For 'more attention to practical matters' is what many wanted. This fitted in well with the contemporary intellectual current that dominated as the 1970s turned into the 1980s: back to the emotions, to the demands of the individual, the celebration of moving experiences at all costs: away from top-heaviness and theory. The more this orientation turned its back on theory, however, the less significant it became for the history of educational science. It was an episode, one concept among many others.

The period up to around the mid 1980s is thus characterised by this multiplicity, the plurality of concepts. No longer could any theoretical path claim for itself the right of sole representation. Educational theory became rapidly differentiated. Its representatives got into considerable difficulties when referring back to their own pedagogical traditions. For the silent deflation of Critical Educational Science, the grandchild, so to speak, of the Pedagogics of the Human Sciences, seemed to prevent recourse to this fundamental tradition in educational science. So it is no surprise that the numerous educational concepts of the 1980s did their borrowing elsewhere. I should like to make a distinction between those concepts referring to other historical traditions outside educational science, that is to say to traditions within the German history of the human mind. These are Materialistic Pedagogics, Psychoanalytical Pedagogics, Phenomenological Pedagogics and Praxeological Pedagogics. Other attempts to place educational science on a new theoretical foundation had recourse to interactionism, structuralism or system theory, that is to say, they drew on contemporary rather than historical conceptions from outside Germany.

Materialistic Educational Science or, rather, Educational Theory was, at least in its German version, a critical theory of bourgeois education. In contrast to neo-Marxist critical educational science, it had its roots closer to Marx insofar as it assimilated, in principle, Marx's theory of society and history. From its standpoint it criticised 'bourgeois' pedagogics for affirming the existing bourgeois state of affairs insofar as bourgeois pedagogics was based on the existence of moral standards in the practice of human living which guaranteed a gradual improvement in living conditions. This attitude, it was said, disregarded the fact that social reality produced contradictions which stood in the way of the realisation of this goal. It was thus the task of Materialistic Educational Science to criticise these conditions as part of a revolutionary, i.e., modificatory, process. The main thing, so it was said, was to show that education was a social, not a private matter, that the educational system was biased towards certain social classes and that this was the reason why a concept of education should be promoted which, like the polytechnical educational system in the GDR, would make resistance to this bourgeois reality possible. Furthermore, both education and educational science were seen as part of a practical revolution far greater than their own narrow individual tasks which would abolish capitalist production methods and their fateful consequences. It is easy to see that the arguments for this approach originated from the standpoint of the capitalist West, whose economic circumstances appeared in need of revolutionising. Following the collapse of the GDR, this conception no longer provides a serious basis for discussion, at least not at present. The significance of this conception for the history of educational theory is the fact that it goes back beyond Dilthey as it were, to Marx.

Another attempt to circumvent traditional human sciences was the revival of the phenomenological tradition. Its supporters did not purposefully go back to beyond the human-science tradition, but to a conception that had existed alongside it. Phenomenology is opposed to the intention of the pedagogics of the human sciences, which aims at explaining the sense of the active educator and teacher. Phenomenological Pedagogics does not deny the possibility of such a sense, but tries to 'insert' its own sense into the actions. The implication is that while a phenomenological viewpoint does not deny the existence of the actor's consciousness (on the contrary, phenomenological description is based on processes of consciousness), it does claim that the actions do not have a subjective meaning and intention in and of themselves. In other words, meaning cannot be recognised in the actions themselves.

The attempt to resuscitate Psychoanalytical Pedagogics also represented recourse to a movement *parallel* to the 'Geisteswissenschaftliche Pädagogik'. This approach is by no means on the same level as the others. While not denying the existence of a sense in human actions, this sense is seen, by contrast to the 'Geisteswissenschaftliche Pädagogik', not as a collective sense but as an individual sense. The history reconstructed here is not the history of a culture but that of an individual, his or her own personal story of life and sufferings. Attention is directed towards the role of the unconscious. Insofar as this unconscious is always a product of an individual and thus intentionally controlled life history, a human being must in the end be conceived as a subject (Bittner 1972).

The renaissance of praxeological impulses in the works of Derbolav and Benner is, finally, the revival of a conception which lies not only further back than Dilthey but goes back in time even beyond Marx, to Kant in fact. According to the independent action-oriented theory of Benner (1987:47), derived from the praxeological impulses of Derbolav, there are four principles behind the question of education which, in his opinion, are suited to systematically 'establish pedagogical practice and the creation of educational theory'. These are:

- educability as the determinability of human beings towards productive leisure time *(Bildsamkeit)*,
- the call to independent action *(Aufforderung zur Selbsttätigkeit)*,
- the transformation of social determination into pedagogical determination and
- the concentration of all human activity on the task of developing humanity to an even higher level *(Höherbildung der Menschheit)* (see Benner 1987, 1991).

With these principles Benner intends to combat the threatening decay of educational science, as these principles are, in his opinion, suitable for concentrating the discussion on pedagogics proper. Even his last principle shows that, with the categories which he has reconstructed from the history of pedagogics, he is dedicated to a progress-oriented philosophy of history which has an eye not only to the progress of the individual but also to that of the entire species, considering such progress as a task for education. This progress does not, however, come about by some automatic agency of its own, it has to be striven for and produced by action in both social and pedagogical practice, i.e., by active subjects. His conception may be considered very elaborate in theory. However, like the others it is unable to take over the leadership in an age of theoretical pluralism. In addition, the complicated concepts involved preclude broad accessibility to his thinking. The list of approaches within this block of conceptions based on German traditions outside the human sciences is incomplete. There are certainly others, such as the transcendental-critical approach or that of communicative pedagogics which is, however, very close to Critical Educational Science. The second block, by contrast, contains those conceptions fed by theories from the Anglo-American or French traditions. We should begin by mentioning Interactionist Pedagogics. This is in fact much closer to the pedagogics of communication. For the concept of interaction can be understood as an extended equivalent of the concept of communication. The important feature of this conception is the assumption of the existence of an 'ego identity'. Interactionism is thus closely related to psychoanalysis. Interactionism represents a programme based on action theory, assuming intersubjectivity, which proceeds on the basis of understanding, is self-related and normatively sociological (Brumlik 1989:769). Interactionist educational science is based on action theory because it assumes that, in the end, 'all social phenomena are attributable to intentional activities of human beings' (Brumlik 1989:770). Insofar as human beings act on the basis of their understanding of meanings, interactionist educational science sees its task in understanding these meanings. The theory is self-related because it selects everyday matters for its subject and uses everyday language. The normative aspect of interactionism will be found in its fundamental target category of the 'ego identity'. Correspondingly, the target in interactionist educational science is also selected as a functional equivalent for the older concept of education. Accordingly, it is the subject which disposes of this 'ego identity'. The task of educational processes is thus to make possible the development of the 'ego identity' and to promote the preservation of a balance of identity in the individual's life. This conception owes a particular debt to Mead and thus to the U.S. adaptation of psychoanalytical and thus, in the long run, German theoretical traditions dating from before 1933.

This applies to System Theory Pedagogics in particular. Externally, this development owes its existence to an extra-pedagogical conflict between Critical Social Theory and System Theory. This extra-pedagogical argument involved Jürgen Habermas and Niklas Luhmann (1971) in the early 1970s. This may have led to educationalists in Germany devoting more attention to system theory. In fact the concept of system is far older and caused a great stir outside educational science directly after the Second

World War, as the reception of Parsons' work showed. If one defines a system as a set of objects, together with relations between those objects and their attributes, it is also possible to understand pedagogics as a system. Correspondingly, the attempt is then made to interpret certain attributes of pedagogics as not belonging to the subject by intention, but being a product of the system's own dynamism. The efforts made by educationalists to achieve autonomy are, for example, understood as 'a problem consequent to social differentiation'. This attitude clearly demonstrates that the Pedagogics of System Theory places itself alongside pedagogics, analysing, so to speak, the latter's systematic character. In this way it cannot help becoming the target of a critical socio-theoretical point of view. From the standpoint occupied by Critical Educational Science it was accused of devaluing the active subject, the educator, the teacher, the educational scientist to a mere element in the complex systematic structure of social part-systems. System Theory Pedagogics was accused of relativising or even denying its intentions, the sense of its actions, its liberty (Luhmann and Schorr 1979).

In the question of the belief in the existence of a subject, System Theory Pedagogics is very close to Structuralist Pedagogics, though the latter is derived from an entirely different theoretical context. Structuralism represents a collective concept for various theoretical applications, drawing from a series of at least six traditions ranging from cultural anthropology to linguistics. The common ground of these approaches is in fact to be found in what has been described as structuralist activity. The main point here is to reconstruct structures in the depths which are assumed to form the foundation of the structures on the surface, the phenomena as they manifest themselves to us. This is what structuralism is interested in. It is assumed that the reduction of variety at the surface to elementary structures in the depths permits, speaking in terms of system theory, simplification, a reduction in complexity. There have only been fragmentary attempts to construct a Structuralist Educational Science. The decisive theory behind them was the attempt to reduce the complex phenomena of educational action via structuralist activity to deep structures. The resultant descriptions were then to permit the reconstruction of an educational method which could have become the object of training measures. It has been shown that this conception can get along without the necessity of assuming a subject because, in the final analysis, the deeper structures are accepted as effective, not the intentions of the 'actors' (Lenzen 1973, 1989).

Phenomenological Pedagogics, System Theory Pedagogics and Structuralist Educational Science mark those spots where, even in the 1980s, the fourth crisis of educational science in Germany was becoming visible.

I should like to designate it as the Crisis of the Subject. The reception of discussion on so-called post-modernism dates, at the latest, from the mid 1980s. Put very simply, this discussion mainly involved seeing the dialectics of Enlightenment as the main reason for the disaster of the close of the twentieth century. Modernism was understood as the expression of a perverted Enlightenment giving birth, logically, to a post-modernist era not described in detail. Determining this era's contents was deliberately avoided since people were convinced that there could no longer be any great theory which would suffice to legitimise all possible actions in all fields of culture. For this is one of the essential aspects of the criticism of today's production of theories. That its aim, in general, is to pursue a doctrine of salvation, some 'great story' as Lyotard (1982:71) has called it, which nobody is able to believe in any more. The last great story is said to have been the 'story of emancipation' (Lyotard 1982:71), which is said to have disavowed itself from the horrors of Stalinism right up to the dictatorship of the GDR. But if there no longer exists an emancipatory theory which all are able to follow, this necessarily means that either a lack of theoretical principles and consequently a lack of orientation is gaining ground, or that there is a plurality of theories permitting one group of people to orient themselves in one direction and the remainder in some other.

In its final form this has far-reaching consequences for pedagogics. In its own way, pedagogics is a child of Enlightenment. It owes its existence not only to a great story but is, for much of the way, identical with that story. If the theory of education lays claim to 'the education of humanity to higher things', to establish progress, in fact it cannot do this without a philosophy of history which permits it to distinguish actions serving this progress from those which do not serve this aim. In other words: it must have a vision of the direction in which everything is to move. But if it is impossible to achieve agreement because Enlightenment has swept away a common philosophy of life such as that of Christianity, then pedagogics as a science of action will finally have to throw in the towel as far as everyone is concerned. It no longer has a binding justification. One could of course draw from this the conclusion that this science should be abolished. This consequence would, however, be as unrealistic as it would be foolish. Unrealistic because an academic subject and its corresponding practical applications cannot be abolished so easily. Foolish because this consequence would fail to understand what the impossibility of justifying total theories really means: the abolition of education distinguishes itself in its totality and its intolerance in no way from the totalitarianism of racist, religious-fundamentalist or Marxist origins.

For reasons of democracy alone it must therefore be assumed that education, the forces that guide it and educational institutions, will continue to exist, as will educational theories. If this is so, the question arises as to who will protect the possible victims of education from its consequences. The answer to this question is difficult: on the one hand there can, under the conditions of post-modernism, be no instance outside of culture which provides an extramundane reason for justifying the interventions of education. Thus protection can only come from those who are themselves involved in the process of education. To provide them with guidance on the implications of their actions, their omissions and their permissions it would be necessary, in addition to unavoidable, action-oriented pedagogics telling them what to do, to have a second form of pedagogics for which I would like to put in a plea: I mean a type of pedagogics which is reflexively concerned with the consequences of education, if action-oriented pedagogics itself does not wish to become involved because it has always believed that right, history and the future, in the form of the young people involved, are on its side.

Perhaps such a suggestion demonstrates once more that the head-on stance taken up between the empirico-analytical and hermeneutic approaches to the phenomena of educational reality, so characteristic of discussions here in Germany, is unnecessary. Both methods of access are required, not only for a reflexive but also for an action-oriented conception of educational science. This insight is significant for the joint undertaking involving Amsterdam and Berlin. For as far as I can see, there are certainly different points of main emphasis in our two faculties, a clearly empirical and maybe also action-oriented accent in Amsterdam and, perhaps contrasting with it, a somewhat stronger emphasis – without being a bias – on questions concerning philosophy and social theory in Berlin, together with a simultaneous appreciation of the nomological approach in both places. I am thus eager to see what we can learn from each other under this constellation, and hope that our joint conference will, in this sense, be a great success.

References

Adorno, W. Th. (1970), *Erziehung zur Mündigkeit. Vorträge und Gespräche mit Hellmut Becker*, Frankfurt/Main.

Benner, D. (1987), *Allgemeine Pädagogik*, Weinheim/München.

Benner, D. (1991), Hauptströmungen der Erziehungswissenschaft, Weinheim.

Bittner, G. (1972), *Psychoanalyse und soziale Erziehung*, München.

Brumlik, M. (1989), 'Interaktionismus, Symbolischer', in D. Lenzen, (ed.), *Pädagogische Grundbegriffe*, vol. 1, Reinbek/Hamburg, pp. 764-781.

Dahmer I. and Klafki, W. (eds) (1968), *Geisteswissenschaftliche Pädagogik am Ausgang ihrer Epoche – Erich Weniger*, Weinheim.

Dilthey, W. (1959), 'Die Geisteswissenschaften ein selbstständiges Ganzes neben den Naturwissenschaften', in *Gesammelte Schriften*. vol. 1, Stuttgart, pp. 4-14.

Dilthey, W. (1961), 'Die Entstehung der Hermeneutik', in *Gesammelte Schriften*, vol. 5, Stuttgart, pp. 317-338.

Habermas, J. (1973), *Erkenntnis und Interesse*, Frankfurt/ Main.

Habermas, J. and Luhman, N. (1971), *Theorie der Gesellschaft oder Sozialtechnologie – Was leistet die Systemforschung?*, Frankfurt/ Main.

Klafki, W. (1976), *Aspekte kritisch-konstruktiver Erziehungswissenschaft*, Weinheim/Basel.

Kunzmann, P., Burkard, F.-P. and Wiedmann, F. (1991), *dtv-Atlas zur Philosophie*, München.

Lenzen, D. (1973), *Didaktik und Kommunikation*, Frankfurt/Main.

Lenzen, D. (ed.) (1980), *Pädagogik und Alltag*, Stuttgart.

Lenzen, D. (1989), 'Struktur', in D. Lenzen (ed.), *Pädagogische Grundbegriffe*, vol. 2. Reinbek/ Hamburg, pp. 1,458-1,471.

Luhmann, N. and Schorr, K.-E. (1979), *Reflexionsprobleme im Erziehungssystem*, Stuttgart.

Lyotard, J.-F. (1982), *Das postmoderne Wissen*, Bremen.

Mollenhauer, K. (1972), *Theorien zum Erziehungsprozeß*, München.

Chapter 2

A PARADOXICAL PROFESSION

The Educational Sciences in the Netherlands

Ernst Mulder

1.

Now that the fragmentation of the social sciences seems almost complete, and empirical science is claiming the victory of neutral and value-free research, social theory is still being invoked to give direction to education, social action, and politics. This paradox lies at the heart of the present state of the educational sciences. Educational scientists have to abstain from ethical and political values and produce hard and reliable data, and at the same time they are expected to solve ethical questions and policy problems. What good is a science that merely questions the facts but gives us no clues what to do?

In this chapter I intend to give a picture of the state of the educational sciences in the Netherlands. Of course it is entirely legitimate to want to inform colleagues and fellow scholars about the educational sciences in a national context. Yet at the same time it is impossible to identify *the* state of affairs, if only because the field is so large and diversity so great. To strive for an exhaustive description would then be a little quixotic. So, depicting the educational or any other sciences, requires a certain level of abstraction or aggregation, and a certain point of view.

As an historian of education with a special interest in the history of science and social thought, I will devote a good deal of this article to the *history* of the educational sciences in the Netherlands. That is, I will not try to discover a supposed 'state' of the educational sciences, let alone *the* state, but I will write about states in the plural, concentrating on *developments* in the educational sciences over the last hundred years. This is necessary, because it is not really possible to understand what is going on in the educational sciences, or in any science for that matter, without looking at the historical antecedents of recent states of affairs.[1] Moreover, the current differentiation in educational sciences can best be illustrated by the variety of articles in this volume.

So my approach will be historical, and I will present the development of Dutch educational science along the following lines. Firstly, I will suggest a central theme. Secondly, I will say something about the origins of the modern sciences of man and society. Thirdly, I will picture early pedagogy in the Netherlands, with some reference to German pedagogy; and fourthly, I will outline the development of Dutch educational science or pedagogy in the twentieth century.

2.

In recent years there have only been three attempts to give a coherent picture of the educational sciences in the Netherlands (see Wirtz 1987, van der Geld 1990 and Pennings 1991). They all seem to accept the diversity and even incompatibility of the various branches of educational science. They present separate contributions on a variety of topics which, taken together, are more or less representative of the field as a whole. Very few of the authors have really tried to relate his or her subject to any of the others. Also remarkable is the almost complete silence with which these three books were received: only three reviews in the six most prominent professional journals over a period of five or six years, and all of them summaries rather than reviews (de Groot 1987:474-476, Pols 1988:343-358 and van Setten 1992:458-462). The very few authors in these books who did try to say more about the educational sciences as a whole – just two of them it seems who were invited to do so (Creemers 1987, 1991 and Imelman 1990, 1991) – laid bare a long-standing conflict which has haunted the educational, and in fact all of the social sciences, since the days of their conception. This is the conflict between fact and value, and stemming from this, the conflict over the malleability of children, the psyche and society.

In a recent article on science studies and the development of Dutch pedagogy, Biesta and Miedema tried to analyse this development from the

1. 'There is nothing more necessary to the man of science than its history, and the logic of discovery ...' Lord Acton quoted in Popper 1975:14.

perspective of the relationship between facts and values (Biesta and Miedema 1992:396-411). They gave five valid reasons for choosing this very theme. First, the distinction between facts and values is central to philosophical and sociological discussions on the demarcation between science and non-science, on value-free science, objectivity and the problem of means and ends. They stressed that the separation of facts and values is not inevitable, but the result of social and scientific processes. This prevents an over-simplified idea of scientific progress, and leaves the process of this separation open to further investigation. Second, the problem of facts and values has special relevance for the identity of educational science. Where emphasis is firmly placed on empirical phenomena and research, it is indistinguishable from the other social sciences; where the main emphasis is on values, its acceptance as a science is at risk. Third, in much historiography of Dutch pedagogy the development of educational science is described in terms of the vanishing of values and the victory of facts. However, as the history of psychology in the Netherlands has shown, this picture is too simple (Dehue 1995). Fourth, the segmentation of Dutch society in the twentieth century along denominational lines has had a pervasive influence on education, youth care, social work, and educational science. Finally, there has recently been a growing feeling that a pluralistic society creates special problems in moral socialisation, to which educational scientists should have some answers. I hope to demonstrate that all these factors have played a part in the development of the Dutch educational sciences.

3.

The modern sciences of man and society are children of the eighteenth-century Enlightenment and nineteenth-century Romanticism. This is also true for the science of education or pedagogy (to use this rather awkward word). The historian Peter Gay (1973:499) even called education 'the logic of enlightenment: if most men are not yet ready for autonomy, they must be *made* ready for it.' Autonomy was a social, psychological, and ethical, in short a pedagogical ideal, and has remained so to this day. The ideal of autonomy is a legacy left by the philosophers of the Enlightenment, which pedagogues, in particular, would not easily forget. For autonomy could only be achieved by purposeful upbringing and education, which would restrict eventual independence. Thus autonomy turned out to be a very precarious project indeed which at any rate would involve not only experience, that is empirical facts, but also values. At the same time, education and socialisation of the young was seen as inevitable and, as such, the responsibility of educators and pedagogues. This, however, presupposed the malleability of children – which, ever since Rousseau, has been seen as rooted in a natural developmental pattern of children, often silently taken for granted (Morss 1990).

From the end of the nineteenth century a reorientation in Western social thought can be observed, which H. Stuart Hughes characterised as a 'revolt against positivism'. Great social theorists, from Weber to Freud and from James to Groce to Durkheim, expressed their opposition to the dominant mode of thought in the second half of the nineteenth century as they saw it, using the terms materialism, naturalism, and positivism interchangeably (see Hughes 1961:36-39, 112-113, White 1973:41-67, Ringer 1969:314-315 and Jonker 1988:30ff.). However, this revolt did not result in the abandoning of faith in strict scientific procedures, nor did it mean a return to the idealism of the beginning of the nineteenth century. Rather it brought about something of a synthesis between the legacy of the Enlightenment, which by the second half of the century had often degenerated into sterile positivism, and certain idealistic notions (Hughes 1961:28-30, 429, Haskell 1977:5-8, Seidman 1983:11 and Mandelbaum 1971:5ff.). Human beings were not as self-confident and rational as the inheritors of the eighteenth century would have it, nor were they totally determined by endowment or environment. A better understanding of social life, on the other hand, could only be obtained by the study of concrete historical phenomena, taken not as expression of a superhuman spirit or mind, but nevertheless shaped by the consciousness of both the actors themselves and the investigators. Thus the social thinkers of the turn of the century admitted a twofold subjectivity: of the investigator, whose values would limit the objectivity of his observations and theories; and of the people under investigation, whose actions turned out to be determined more by non-rational values than by purely logical considerations. It was at this time that Max Weber presented his classical and authoritative formulation of the problem of values in the social sciences.

Of course, epistemological problems date further back than the end of the nineteenth century, but in the decades around the turn of the century they were not only worrying philosophers, but also natural and social scientists. Thus while some social-evolutionary conceptions of Darwinism led to a rather rigid determinism, in other interpretations the emphasis on change and variation implied a low level of fixed rules in human societies. Sometime later the ideas of Mach and Poincaré about the hypothetical character of knowledge made a lasting impression even beyond the borders of the exact sciences, and developments in physics led to a growing tolerance of relativistic theories. Finally, with the *Principia Mathematica* of Russell and Whitehead it became commonly accepted that even in mathematics different systems of axioms were possible. Sometimes this was held to be true for every mental activity, which led some to the conclusion that every system of thought, and by implication also every value system, should have an equal right to admission (Hughes 1961:38-39, 106-110, Haskell 1977:244, Soffer 1978:5-6 and Lichtheim 1974:91-93). Even so, at least social philosophers and scientists began to realise that their knowledge of human social and psychic life was relative to a certain, probably high, degree, and that it was therefore hypothetical, provisional, and highly dependent on the values of the investigator.

4.

Educational science or pedagogy in the Netherlands only entered the universities in the first decades of the twentieth century. It therefore acquired a different status from the *Pädagogik* in Germany. In the Netherlands there had been no famous philosopher in the eighteenth or nineteenth centuries systematically addressing fundamental theoretical questions in pedagogy or education. There had been no Kant or Von Humboldt, no Schleiermacher, or Herbart. On the contrary, until the twentieth century all but one of the professors at the Dutch universities had refused to teach any pedagogy or philosophy of education, even though lectures on the subject had been obligatory for students who wanted to teach at one of the gymnasia since 1827 (Mulder 1989:14-15). This also means that Dutch educational science had no traditional roots in idealistic conceptions of a cultural science (a 'Geisteswissenschaft' in German, which is difficult to render exactly in translation [see Lenzen this volume, Hughes 1961:chap. 6]), although some of the early professors of pedagogy used related notions and methods, like 'Verstehen' (literally: understanding, meaning the interpretation of cultural phenomena, Hughes 1961:310-312).

Academic recognition, though fairly slow in coming, benefited from the favourable circumstances of the reorientation of the social sciences around the turn of the century. The coincidence of greater tolerance of value-related aspects of (social) science, the recognition of the irrational sides of social and psychic life, and the epistemological relativity paved the way for a normative approach to educational questions in an academic atmosphere. After all, pedagogy was considered to be a practical science, which implied that practitioners should operate in a goal-oriented, ethical way. The growing interdependence in modern society, which social scientists thought they could observe, appeared to make it inevitable that these problems be tackled professionally (Mulder 1989:

12-14). The first representatives of Dutch educational science, the professors in pedagogy, observed the reorientation of the social sciences, and perceived a need for a pedagogical profession. They used this as an argument in favour of their new discipline, which they conceived as ethical, even normative, to the core. In this respect at least, they resembled their German colleagues (Ringer 1969:334, 404ff.). Most of the Dutch professors in pedagogy considered the ethical, value-laden character of their discipline to be crucial. For them it was the central criterion by which they could distinguish educational science from the adjacent domains of psychology and sociology in particular, but also from medicine and psychiatry (Mulder 1989:247). So while other social sciences were trying to emancipate and dissociate themselves from philosophy, pedagogy was moving in the very opposite direction. As the leading professor of the time, Kohnstamm, declared: 'Pedagogy will be philosophical, or will not be at all' (1929:21). A value-free pedagogy or educational science was inconceivable to them – and to almost everyone else, including advocates of experimental or empirical pedagogy, like Brugmans at the University of Groningen (Mulder 1989:229-234).

5.

So despite the fact that they had inherited a different intellectual legacy, German and Dutch educational scientists or pedagogues both put the issue of values at the heart of their discipline. In the Netherlands this tendency has been strengthened by a social and political peculiarity which deserves some explanation: the so-called pillarisation (in Dutch: 'verzuiling').[2] In the nineteenth century a struggle broke out over the religious character of primary education between the ruling elite of liberal, moderate, enlightened Protestants on the one hand, and the orthodox Protestant, Calvinist minority on the other. In the second half of the century in particular, they argued vehemently about the control and financing of denominational primary schools. In that political fight, known in Dutch historiography as the school struggle, the Roman Catholics took the side of the orthodox Protestants. Together they strove for maximum subsidy and minimum interference from the government. This struggle also played an important role in the political emancipation of orthodox Protestants and Roman Catholics.

Gradually the liberals began to realise that the privately founded denominational schools were providing for the wants of large groups of

2. The classical formulation of the political process of pillarisation in the Netherlands is Lijphart 1975.

religious people and they began to think about concessions. At the same time their power was waning so they had to reckon with the other (denominational) political parties. In a new Education Act of 1889 the denominational schools were granted some state aid and the amount was increased during the following decades. Having accepted the principle of subsidy of private education the liberals' main goal became the introduction of compulsory education (from the ages of six to twelve years), which they achieved in 1900. In 1917 a new constitution was passed which stipulated that the government should take care of *all* primary education and that public and denominational education were to be financed equally by the state. Eventually this meant a victory for the denominational political parties of the right. However, there was a cost: universal suffrage, which was a demand of the parties of the left, the liberals and the socialists. This deal put an end to some eighty years of political struggle and solved two protracted problems in Dutch political life. It is known as the 'pacification' of Dutch politics. The Primary Education Act of 1920 sealed the so-called financial equalisation of public and denominational education (see Mulder 1992:373-381, Kwaasteniet 1990, Heyting and Tenorth 1994:5-243).

The settlement of educational affairs in the constitution of 1917 meant the consolidation and sanctioning of a Dutch system of primary education divided up into rather autonomous religious spheres. This system has been cherished by Protestants and Roman Catholics alike and it is called the 'verzuiling' (literally: pillarisation) of education. In fact, the process of pillarisation was not limited to education but has affected many sectors of Dutch society in the twentieth century. As one Dutch historian described it, pillarisation meant 'the system of institutionalised segmentation by which each religious or quasi-religious group, Protestant, Catholic, or humanist, was encouraged and subsidised by the state to create its own social world, encompassing the entire existence of an individual from nursery school via sports club, trade union, university, hospital, broadcasting and television corporation, to the burial society' (Kossmann 1978:304). The system of pillarisation has existed to this day and is especially firmly entrenched in Dutch education.

This was the important background against which Dutch pedagogy became established at the universities. Pillarisation also applied to this new discipline. Within the few years from 1918 to 1926 each of the six universities had appointed a professor of pedagogy, including the two denominational ones (one orthodox Protestant, and one Roman Catholic). Moreover, as I have pointed out, all the professors, including the ones at the non-denominational universities, acknowledged the central importance of values in their discipline. Some of them even tried to develop a specific Roman Catholic, or orthodox Protestant scientific pedagogy.[3] Notably, the Calvinist Jan Waterink justified these attempts with reference to the axiomatic foundation of mathematics, which he compared with the systems of values, religious convictions and world views on which different scientific pedagogies were supposed to be built (Mulder 1989:210ff.). Although most of the early academic educational scientists did not go as far as this, obviously different pedagogies were possible as soon as they admitted the importance of values as the constituting core of their discipline. But in accordance with the politics of accommodation which took shape during the process of pacification, the academic representatives of pedagogy never questioned each other's ethical or religious points of view. On pedagogical and educational topics they rarely disagreed.

Actually there was only one exception: Kohnstamm, who was Professor of Pedagogy at the University of Amsterdam. A physicist by training, he originally held a chair in thermo-dynamics. Well versed in scientific research, he founded empirical research in pedagogical and educational problems in Amsterdam, but he was absolutely not a narrow-minded positivist or empiricist. As he once wrote, it was his very acquaintance with natural science that showed him the limits of scientific research (Mulder 1989:96). And although he was by no means the only empirical scientist in the field of education and pedagogy, as Marc Depaepe so thoroughly demonstrated (1993), in this respect he differed from most of them. It must also be remembered that in his opinion pedagogy should be not only an empirical, but above all an ethical science. Empirical pedagogical research should always serve to further the development of children's potential, and educational ends of this kind necessarily involve moral considerations and hence a world view. Kohnstamm, therefore, developed his pedagogy as part of his philosophy of Biblical Personalism. His own research concerned the transition from primary to secondary schools and particularly cognitive learning processes and didactics (Mulder 1989:chap.3). Another professor of pedagogy who promoted empirical research was the Calvinist Waterink. He became director of a psychotechnical laboratory and of an institute for the treatment of mentally disturbed children. His most important work was in the counselling and treatment of children with learning and behavioural difficulties and in advising on matters of education and occupation. Waterink tried to found a Calvinistic pedagogy. In this he was, however, less successful than in his practical work (Mulder 1989:191ff.).

3. Respectively J.H.E.J. Hoogveld at the Roman Catholic University of Nijmegen and J. Waterink at the Free University in Amsterdam; see Mulder 1989:chaps 5,6.

After the Second World War a new generation of professors of pedagogy and educational science entered the universities. At first they continued the work of the first generation, but as a process of depillarisation (Dutch: 'ontzuiling') developed in Dutch society in the 1950s and 1960s, the ethical basis of the discipline became more and more invisible. This process can be clearly seen in the dominant educational scientist of these decades: Langeveld (see Homann 1971). He was a pupil of Kohnstamm, but gradually tried to accommodate his theories to the new socio-cultural circumstances. He called his pedagogy 'phenomenological',[4] by which he indicated his attitude of avoiding preconceptions in his approach of children. He moved away from normative pedagogy, and towards 'factual', that is experienced, educational phenomena. This was also a sign of the growing autonomy of educational science. Nevertheless, Langeveld was convinced that education and upbringing are necessarily cultural, and therefore value-related activities. This became very clear in the early 1950s, when he wrote the concluding report to an extensive investigation commissioned by the government into the post-war youth problem, considered an enormous threat to social stability at the time. He not only referred to the huge amount of data gathered, but also did not hesitate to blame the supposed decline of traditional values for creating socially disturbed youth and to recommend a Protestant-inspired ethic of responsibility.[5] It seems fair to see Langeveld as trying to overcome the boundaries of pillarisation which, in education, youth care, and social work in particular, have remained pervasive, even to this day. He strove for a synthesis of a more ethical and an empirical approach, of value and fact.[6]

In the meantime the educational sciences went through a process of differentiation and specialisation. During the 1950s at least four pedagogical subdisciplines emerged. They were: 1) youth care and special education, including the treatment and training of criminal youth, learning problems, and diagnosis and treatment of physically and mentally handicapped children; 2) educational research into issues like didactics, school systems, the effectiveness of educational programs, and educational and social mobility; 3) social pedagogy, the study of youth, and later also of adults, outside educational institutions, and of social work; and finally, 4) general theoretical, often philosophical, epistemological, and historical

4. He was indeed impressed by existentialism and by Husserl.

5. His diagnosis and his cure, sounded a little frantic and pedantic, even in the 1950s; see for the whole project on socially disturbed youth and the role of Langeveld: Meijers and du Bois Reymond 1987.

6. See Biesta and Miedema 1992: 401ff. For a somewhat different interpretation: Weijers 1995:61-72.

reflection on, and analysis of, pedagogical phenomena. Each of these descendants of the pedagogical ancestor received its own chair at most of the Dutch universities.

This however, was only the beginning of a process of unprecedented proliferation that has taken place since the end of the 1960s, whereby each of the subdisciplines mentioned above has broken up into more specialised subjects.[7] A look at the three books mentioned earlier, or a glance at the professional journals, reveals a host of divergent subjects: youth and sexuality, working mothers and attachment, computerised reading tests, John Dewey, game-simulation as a supportive system in organisations, observation of non-verbal behaviour of teachers, paradoxical therapy, self-esteem of adopted children from India, phonological encoding by children with severe reading problems, and so on. Pedagogy as a discipline has given way to a great variety of subjects which are being investigated analytically or empirically, and are at best concentrated in research groups. Some of these have proved to be very successful in terms of coherence and theoretical and methodological progress, like research programs as Lakatos mentioned them. Examples of such programs are an extensive project on Bowlby's attachment theories at the University of Leiden (e.g., IJzendoorn and Bakermans-Kranenburg 1994:1-24); and a research tradition established around the theme of education and social mobility, which in some respects harks back to Kohnstamm, and certainly to sociological research on education in the 1950s (see Habers 1986). Both are also examples of the tendency Biesta and Miedema pointed out, that a strong emphasis on empirical phenomena and research makes educational sciences indistinguishable from other sciences, in these cases psychology and sociology.

There seems to be no unifying idea in the educational sciences, let alone a theory. This also means that since the reign of Langeveld, the problem of values has scarcely received any systematic attention, except in some conceptual analyses and in some empirical research on moral development and education. Advocates of value-free empirical research and of value-related pedagogy both agree on this conclusion (Creemers 1991, Imelman 1991). Nevertheless, in actual education and upbringing values keep playing a part, if only because educational and pedagogical organisations and institutions have not been depillarised to the same degree as academic educational science and higher learning. However, in non-denominational circles too, people sometimes worry about the lack of moral socialisation and ask for a re-valuation of education and family

7. This process is described for the University of Amsterdam in Mulder, Hetterschijt and Sinkeldam 1994.

life, as the Dutch Minister of Education has done (Ritzen 1992, Spiecker, et. al. 1992:90-95). Educational science however, seems to be unable, and even refuses, to give quick and ready-made solutions.

Educational scientists appear to be hesitating between mourning the loss of values, and celebrating the victory of facts. When asked for advice, they seem to strive for balanced judgements, involving social or personal values, firmly grounded in empirical knowledge. This almost sounds like the intentions and programmes of Kohnstamm and Langeveld put into practice. But neither of the research groups I mentioned earlier is explicitly and directly treating the problem of values. Values are, nevertheless, implied in their research and its applications, as the Enlightenment philosophers already knew, and the Minister of Education suspects. This, in conjunction with present-day theoretical pluralism, gives much reason for reflection on the discipline of educational science.

References

Biesta, G./S. Miedema, 'Feiten en waarden in de ontwikkeling van de Nederlandse academische pedagogiek. Een opmaat voor pedagogisch wetenschapsonderzoek' *Pedagogisch Tijdschrift* 17(1992).

Creemers, B.P.M., (1987) 'Onderwijskunde tussen droom en werkelijkheid' in: Wirtz et al.1987.

Creemers, B.P.M., (1991) 'Ouder en wijzer? Reflecties over onderzoek in de pedagogiek, andragogiek en onderwijskunde' in Pennings et al. 1991.

Dehue, Trudy, (1995) *Changing the Rules: Psychology in the Netherlands, 1900-1985*, Cambridge.

Depaepe, Marc, (1993) *Zum Wohl des Kindes? Pädologie, pädagogische Psychologie und experimentelle Pädagogik in Europa und den USA, 1890-1940*. Weinheim.

Gay, Peter, (1973) *The Enlightenment. An Interpretation. Vol. II: The Science of Freedom*, London.

Geld, A.M.C. van der, and A.F.D. van Veen (eds), (1990) *Pedagogiek in beweging*, Amsterdam.

Groot, R. de, (1987) 'Boekbespreking van *Stilstaan bij vooruitgang*, F.D. Wirtz et al. (ed.)', *Tijdschrift voor Orthopedagogiek* 26.

Harbers, Hans, (1986) *Sociale wetenschappen en hun speelruimte. Een onderzoek naar de relatie tussen wetenschap en maatschappij aan de hand van ontwikkelingen in de onderwijssociologie en het politieke debat over ongelijke onderwijskansen*, Groningen.

Haskell, Th.L., (1977) *The Emergence of Professional Social Science. The American Social Science Association and the Nineteenth Century Crisis of Authority*, Urbana/Chicago/London.
Heyting, G.F., and H.E. Tenorth, (1994) 'Pädagogik und Pluralismus. Zur Einleitung in diesen Band' in F. Heyting and H.E. Tenorth, *Pädagogik und Pluralismus. Deutsche und Niederländische Erfahrungen im Umgang mit Pluralität in Erziehung und Erziehungswissenschaft*, Weinheim.
Homann, M., (1971) *Die Pädagogik M.J. Langevelds*, Bochum.
Hughes, H. Stuart, (1961) *Consciousness and Society. The Reorientation of European Social Thought, 1890-1930*, New York.
IJzendoorn, M.H. van, and M.J. Bakermans-Kranenburg, (1994) 'Intergenerationele overdracht van gehechtheid' *Kind en Adolescent* 15.
Imelman, J.D., (1990) 'Pedgagogiek in Nederland: bedreigde wetenschap, bedreigde opleiding?' in Van der Geld and Van Veen 1990.
Imelman, J.D., (1991) 'Geen ding betert door ouderdom, zeker een gedateerde opvatting over wetenschap niet' in Pennings et al. (1991).
Jonker, E., (1988) *De sociologische verleiding. Sociologie, sociaal-democratie en de welvaartsstaat*, Groningen.
Kohnstamm, P.A., (1929) 'Staatspaedagogiek of persoonlijkheidspaedagogiek' in P.A. Kohnstamm, *Individu en gemeenschap. Verzamelde sociaal-paedagogische opstellen*, Gravenhage, original edition 1919.
Kossmann, E.H., (1978) *The Low Countries, 1780-1940*, Oxford.
Kwaasteniet, Marjanne de, (1990) *Denomination and Primary Education in the Netherlands (1870-1984). A Spatial Diffusion Perspective*, Amsterdam.
Lichtheim, G., (1974) *Europe in the Twentieth Century*, London.
Lijphart, A., (1975)*The Politics of Accomodation: Pluralism and Democracy in the Netherlands*, Berkeley.
Mandelbaum, M., (1971) *History, Man and Reason. A Study in 19th Century Thought*, Baltimore/London.
Meijers, F., and M. du Bois Reymond (eds), (1987) *Op zoek naar een moderne pedagogische norm. Beeldvorming over jeugd in de jaren vijftig: het massajeugdonderzoek (1948-1952)*, Amersfoort/Leuven.
Morss, John R., (1990) *The Biologising of Childhood. Developmental Psychology and the Darwinian Myth*, Hove/London/Hillsdale.
Mulder, Ernst, (1992) 'The Development of Primary Education in the Netherlands' in: Gary A. Woodill, Judith Bernard, Lawrence Prochner (eds), (1992) *International Handbook of Early Childhood Education*. New York/London.
Mulder, Ernst, (1989) *Beginsel en beroep. Pedagogiek aan de universiteit in Nederland, 1900-1940*, Amsterdam.
Mulder, Ernst, Caroline Hetterschijt, Ilonka Sinkeldam, (1994) *75 jaar pedagogiek aan de Universiteit van Amsterdam, 1919-1994*, Amsterdam.
Pennings, A., et al. (eds), (1991) *Bijdragen aan pedagogisch onderzoek 1990*, Amersfoort/Leuven.
Pols, Wouter, (1988) 'De ontnuchterende beweging van de pas op de plaats' *Comenius* 31.
Popper, Karl N., (1975) *The Logic of Scientific Discovery*, London.

Ringer, F.K., (1969) *The Decline of the German Mandarins. The German Academic Community, 1890-1930*, Cambridge, Mass.

Ritzen, J.M.M., (1992) *De pedagogische opdracht van het onderwijs. Een uitnodiging tot gezamenlijke actie*, Zoetermeer.

Seidman, S., (1983)*Liberalism and the Origins of European Social Theory*, Oxford.

Setten, Henk van, (1992) 'De armoede van de pedagogiek' *Comenius* 48.

Soffer, R.N., (1978) *Ethics and Society in England. The Revolution in the Social Sciences*, Berkeley/Los Angeles/London.

Spiecker, B., A.W. van Haaften, and J.D. Imelman, (1992) 'Stellingen bij de voordracht van de Minister"*Pedagogisch Tijdschrift* 17.

Weijers, Ido, (1995) 'Mündige Bürger. Eine kulturhistorische Platzbestimmung der Pädagogik des M.J. Langeveld' *Pädagogische Rundschau* 49.

White, M., 'The revolt against formalism in American social thought of the twentieth century' in M. White, (1973) *Pragmatism and the American Mind. Essays and Reviews in Philosophy and Intellectual History*, New York.

Wirtz, F.D., et al. (eds), (1987) *Stilstaan bij vooruitgang. Beweging en tegenbeweging in opvoeding, vorming en onderwijs*, Nijmegen.

Chapter 3

EDUCATION IN URBAN ENVIRONMENTS

Amsterdam Youth Policy in the Context of Reflexive Modernisation

Frieda Heyting

1. The City as a Danger to Education

Rousseau thought it wise for Emile to develop a sense of discretion before sending him off to the city of Paris, in order that he develop a fine sense of taste. As long as he was incapable of dealing with town ways in an autonomous and reflexive way, the overwhelming impressions could make him an 'esclave de l'opinion' and in that sense be a threat to his moral development (Rousseau, 1762:666 ff.).[1]

The fear of the city as an educational environment has not decreased over the centuries. Today, educational scientists still consider urban environments a threat to child development in various respects. The specific threats that are observed vary with time and place, depending on the perspective from which education in large cities is approached. I will analyse Amsterdam youth policy as an example and subsequently try to explain one of its main premises from broader social and cultural developments. To set the stage, I will first clarify the perspectives from which urban educational opportunities and limitations can be assessed, referring to the various meanings cities can have in society.

1. I thank Mirjam Zaat, Marian de Graaf and Jan Jongkind for helping me with illuminating discussions, illustrative examples and data.

In the case of Emile, Rousseau emphasised the aspects of culture and fine taste in urban life, he also thought that the temptations of the omnipresent stimulation of the senses would be a threat to Emile's autonomy of judgement. Other educationalists did, or do, consider the city a threat to moral development for quite different reasons. In the eyes of many 'Reformpädagogen' (the German and Dutch new education movement at the turn of the century), moral development requires a closely-knit community in which to grow up. They found this kind of community to be lacking in urban environments and many of them sought the solution to this problem in the establishment of educational communities in the countryside ('Landerziehungsheime'; see Mennicke 1937). The Dutch new educationalist Kees Boeke (1884-1966) thought likewise. Together with his wife Beatrice Cadbury he founded the Werkplaats Kindergemeenschap (Workshop Children's Community), where the present Dutch Queen Beatrix was one of the pupils during her elementary school years (see Kuipers 1992).

Others have stressed the bad influences of the spatial characteristics of cities. Of course, the amount of traffic is often mentioned in this context, and not only because it creates serious physical dangers. To educationalists, traffic density means serious limitations to explorative behaviour. Martinus Langeveld has written about this subject (Langeveld 1964:183 ff.) as, more recently, have Hans Bleeker and Karel Mulderij (1978). They emphasise the decreased opportunities for children to develop their imaginations in an urban environment. Mieke van der Spek and Rogier Noyon also note the limitations to children's freedom of action. In Amsterdam, children have to wait a year or two longer than children living in the countryside before they are allowed to go outside on their own (Van der Spek and Noyon 1993:67). Els Lodewijks-Frencken (1989) considers those limited opportunities following from the spatial characteristics of cities to be a sign of lack of concern for the welfare of children in our modern society.

In addition to the perspectives on cities as centres of high culture, as (faulty) moral communities, or as unities of spatial organisation and planning, cities can also be described as contexts for production, consumption and reproduction (see Saunders 1986). Though some educationalists stressed the educational relevance of the productive aspect of cities, these days a connection is mostly seen between educational disadvantage and the socio-economic position of workers in disadvantaged urban areas (Carta 1992:71-86). Furthermore, as we will see, there is a growing tendency to look at urban educational environments from a (sub)cultural point of view, rather than from an economic stance.

2. The Social Construction of Urban Meaning

I could go on describing examples of how characteristics of cities have been connected with child development. The examples mentioned show clearly enough, however, that it is not the urban environment itself but rather the perspective from which it is described, evaluated, and related to child development, that explains how educationalists assess cities as educational environments. Manuel Castells, an urban sociologist, extends this principle to the social process of meaning construction in society as a whole. He states, that the definition of urban meaning should be seen as the result of an 'endless historical struggle … by antagonist social actors who oppose their interests, values and projects.' (Castells 1983:335). Closely associated with this view is the notion that city ways of life should not necessarily be explained through the spatial characteristics of urban environments, but rather through the meaning they have to those concerned.[2] In this view, city ways of life should be seen as exponents of broader developments in society.[3]

The process of defining urban meaning reflects then, on the one hand, the processes which underlie major changes in society as a whole. For example, during the course of this century attention has been shifted from the city as a centre of production to the city as a centre of consumption. As an illustration, Castells (1983:27 ff.) describes the Glasgow Rent Strike of 1915, in which for the first time workers successfully defined and defended their interests in terms of consumption rather than in the context of production.

Though the 'social construction of urban meaning' (Savage and Warde 1993:129) can be seen as reflecting broader developments in society, it implies, on the other hand, that different groups can attach different meanings to urban environments. The Glasgow Rent Strike can serve as an example of this view as well. Every description of an urban educational environment can thus be seen as a product of a specific perspective on the position and opportunities of children in the city, which in its turn can be considered as both reflecting and shaping developments in society as a whole.

In examining the characteristics of Amsterdam youth policy, I will concentrate on some common aspects of the perspectives from which those descriptions arise. I will also try to connect those aspects with views

2. The spatial foundation of urban ways of life was a classic view in urban sociology, and first formulated by Louis Wirth in 1938; see Mike Savage and Alan Warde 1993.

3. Savage and Warde (1993:97) consider Georg Simmel to be the founding father of this view. Simmel did not, like Wirth, contrast the city with the countryside, but with earlier periods in the development of society.

on broader social developments on the one hand, and with the specific position of the development of children in this context on the other.

3. The Construction of the City in Amsterdam Youth Policy

Youth policy in Amsterdam is de-centralised to the level of area councils. The various reports and plans of the different councils do not, however, differ fundamentally, neither with respect to the kinds of problems they mention, nor with respect to the kinds of intervention they recommend. Above all, attention is focused on the risks of children and young people getting involved in criminality and drugs, as well as on the risks of educational disadvantage and unemployment.

The concern about criminality and drugs is not a response to increasing offence rates. Quite the opposite is the case. The occurrence of both youth violence and vandalism is showing a downward trend (Jansen and Faas 1995). While the identification of risk groups used to run along the lines of socio-economic positions, now distinctions are most often made between ethnic groups, despite the fact that this does not always seem the most illuminating perspective. The office for ethnic minority policy (Bureau voor strategisch minderhedenbeleid, BSM), for example, investigated the occurrence of criminal behaviour among youngsters of various minority groups. As for vandalism, theft and fare dodging, they found very few differences between Moroccan, Turkish, Dutch, Surinam/Antillean and other groups of youngsters. The Turkish group reported the fewest offences, whereas the Moroccan youngsters had fewer experiences with drugs (BSM 1993:22 ff.).

With respect to educational disadvantage, policy makers largely follow the same pattern. Though the socio-economic situation of the family, language and (sub)cultural barriers are often mentioned to explain underachievement and dropout in school education, causes are first sought in immigrant backgrounds. The comparatively low participation of children from ethnic minority groups in cultural and social activities (such as artistic and musical education) are proposed to explain the connection (DSV 1993). The office for ethnic minority policy (BSM) conducted further studies on Moroccan children. In primary education they were significantly behind, but between fourteen and sixteen years of age they appeared to have caught up with the Dutch group. The proportion of Moroccan children attending schools for special education is equal to that of the Dutch children, though their level of education is comparatively low and they leave school at an earlier age. There is no evidence whatsoever indicating that this situation relates to specific characteristics of Moroccans.

It is not only criminality and underachievement in school that are described along ethnic lines. The independence of children outdoors has also been investigated on this basis. Van der Spek and Noyon (1993:65 ff.) conclude that children from immigrant backgrounds play outside, visit friends and join clubs less often. They also make less use of bicycles as a means of transport than Dutch children [sic]. Within the broad spectrum of immigrant children, however, somewhat larger differences can be seen. Some children go out with hardly any restrictions, while others have to be escorted almost everywhere. Girls in particular experience more restrictions. Gender (perhaps in combination with religious backgrounds) seems to offer a better explanation for this than ethnic differences.

Despite the fact that many city councillors object to this kind of policy, intervention and prevention strategies are also often aimed at ethnically specific target groups (BSM 1993:28). For Moroccan boys, there is a special penitentiary with Moroccan staff (De Groot 1993:6). Frank Bovenkerk, a criminologist, has advocated a policy in which the Moroccan community would rehabilitate its own delinquent youngsters (Van der Meer 1993, 16). Many experiments, aimed at the improvement of educational opportunities by means of intervention in family contexts as well as in school contexts, make use of para-professionals from the specific ethnic group (BSM 1993).

This kind of approach might seem obvious. On the other hand, it becomes less so if we realise how small a proportion of the problems is explained by differences between the various ethnic groups, especially in the field of crime, and how poorly founded is the definition of 'ethnic minorities'. In Amsterdam, for someone to be classified as a member of an ethnic group, either the particular person or one of his/her parents has to be born in a foreign country. Furthermore, the categorisation of ethnic groups appears to be based beforehand on the expectation of the presence or absence of disadvantage and deprivation in that group. Children are divided into three categories: the Dutch, people from other rich countries who are not a target for special policies, and the ethnic groups which have the potential to show disadvantage (AC 1994:466).[4]

If differences in the incidence of problems cannot fully explain the strong tendency to perceive youth problems in terms of ethnicity, differences in cultural and family background might still justify an ethnic differentiation of intervention projects. In general terms this aspect is often mentioned, but I have found very few concrete underpinnings for this

4. According to this definition, 31 percent of the population of Amsterdam belongs to ethnic groups (AC 1993:10); ± 35 percent of the population between 15 and 21 years of age belongs to ethnic groups (BSM 1993:14); expectations are that in 2005 55 percent of the population will be non-Dutch (BSM 1993:5).

view. Sometimes a need for knowledge is explicitly formulated. For example, the office for ethnic minority policy (BSM) has argued in favour of a monitoring system to obtain more detailed knowledge of the way Moroccan children live their lives and of the effects of intervention projects aimed at this group (BSM 1993:34). Martin de Groot (1993:8) mentions some characteristic problems which could lead to delinquency among various groups of youngsters, but these are hardly sufficient to account for a different treatment of those groups. De Groot mentions Moroccan children growing up with very austere parents, Antillean children often growing up in incomplete families, and Turkish children who have the opportunity to participate in the organised criminality which appears to exist in the Turkish community.

This description of background problems – which in itself can hardly be called specific – does not even mention the problems that are supposed to cause delinquency among Dutch children. This strengthens the impression that a presupposed 'Dutch' culture could serve as a hidden standard. An implicit standardisation of Dutch culture also appears to be involved where educational underachievement is explained in terms of low cultural participation by ethnic groups and people at a minimum income level. This is the case in a major school intervention project, which tries to compensate for low participation by means of a so-called 'extended school day'. The extra hours in school will offer the opportunity for the children to participate in cultural and social activities in the neighbourhood via the school.

Summarising, it may be said that the Amsterdam youth policy was constructed from the perspective of the constitutive relevance of ethnic differences, together with a tendency to consider a presupposed 'Dutch' culture as a standard for a developmental context offering good prospects. It is not my intention to condemn this policy, or its founding perspectives, as wrong. However shaky the foundations of the policy, this does not prove it wrong or right. This short analysis only illuminates the premises on which it is based. As already stated, my aim is to understand those premises as expressions of broader social and cultural developments and subsequently confront them with some views of child development.

4. Globalising Tendencies and Tocal Identities

It is obvious that Amsterdam youth policy is founded on a consciousness of what is often called a 'multicultural society'. (Sub)cultural diversity, however, can hardly be considered a new phenomenon in the city of Amsterdam. Though the most flourishing period was in the seventeenth century, as a trading centre Amsterdam has always been confronted with a large numbers of foreigners.[5] I believe that the prominent position of ethnic differences in youth policy cannot be fully explained by the number of immigrant youngsters alone. A starting point could perhaps be found in a remark by Kreukels on the changing position of cities. He characterises the current situation in terms of contradictory developments. On the one hand, urban areas can be seen as communicative junctions in a world-wide network, whereas, on the other hand, as social junctions they seem to be characterised by growing disintegration (Kreukels 1993:14).

On closer inspection, many authors consider comparable contradictory developments to be a major characteristic of present (world) society. Castells (1989), also reflecting on the position of cities, considers these contradictions to be a reaction to the loss of the significance of place as a result of economic developments. Whereas economically based power structures tend to develop on a global level, Castells sees a tendency of societies 'to fragment themselves into tribes, easily prone to a fundamentalist affirmation of their identity' (Castells 1989:350). Globalisation and tribalisation are two sides of the same coin. At the cultural level, local communities tend to preserve their identities, regardless of their dependence on world-wide economics and power flows (Ibid.).

A comparable opposition can be found in Giddens' (1994) description of major developments in present society. He too emphasises the simultaneous occurrence of globalising tendencies and tendencies to stress local identities. In his view, the process of globalisation is even wider in scope than the concentration of economic power on a world scale alone. A complex of developments, including economic structures, mobility and media, brings about a situation in which one can no longer isolate or dissociate oneself from an emerging global cosmopolitan order. In this sense, according to Giddens, the meaning of place disappears, for in this situation cultural diversity no longer has a direct connection to geographic segregation (Giddens 1994:84). Like Castells, Giddens observes a new longing for diversity, lost traditions, and local identities as a result of this globalisation. Under the present circumstances, however, local identities cannot be restored just like that. As almost no-one can escape from the process of globalisation, even the preservation of traditions requires a more or less conscious decision. A form of reflexivity becomes indispensable in society, which was previously unknown. We can no longer simply keep our habits and traditions, we have to make a choice and decide about anything we do. This does not mean, that all traditions disappear. Rather the status of traditions is changing. They are no longer self-evident truths; nowadays traditions must constantly declare themselves.

5. In the seventeenth century, over 50 percent of the population of Amsterdam was of foreign origin (see Van Deursen 1991:44).

In Giddens's view, then, the required reflexivity is at the core of the process; that is why he speaks of 'reflexive modernisation', in contrast to 'simple modernisation', and of 'post-traditional' in contrast to 'traditional' societies (Giddens 1994:78 ff.). Simple modernisation can be understood as the complex reactions in society to the development of industrial order. Though this process brought much uncertainty, the process itself was assumed to have a clear and predictable direction in which authority could be ascribed to science and technological advances. The slogan 'more knowledge, more control', however, no longer appears to apply (Giddens 1994:4). According to Giddens, we find ourselves robbed of the very concept of unquestioned certainty. The globalisation of this period of reflexive modernisation does not alter this by inducing integration. On the contrary, integration seems rather to be undermined by it (Kreukels 1993). Perhaps this can explain, as Giddens suggests, why traditions and local identities are sometimes defended so rigorously these days. In such cases, the defence is often not built on arguments – as reflexive modernisation would require – but on a simple (traditional) assertion of ritual truth. Giddens calls this kind of defence of traditions 'fundamentalism' (1994:85) which, in his opinion, can refer to every aspect of a culture.

It is clear that the contrasting globalising and 'tribalising' (Castells) tendencies, which are at the basis of reflexive modernity, have put their stamp on urban areas. Urban areas are seen as the first areas to reflect the processes which are supposed to prepare tomorrow's society as a whole. This fits the picture of today's Amsterdam youth policy very well. The great importance attached by policy makers to (sub)cultural and ethnic differences is one side of the picture, of which the uncertain and questioned, but still visible tendency to view Dutch customs and traditions as a standard forms the other.

Current youth policy can be understood as an expression of major developments in present society. A question still remains, how we can describe the development of children in the context of these contradictory developments in order to get some idea of their educational problems and opportunities? For an answer to this question, I would like to refer to the way Adalbert Rang (1989) analysed the reactions of educationalists to the changes in society at the turn of this century.

5. Double Strategies in Educational Reactions to a Changing Society

At the turn of this century Western societies were also engaged in a process of radical change. The educational question at that time seemed to be: how could children be brought up in a culture where confusing multiplicity seemed to end in formlessness and non-commitment? (Rang 1989:122) The phenomenon of diversity seemed also to be an issue. As is also the case today, this emphasis on plurality can probably best be understood as an expression of traditional structuring principles becoming out of date. Educational views at that time also seemed to simultaneously recognise and deny the changes taking place in society. In this context Rang observes a 'double strategy' (1989:122) in educational reflection in those days. Whereas on the one hand the uniqueness of the developing subject was stressed, on the other hand the concept of 'Gemeinschaft' served as an homogeneous counterpart to the observed vague and plural culture.

In a similar way, recognition and respect for the plurality of (sub)cultural identities is stressed nowadays, while at the same time it is proving difficult to leave behind the idea of the universal validity of Western culture. This ambivalence or equivocality is not restricted to educational contexts. Perhaps, then, we cannot expect an easy and univocal solution to the educational problems in the cities of today. A closer analysis of some presuppositions of the discussed strategies, however, could give us a clue.

While the diversity of (sub)cultural positions seems to be at the core of educational policy today, the consequences of the fact that cultural diversity no longer directly refers to geographic segregation (Giddens 1994:84) seem less often recognised. In some respects, (sub)cultural communities are still seen as relatively closed and fully encompassing individual lives. This contradicts Giddens' observation that nobody can escape from globalising processes. In particular, children in urban areas no longer live in culturally homogeneous environments, and that applies equally to all categories of the population. Even if their peer groups outside the family are still ethnically homogeneous, children are confronted with many heterogeneous contexts: in school, in medical and legal contexts, in shops, in the streets and so on. Children live their lives in complex and varying participation contexts. This would appear to account for their development and opportunities, rather than their ethnic backgrounds alone (Alba 1988). Multiple participations and 'fractional relations' (Gergen 1991) break the ethnic homogeneity of children's environments. In addition, each of those participation contexts is partly shaped by reflexive modernisation, in that the retention, rejection or recreation of customs and habits have become a matter of choice and decision for all of us.

This enforced reflexivity seems problematic to educators. Sometimes they seem to project the perceived lack of naturalness onto their evaluation of the position of (urban) youth in society. Despite decreasing offence rates, for example, youngsters are often described as morally rudderless (Boutelier 1993:217). This position seems to reflect the problems of the educators themselves, who perceive moral indeterminacy in society at large, rather than those of the children.

Apart from the (ambivalent) way cultural plurality is dealt with, educationalists' reactions to the present situation also resemble those of educators at the turn of the century in a second respect. Rang's (1989:104-135) analysis of the German new education movement at the turn of the century, which can also apply to the Dutch movement, leads to another perspective from which the central concepts of this movement ('subject' and 'Gemeinschaft') can be seen as a reaction to developments in society. According to Rang, the specific combination of concepts they used seems to reflect precisely the kind of flexible and adaptable people who were useful in a technologically and industrially developing society. Lacking every sociological and political analysis, their concept of education turned out to be a concept of adjustment. Rang is not surprised, then, that certain versions of this new education movement could easily be adapted to dangerous developments in pre-war German and Dutch societies.

Rang's analytical observation presents us with a similar question today. We must ask ourselves what could possibly be the effects of the 'double strategy' in our present views on and approaches to urban education. In particular, we must ask ourselves, whether and in which respects our educational practices and beliefs reflect or even confirm and reinforce the 'fundamentalist' (in Giddens' sense) tendencies which are now part of our world. Ethnic definitions of educational problems could be part of such a reflection of social tendencies.

6. Indeterminacy, Reflexivity and Education

At this point, the question remains whether, and how, the indeterminacy in present society constitutes a real threat to child development and education. Does the 'saturated self', which according to Gergen (1991) results from the many diverging options we are continually facing, offer good prospects for developing children? In dealing with this question, I will restrict myself to the example of moral education and development.

It will not come as a surprise that many educators object to the view that young children should be confronted with the full complexity of society. Michael Winkler (1994) thinks it impossible for children to develop a sound sense of subjectivity in a society composed of functionally fragmented participation contexts and a plurality of norms and values. Referring to the new education movement, he argues once again in favour of an 'educational province' ('pädagogische Provinz') where children can learn to handle rules. In Winkler's view children need the certainties and boundaries of an educational community to learn how to act socially and morally and to develop subjectivity. Others hold a similar opinion. Andreas Flitner, for example, thinks that a certain amount of 'regression' must be part of education if we do not want to overburden children (Flitner 1992:234).

So, uncertainty and the absence of fixed rules still seem to be incompatible with educating young children. However, there are also other voices. Lynda Stone even calls out for the introduction of dissonance in education. By 'dissonance' she means the recognition of the diversity of opinions and a procedure of exchange and communication which does not aim at one true answer – a procedure which has to be distinguished from tolerating each and every opinion (Stone 1994:60). Stone considers our present dominating yearning for consonance as a sign of nostalgia for bygone times. The question is, however, whether moral judgement does not require the ability to handle rules and principles, even if we want people to make autonomous moral decisions and choices. In that case, Stone should postpone her wish for dissonance. Are we not forced to assume a standard, be it derived from Dutch culture or from any other one?

Though influential theories of moral judgement and development (e.g., that of Kohlberg) lean heavily on the concept of principle-based decisions, this view is also open to question (Gergen 1991; Bauman 1993; Lash 1994; Giddens 1994). Gergen looks at the instability and uncertainty of today as a transitory phase in a process in which we will learn to deal with a morality of discourse instead of a morality of principles (Gergen 1991:252). Such a morality does not ask for universal (moral) truth. Giddens even considers the present principle-based moralities a danger, especially to the required reflexive cosmopolitanism. In his opinion, such moralities can only lead to 'a world of multiple fundamentalisms' (Giddens 1994:252). Like Gergen, Giddens opts for a discursive engagement. If ever we want to formulate a universal principle, in this view, it can only refer to the dynamics of discourse and discursive justification (1994:253). Or, as Gergen puts it, a relational morality will emerge, in which moral decisions are not considered as derivatives of principles, but as the results of interactions (Gergen 1991:256). Gergen also holds the opinion that principles will not solve the problems in this field (1991:252) and he too observes a development in which emphasis shifts from principles to socially embedded discourse (1991:250).

To the question whether it can be considered wise to expose children to these complex ethical discourses, an answer can be formulated in association with Jürgen Oelkers (1994). In his opinion, education should be *defined* as a process of moral communication, as 'processes of negotiating (...) which deal with "morality", i.e., with normative demarcations within the framework of social groups'. (Oelkers 1994:103). In this view, moral education does not refer to the development of ever-higher predefined levels of morality in children, but rather to the acquisition of the conditions of participation in moral communication. Oelkers continues: 'All moral terms (...) are always questionable entities and can never be internalised as stable qualities of the good.' If we apply this to the problems of city education, for which cultural fragmentation seems so characteristic, there seems to be no need, then, to create homogeneity, neither by supposed homogeneous ethnic categories, nor by assuming the universal validity of one (hidden) standard. From this view, we could perhaps better adjust our educational thoughts and practices to the dynamics of heterogenous discourse.

From such a dynamic and socially embedded perspective on education, Rousseau should have sent Emile to Paris right from the beginning, just to prevent him from developing an autonomous morality of principles and from putting himself outside of moral discourse.

References

Amsterdam in Cijfers (AC), (1994). Amsterdams Bureau voor Onderzoek en Statistiek.

Alba, R.D. (1988). 'Cohorts and the Dynamics of Ethnic Change'. In M. White Riley (ed.), *Social Structures and Human Lives*. London.

Bauman, Z. (1993). *Postmodern Ethics*. Oxford.

Bleeker, H. and K. Mulderij (1978). *Kinderen buiten spel. Op zoek naar een vriendelijke woonomgeving voor kinderen*. Meppel.

Boutelier, H. (1993). *Solidariteit en slachtofferschap. De morele betekenis van criminaliteit in een postmoderne cultuur*. Nijmegen.

Bureau voor Strategisch Minderhedenbeleid Gemeente Amsterdam, (BSM) (1993). *Hoe stevig is de handgreep nog? Plan van aanpak voor de problematiek van Marokkaanse jongeren in Amsterdam*. Amsterdam.

Burgers, J.P.L. (1990). 'De stad van de jaren negentig: postmoderne nederzetting?' *Sociologische Gids*, no. 37.

Carta, J.J. (1992). 'Education for Young Children in Inner-City Classrooms'. In T. Thompson and S.C. Hupp (eds), *Saving Children at Risk*, London.

Castells, M. (1983). *The City and the Grassroots*. London.
Castells, M. (1989). *The Informational City. Information Technology, Economic Restructuring, and the Urban-Regional Process*. Oxford.
Deursen, A.T.H. van (1991). *Mensen van klein vermogen. Het 'kopergeld' van de Gouden Eeuw*. Amsterdam.
DSV (1993). 'Concept Discussiestuk Sociale Vernieuwing – Onderwijs'. Slotervaart/ Overtoomseveld
Flitner, A. (1992). *Reform der Erziehung. Impulse des 20. Jahrhunderts*. München: Piper.
Frampton, K. (1993). 'Toward a Critical Regionalism: Six points for an a-rchitecture of resistance'. In T. Docherty (ed.), *Postmodernism. A Reader*. New York.
Gergen, K.J. (1991). *The Saturated Self. Dilemmas of Identity in Contemporary Life*. New York.
Giddens, A. (1994). *Beyond Left and Right. The Future of Radical Politics*. Cambridge.
Groot, de, M. (1993). 'Amal leert Marokkaanse jongens Nederlandse mores'. In *Kans of straf; dadergerichte criminaliteitspreventie*. Amsterdam.
Jansen, K. and A. Faas (1995). 'Jong zijn gaat vanzelf over'. *SEC, tijdschrift over samenleving en criminaliteitspreventie*, 1.
Jencks, C. (1993). 'The Emergent Rules'. In T. Docherty (ed.), *Postmodernism. A Reader*. New York.
Kreukels, A. (1993). 'Stedelijk Nederland: de actuele positie vanuit sociaal-wetenschappelijk gezichtspunt'. In J. Burgers, A. Kreukels and M. Mentzel (eds), *Stedelijk Nederland in de jaren negentig*. Utrecht.
Kuipers, H.J. (1992). *De wereld als werkplaats. Over de vorming van Kees Boeke en Beatrice Cadbury*. Amsterdam.
Langeveld, M.J. (1964). *Studien zur Anthropologie des Kindes*. Tübingen.
Lash, S. (1994). 'Reflexivity and its Doubles: Structures Aesthetics, Community'. In U. Beck, A. Giddens and S. Lash, *Reflexive Modernization. Politics, Tradition and Aesthetics in the Modern Social Order*. Cambridge.
Lodewijks-Frencken, E. (1989). *Op opvoeding aangewezen. Een kritiek op de wijze van omgaan met kinderen in onze cultuur*. Baarn.
Meer, F. van der (1993). 'Laat de Marokkanen hun kinderen zelf helpen'. In *Kans of straf; dadergerichte criminaliteitspreventie*. Amsterdam.
Mennicke, C.A. (1937). *Hervorming van opvoeding en onderwijs*. Rotterdam.
Oelkers, J. (1993/94). 'Influence and Development: Two Basic Paradigms of Education'. *Studies in Philosophy and Education*, 13.
Rang, A. (1989). 'Zum Bildungskonzept der Reformpädagogik'. In O. Hansmann and W. Marotzki (eds), *Diskurs Bildungstheorie II: Problemgeschichtliche Orientierungen*. Weinheim.
Richard, N. (1993). 'Postmodernism and Periphery'. In T. Docherty (ed.), *Postmodernism. A Reader*. New York..
Rousseau, J.J. (1762). *Émile. Oeuvres complètes IV*. Édition publiée sous la direction de Bernard Gagnebin et Marcel Raymond. Paris 1969.
Saunders, P. (1986). *Social Theory and the Urban Question*. London.

Savage, M. and A. Warde. (1993). *Urban Sociology, Capitalism and Modernity*. London.

Spek, van der, M. and R. Noyon. (1993). *Uitgeknikkerd, opgehoepeld. Een onderzoek naar de bewegingsvrijheid van kinderen op straat*. Amsterdam.

Stone, L. (1994). 'Modern to Postmodern: Social Construction, Dissonanca, and Education'. *Studies in Philosophy and Education*, 13.

Winkler, M. (1994). 'Vom Verschwinden in der Vielfalt. Eine Skizze über Pluralität als Bedingung für Realität und Auflösung der Sozialpädagogik'. In F. Heyting and H.-E. Tenorth (eds), *Pädagogik und Pluralismus*. Weinheim

Chapter 4

THE CURRENT 'AESTHETICS' DISCOURSE AND EDUCATIONAL SCIENCE

Yvonne Ehrenspeck

1. The Promises of Aesthetics

In recent discussions of the criticism and self-criticism of modernism in the discourse of so-called post-modernism, one concept that stands equally for the dilemma and for the possible opportunities of the current and interdisciplinary formation of theories in the fields of philosophy and the social sciences[1] has again come to the fore: aesthetics.[2]

In many cases 'aesthetics' stands for the hoped-for possibility of breaking open 'hardened' rationality patterns of individual perception and social communication, as well as for the admission of the physical and affective parts of experience repressed by 'instrumental reason'. 'Aesthetic thinking' or aesthetic experience is said to sensitise and differentiate the individual not only for his/her own, mostly suppressed, wishes and needs but also for those of other people or for the artefacts of culture and, last but not least, for an unabbreviated 'holistic' experience of nature. Sensu-

1. In the following the current reception of aesthetics in pedagogics/educational science is in the foreground. For the use of concepts see note 3.

2. Great expectations have always been associated with the 'aesthetic' dimension. In his *Letters on the Aesthetic Education of Mankind*, Schiller expected aesthetic education to provide total salvation, and German Idealism constructed, in the dimension of aesthetics, the lost unity of experience. This construction has continued to exert its influence right up until the present day.

ality is listed under this rubric alongside feeling, perception, art, creativity, fiction, creation and lifestyle. Aesthetic thinking is reported to be equally qualified for political, ethical and ecological requirements. More sensuality, more art, more aesthetic experience, more perception – this is what is called for. The sociologist Ulrich Beck, for instance, places his hopes in this context on the possibility of culturally re-establishing the lost capacity for perceiving dangers and risks in order to gain the competence of one's own judgement (Beck 1988:293). The philosopher Wolfgang Welsch is certain that aesthetic thought is at present the only realistic type of thinking, as conceptual thought is no longer sufficient for the present-day problems of a pluralistic society with its claims to individualisation and with the fictionalisation of the world, via the much-quoted power of the media: diagnostics and orientation, it is said, can only be expected from art and 'aesthetic thought'. This type of thinking is said to be chiefly perceivable and associated with perception. Perception is said to make one sensitive to differences; thus this function of feeling, noticing and perceiving is of particular importance for the political culture of plurality (Welsch 1990).

The educationalist Horst Rumpf, on the other hand, suggests adding to these considerations a concept of holistic learning in which the previously repressed sensual-emotional coenaesthetic potentials would once more be given greater consideration ahead of the diacritical, analytical, linguistic and cognitive potentials (1987).

2. Functions of the Promises

This list could be extended almost ad infinitum since the concept of 'aesthetics' or 'aesthetic thinking' is also used in pedagogics/educational science[3] as a collective concept for differing thematic fields, expectations and promises. Even the list of fields and problems subsumed under this category makes it clear that aesthetics is not so much to be given an analytical or systematic value but, rather, that at first glance this is once again one of those adaptations of theories and concepts which Ewald Terhart once appositely described, in the case of educational science, as a cycle of expression in linguistic terms, promises, disappointments and new promises.[4]

3. The concepts 'pedagogics' and 'educational science' may be used as synonyms in this context as the position of these two concepts with regard to 'aesthetics' as an object do not differ systematically.

4. Terhart, (1992) 'The process of the rapid adaptation of the latest fashions in theory from the fields of philosophy, the social sciences, psychology etc., always follows a similar pattern. Every new change begins with new expressions in linguistic form which, at the same

There is no doubt that new semantics such as aesthetics are eminently suited to stabilise or even promote the production of theories and discourse within the relevant specialised field. But analysis of the function of such semantic shifts says little about the extent of the adapted questions in the case of an (apparently) successful correlation with questions of educational science, pedagogics or the theory of education. So when questions are asked about the systematic meaning of the discourse on 'aesthetics' in educational science, it is advisable to check whether these concepts can be of significance for the further development of particular means of educational-science theory.

So, apart from the 'indeterminacy principle' of the concepts as a prerequisite for their ability to trigger discursive turbulence and to be attachable to the most varied discourses, one may, in the case of aesthetics, follow the call of W. Welsch (1990) that an adequate thematicisation of the aesthetic today has a long way to go, as the aesthetic no longer primarily or exclusively has its home in art but will increasingly extend beyond the bounds of art. Such an extension of the thematicisation of the aesthetic can also be observed in pedagogics/educational science. This concept thus no longer refers exclusively to education in the fine arts or to the question of the importance of the aesthetic experience for the educational process or 'subjectivisation'.

In order to get a better view of this thematic extension, a systematisation by categories of the most important received threads of discourse regarding with aesthetics in educational science over the past fifteen years is suggested in the following, once the logical procedure of the argumentation has been presented.

3. Conceptual Systematisation of the Discourse Field of 'Aesthetics'

The evaluation of 'aesthetics' is extremely closely linked with the conceptual texture of 'reason', 'the senses/sensual/sensuality', 'perception' and 'recognition'. If the discourse on recognition and reason changes, the evaluations of aesthetics or of the semantic field attached to it will always behave in relation to these changes, and vice versa. This relationality is by no means in contradiction to the 'inherent logic' of the

---

time, contain new promises. In the course of the realisation process these promises are then partially disappointed or relativised, quite automatically awakening the desire for new promises. The result is the extension at the theoretical level of a basically optimistic attitude, a trust in the constantly offered opportunity to begin again that is characteristic and indeed clearly essential for successful pedagogical activity in educational practice.'

aesthetic, but is a historical product of modernism only when the above-mentioned sectors are differentiated from one another. Against this background the evaluation over the past fifteen years of the concepts 'aisthesis' or 'perception' also becomes easier to understand. Their relational character implies that they only open up to theoretical reconstruction when accessed in a way that is both systematic and in keeping with the history of concepts.[5] In view of the conglomerate of meanings borne by the concept 'aesthetics', it is indispensable, from the viewpoint of an analysis of the 'aesthetics' discourse and its reception in the field of educational science, to introduce structuring categories and questions which will bundle the most important aspects of discussions on 'aesthetics' and give access to an 'ideally typical' categorisation.[6]

For analysis purposes the aesthetics discourse can be divided up into the four aspects of the problem: aisthesis (3.1), the aesthetic experience with works of art or with the artistically and naturally beautiful and the sublime (3.2), representation, or 'aesthetics' as a quality of representation (3.3) and the connection between aesthetics and ethics/normativity (3.4)[7] These aspects of the problem are illustrated in the following with the help of selected examples of theory.

3.1. Aisthesis

The present meaning of the concept of aisthesis or perception stems from efforts, resulting from the criticism of 'instrumental reason' and scientific

5. The importance of the history of the concepts 'aisthesis' and 'aesthetics' for the allocation of the present revaluation of the concepts 'aisthesis' in philosophy and the social sciences, particularly educational science, has already been pointed out elsewhere. Ehrenspeck 1996:210-231.

6. The usefulness of these categories can also only be examined via a situation of the aesthetics discourse that is systematic and based on the history of concepts. Such examination can, however, only be carried out in a broader analysis of the material.

7. Related topics and questions such as the relationship between art and life, lifestyle, or the media will be excluded here, as they either involve discourses at present adapted from anthropology or sociology (lifestyle analyses) or, as in the case of the media and associated questions such as simulation etc., discourse fields which could equally only be processed in separate analyses. The same applies to the recently revived discussion of the concept of mimesis. These are, rather, anthropological and literary-science questions which could only be associated with aesthetics via the concepts of aisthesis or representation. A survey of the concept of mimesis, however, has already been produced by G. Gebauer and C. Wulf 1992. See especially for educational science Schuhmacher-Chilla 1995:146-155. A further aspect excluded here are the education-sociological considerations on the changes of 'post-modernist modernism' and its culture, which are communicated in pedagogics via the categories 'taste', 'culture' or buzz-words such as 'aestheticisation of life-world'. See, in this context, Liebau 1992. The pre- and post-Kantian version of the category of 'taste' might, admittedly, be added as a fifth problematic aspect of analysing the discourse field 'aesthetics'.

rationality, to extend the traditional concept of reason into various rationalities or, by demonstrating its historicity and the fact that it is tied into physical or practical executions. Against this backdrop it is clear why the media of experience or, respectively, of reason, such as perception, body and language move to the forefront. The dualistic idea of sensuality and reason is circumvented, and the 'body' is attributed its own rationality and sense presentation. This simultaneously re-interprets the concept of recognition and revalues the sphere of pre-scientific experience in which the as-yet depotentised aspects of reason have their roots. In particular it is philosophical anthropology (H. Plessner) – which has been increasingly received[8] by educational science over the past few years – and the body-phenomenological revision of Husserl's theory of consciousness (M. Merleau-Ponty) that are working on a rehabilitation of forgotten foundations of the senses. If Husserl's great contribution was to recognise the tension between concrete perception and formal science and also recognise the dependence of recognition on a life-worldly, pre-conceptual doxa, and if this polarisation of science and life-world meant a further step in the recognition of the 'logos of the aesthetic world' (Husserl), then this revaluation of the aisthetic was still slowed down by the construction principles of a transcendental philosophy of consciousness, which did not really overcome the aporetic structure of the subject in the field of tension between the transcendental and the empirical. Only Merleau-Ponty's body-phenomenological revision of Husserl's theory of consciousness shows how consciousness is based on anonymous, pre-personal and pre-predicative executions of perception. Against the formalisations of clearly distinguishable dimensions of the validity of reason, Merleau-Ponty sets physically founded activities of the senses. By returning the transcendental subject to an existing, incarnate subject, Merleau-Ponty, by analogy with Heidegger's construction of 'being-in-the-world', votes for a philosophy of 'facticity' or of 'existence'. So the aisthesis model stands for an existentially charged, concrete concept of experience embedded in practical executions.

'Experience', 'being-in-the-world' and 'existence' represent, in this context, the counter-model to scientific attempts at operationalisations of what is experienced or of transcendental constructions of the preconditions for recognition. As these models cannot be demonstrated in concrete experience, they are, for Merleau-Ponty, rather 'rationalisations of the life-world'(Waldenfels 1985:94-120) as an adequate possibility for presenting concrete executions of experience (Merleau-Ponty 1966).

8. This reception was not, however, accompanied by any broad results. Only over the past few years have these theories once more been the focus of interest.

Immediately, in the metaphoric and semantic senses, analogous descriptions and differentiations as they have been and still are proposed in connection with the debate on 'explaining and understanding' suggest themselves. This debate is one important thread of the discourse that has contributed to today's criticism of scientism and in consequence of which the concept of the aesthetic and aisthesis have been revalued or gained prominence respectively. The emphatic revaluation of perception as a foundation-laying experience and the precedence of understanding before explaining is, however, merely one result of the interest in aisthesis. 'Aisthesis' is also an important theme in the educational-science discourses oriented towards anthropology, experimental scientific research, or the 'biology of the mind' (Miller-Kipp 1992). In the meantime interfaces have also been formed between phenomenological, anthropological and human-science research,[9] and here, too, Merleau-Ponty's deliberations provide a good example. This is because for him, too, the aisthetic is not obtained just on the basis of phenomenological description or processes involving understanding, but also by reflecting on scientific research. Merleau-Ponty was by no means hostile to science. His investigations into the 'phenomenology of perception' (1966) are to a great extent based on human-science research from the fields of medicine, experimental psychology and physics. Research into aphasia and investigations of those so afflicted are one such link in which (natural) scientific reference is made to the 'body-boundness' of cognitive processes. The reference to the indistinguishable connection between feeling, thinking and perceiving is also more than just a discussion of interest to phenomenology. These questions are directly linked to Anglo-Saxon and American discussions of the 'mind and body problem' oriented towards the (natural) sciences or turned towards linguistic analysis. The colloquial expressions for faculties of the mind are broad abstractions, while 'real' mental phenomena are always mixtures, so that both pure thought and pure feeling, for example, must be regarded as fictions and, indeed, constructions devoid of experience. For this reason Merleau-Ponty translates these scientific findings into the language of philosophy, for his wish is to confront the phenomena which science unearths with the philosophical preconditions of this science, and to illustrate the contradictions which emerge between theory and experience. A good example of this procedure is his discussion of the development psychology of J. Piaget (Merleau-Ponty 1994). Here, however, the limitations of phenomenological research into aisthesis also become apparent, for even if one concedes that the separation of explanation and understanding, for instance, never exists in its

9. See the volume of *Bildung und Erziehung* devoted to this topic, Vol. 4, 1994.

purest form in Merleau-Ponty's theories, it must be noted that although existence is opposed to epistemology, the primate of the interpretation of 'being-in-the-world' is attributed to the representation of concrete executions of experience. This interpretation, influenced by phenomenology, is still, however, far more widespread in educational science than is anthropological, scientific, ethological or neurobiological (basic) research, which has only been increasingly received in recent times.[10] To sum up, the concept of aisthesis in the educational science/pedagogics discourse is thus still, in general, an emphatic concept of experience.

3.2 Aesthetic experience with works of art or with the artificially and naturally beautiful and the sublime

While reflection on aisthesis can boast of a long discourse history going back to ancient philosophy, of which in this context, however, only the discourse since Husserl's 'phenomenological investigations' is pertinent, reflection on the autonomous status of art and on genuine 'aesthetic judgement' is well known to have started only with the reception of Kant's 'Critique of Judgement' and is therefore a phenomenon of modern times (Recki 1988:79ff.). The specific form of 'aesthetic judgement' is produced by turning away from the metaphysical idea of beauty and the transcendental turning point which provides for a separation of empirical psychology, anthropology, transcendental philosophy, epistemology and critique of taste. In his transcendental critique of taste Kant distinguishes between taste, of the senses and reflective taste and thus between sensuality and aesthetics.[11] In the judgement of taste or the judgement of the aesthetically reflecting power of judgement, the judgement of taste refers the representation of an object to the subject and his/her feeling of desire or lack of enthusiasm. It is thus not generally conceptual but subjectively aesthetic and only sensual to the extent sensual as understood by Kant. The particular, subjectively aesthetic feature of these judgements is, however, related to the general in its reflective reference to the *sensus communis*. This reflective relationship is, according to Kant, the foundation of the relationship between aesthetics and ethics – a further connection to ethics which has provoked great interest in present-day discourse can be established via the definitions of the sublime in the 'Critique of Judgement'.[12] Fundamentally, however, it is exclusively the reflective

10. See Beck (1994:227-269) on the problem field 'body -and-mind' and his warning to educational science not to miss the connection to recent fundamental research.

11. For the original semantic distinction between sensuality and aesthetics in Kant 1989:9.

12. See also the reception of Kant in the collection edited by Christine Pries 1989.

judgement – and not, as in the latest discussions, the immediately sensual or perception[13] – which permits the (formal) analogy of aesthetic and ethical reflection judgements. In Kant's writings, the aesthetic is revalued via the aesthetic judgement, but not the aisthetic. Reflections on adding an aesthetic dimension to the concept of reason are undertaken there exclusively on the foil of the transcendental-empirical question of the transition from 'mere nature' into 'freedom'. The same applies in connection with Schiller's concept of 'play'. Both Kant's and Schiller's dualism of sensuality and reason is thus reproduced on another plane. While Kant and Schiller still relate aesthetic judgement to experience with nature and art, the concept of 'aesthetic experience' in movements following on from German Idealism and above all in H.-G. Gadamer's philosophical hermeneutics, is reserved for existential experience with works of art.[14] Gadamer's argumentation is a prominent example of the typical connection of academic criticism, criticism of positivism, hermeneutic philosophy and aesthetic theory on the basis of an emphatic and existentially charged concept of experience.

The debate over 'explaining and understanding' is sharpened in a new way in Gadamer's 'truth and method'. While 'truth and method' is understood as the justification of philosophical hermeneutics, the 'detour' by way of the experience of truth in the aesthetic experience of works of art is, argumentatively, more than just a 'detour'. It has 'method': in his criticism of Kant's model of aesthetic judgement, which as we know has no function of recognition but remains solely within the subject's horizon of feelings, Gadamer shows, by analogy to W. Dilthey's distinction between the natural sciences and the humanities, that aesthetic judgement is an access to knowledge at least equal in value to, if not more privileged than scientific and conceptually theoretical knowledge. Gadamer thus expands Kant's restricted concept of knowledge and experience. The work of art is a medium of experience and knowledge because it offers a truth-happening *sui generis*.

Gadamer refers in this context to Hegel's attribution of art to truth happenings. In Schiller and Kant only philosophical cognition – oriented towards the natural sciences – and logic were concerned with truth, while aesthetics belongs in the field of the beautiful, from which no truth can be gained. Beauty merely contributes – and herein lies its educational

13. In most considerations of the relationship between aesthetics and ethics this differentiation is either overlooked or rejected as a 'restriction' of the sensual by reflection. See, for instance, Welsch 1993:40ff.

14. Gadamer's concept of experience and his hermeneutic presentation of the meaning of aesthetic experience with works of art had a great influence on both the national and the international reception. Mention need only be made of H.R. Jauss and Richard Rorty.

function – towards cultivating the freedom of the mind. As the path to cognition is blocked, aesthetics is restricted to the creation of an area reserved for it alone. The work of art became a specifically aesthetic product, and the experience of art became an aesthetic experience. Thus aesthetic consciousness belongs to the world of appearances – a popular topos even today, used by preference in rationalistic theories frequently employed to point out the superfluousness of such products resulting from the fact that they are not part of reality.

According to Gadamer (1986), this understanding of art is based on the performance of a process of abstraction which he calls 'aesthetic distinction'. In this abstraction, consciousness is directed towards the purely aesthetic experience of the work of art, and it does not consider the extra-aesthetic moments. Gadamer, on the other hand, attributes to the work of art not only esoteric but also exoteric significance. Freely interpreting Hegel, Gadamer considers art to be a mirror of historical truth because historical truth mirrors the history of worldviews. This wins back for art its function in the formation of the 'spirit'. This factor is thus extremely topical from the perspective of educational theory. One further important topos is integration, i.e., the integration of all experience in the self-understanding of the consciousness experience. Here, too, an existential concept of experience once again applies. The relationship between the understanding of being and existence is related, just as Heidegger would have wished, to the fact that all experience of the individual as a finite and historical being turns into self-recognition. The experience of works of art thus becomes, at the same time, an 'educational happening' and an approach to the world of the same status as all other modes of access. Art is thus a sensuous experience as understood by the opening up of a sense that is in each case related to the existential experience of the individual. Under a different sign to that of Gadamer, T.W. Adorno, in his 'Aesthetic Theory', emphasises the autonomy of art in its negative relationship to society. Here the aesthetic owes its power and importance precisely to the independence of the aesthetic in contrast to the social world. A prominent place is also once again reserved for the naturally beautiful, albeit as a metaphor for the 'non-identity' of the final unavailability of the repressed factors of internal and external nature. In the dialectic philosophy of the late 'critical theory', aesthetic experience becomes the representative of truth – the state of a nature reconciled with the adjustments of 'instrumental, identifying' reason.

Thus aesthetic experience is seen as the only form of unpretentious experience. In the latest contributions, this determination of aesthetic experience with works of art as a privileged form of access to the world still shines through, whether in the works of W. Welsch, where it is stylised as a practice model for difference, plurality and individuality, or in those of that representative of the American Gadamer reception Richard Rorty, where it is attributed the sensitising function for cruelty and violence (1991). These deliberations have been pursued with interest, particularly in pedagogics/educational science, for example under the rubric of the question of the 'educative effect of works of art' (Mollenhauer 1990:481-491, 1988:443-461, 1992:17-37) or the possibility of the self-limitation of autopoietic educational processes via sensitisation through works of art (see Lenzen 1994:17-30, Hellekamps 1994:109-125). The connection between sensitisation and self-limitation is, by the way, a further reference to the (possible) connection between aesthetics and ethics.

3.3 Representation: aesthetics as quality of representation

The question concerning the problem of representation has a long tradition. It has its roots in the rhetoric and poetics of the Ancients, and ranges from considerations such as that of the representation of pure concepts of reason or of aesthetic ideas (the problem of the 'indemonstrable' and 'inexponible' in Kant's 'Critique of Pure Reason')[15] to the more recent considerations of Lyotard on the impossibility of representing the sublime (Lyotard 1989:319-348, Nibbrig 1994). Over the past few years the question of the share of the performative, the rhetorical or the creative in the construction of epistemological facts has come more frequently to the fore even with relation to science. Thus, in connection with the revaluation of the concept of experience by comparison with scientific forms of rationality, the classical problem of explaining and understanding, or of the relationship between natural sciences and the humanities has also undergone a shift. This new orientation has brought art and science closer together.

In the classic distinction between explanation and understanding, the former was concerned with the search for laws, the generation of hypotheses, explanations of causes and effects, etc., while the latter was involved with singularities, individualities and occurrences. In present-day discussions, these hair-line divisions are considered out of date. In this context mention need only be made of T. Kuhn and P. Feyerabend, who attribute to science a hermeneutic component; all formation of hypotheses or even changes of paradigms are subject to pre-comprehension and are historical. Thus scientific truths are also subject to history,

15. The problem of representation or 'hypotypos' occurs in Kant's 'Critique of Judgement' in connection with the presentation of concepts of pure reason or aesthetic ideas, and touches the question of beauty as 'symbol of morality' and the 'inexponible' nature of aesthetic experience. R. Gasché 1994:152-175.

and even the methodical work of the natural sciences cannot be absolved from this conditionality. A special relationship to the dimension of the aesthetic is, admittedly, represented by the metaphor of the creative act as the researcher's productive share in the production of the hypothesis. P. Feyerabend, N. Goodman and R. Rorty have drawn the consequences from this and assume an analogy of art and science (see Feyerabend 1984). It must, however, be emphasised in this context that, despite all analogies, scientific research and all the other cognition and sense accesses to world are varying, differentiated fields each of which has its own specific plausibility standards. An 'aesthetic fundamentalism' (W. Welsch) that accepts the analogies at their face value is thus in no way appropriate (see Heyting 1993). Another problem which may be classified as a 'problem of representation' is the question of the representability of feelings, e.g., the unpretentious experience, the authentic experience, the aesthetic experience and the total experience of nature. Here we are dealing with the question of 'what can and what cannot be said', speaking in the metaphors of M. Frank (1980, see also Castoriadis 1978), or with the problem of representation and expression. Representation is not actually 'representation' but, rather, a performative act producing something that did not exist (in that form) previously, or that is only expressed in its representation. In Goodman's 'Ways of world-making' it is, for instance, referred to as 'the invention of facts' and, analogously, in Merleau-Ponty, as 'vérité à faire'.[16] In the same way that Merleau-Ponty brings linguistic and non-linguistic forms of expression into closer contact, Goodman moves the various methods of world-making in perception, the arts and the sciences into an amazingly close proximity to one another (see de Chadarevian 1990).

Here representation has a factor that is, at the same time, creative and futile. As representation can neither touch nor copy anything like 'pure being', an authentic feeling, for instance, it owes itself, so to speak, to an original difference which it desires to annul as a difference yet which reproduces itself at every attempt to annul it. Representation is thus the indefatigably repeated, vain attempt to achieve the presence of something which is constantly withdrawing itself.[17] The question of represen-

16. Many points of contact can be found between Goodman's theory of the making of worlds and Merleau-Ponty's theory of the structuring work done by perception and languages and his division of knowledge into various fields of symbols and orders. This is not by chance, as both refer to Ernst Cassirer's 'theory of symbolic forms'.

17. What appears to be abstract here actually becomes a real problem for education, for how can the 'total' feeling, demanded of a pupil, of being a tree be represented in a concrete learning situation that is often also an evaluation situation? These are some didactic and educational suggestions and some educational-theory considerations connected with the

tation is also posed in another context of research into educational science and, above all, the theory of education. To what extent can fictional texts or other documents hitherto ignored by research, such as works of the fine arts, be integrated into scientific analysis? Do we need different forms of representation to explain the complex interrelationships of an educational process or of a biography? Research into acts of speech and their performance, together with those figures of rhetoric 'that allow something to be understood that cannot be said directly' (Kokemohr 1995) in recent biographical research belong in the field of questions of representation as already dealt with by classical rhetoric and poetics (Baacke and Schulze 1993, Kokemohr and Koller 1995).

3.4. Aesthetics and ethics/normativity

One especially prominent topic over the past fifteen years has been the question of how qualified is aesthetics for the requirements of ethics. This question has a particular tradition especially in educational science/pedagogics. In connection with the question of the 'educative' effect of art or taste, the direct or analogous transfer of aesthetic attitudes, judgements and experiences to ethical behaviour was being discussed in Britain, France and Germany even in the eighteenth century (Baümler 1967). Following Kant's transcendental foundation and definition of the relationship between aesthetics and ethics, and its subsequent radicalisation and transference to pedagogics by Herbart (1964, see also Hellekamps 1993:137-151), this discussion in neo-Humanism reached its zenith before once more withdrawing into the background. Only during the period of modern pedagogical reform and of educational science oriented towards the philosophy of life was the call for a realisation of the 'promises' of aesthetics reiterated, albeit with a different accentuation whereby the category of totality and criticism of the reductionism of science and technology represented the principal point of contact with the relationship between aesthetics and ethics.[18] The resumption or reformulation of this problem in the years from 1980 to the present day

creation of environment. Anyone who has once 'been' a 'tree', goes the thesis of some environmental protectionists and educationalists, will never ever want to fell one. Should pupils then become poets, as Heidegger once recommended that everybody become? For this would be the only adequate form of expressing, i.e., representing such feelings. According to Heidegger, the poetic approach to the world as being-oriented versification and thinking is seen as the 'only true' approach, in contrast to the consequences of 'Seins-Vergessenheit' such as science and technology (the so-called 'Gestell'). As Heidegger puts it 'science does not think'. See Schönherr 1989.

18. This is a topos which was particularly popular primarily at the beginning of this century with the rise of the philosophy of life. See for example G. Simmel 1908.

is, particularly in the field of pedagogics/educational science, due to completely different interests.

On the one hand we are dealing here with the reception of neo-Aristotelian and 'post-structuralist' ethics as part of the debate on post-modernism (see Welsch 1993:38). These reformulations of traditional ethical drafts provide aesthetics with a key role for ethics. Particular attention is given to the analogous structure of judgements reflecting aesthetics and the reflective power of judgement as discussed in connection with the question of the concretisation of moral action.[19] The analogy results from the reflective structure of the judgement of taste which, in referring to the *sensus communis*, transcends the subjective particularity of the feeling of aesthetic desire and relates it to the general. Subsequent to Kant's transcendental-philosophy version of the judgement of taste, the aesthetically reflective judgement is confronted, in Gadamer's philosophical hermeneutics for instance, by its original relationship to the eighteenth-century moral-philosophical tradition of the concept of taste, and placed in proximity to concepts such as phronesis or practical cleverness, but also to concepts such as tact, taste or 'Bildung' (Gadamer 1986, Arendt 1985). In connection with the debate on individualisation and modernisation, too, aesthetic categories such as the concept of style (Müller 1993) have become leading analytical criteria within the framework of analyses of lifestyles and perception. Philosophical and sociological theories, in particular, have here reformed the concept of ethics in order to integrate it, with anthropological or sociological intentions in mind, into the concept 'ethos'. Aesthetics as Ethics becomes an attitude, a standpoint or an exercise, whereby the emphasis now lies rather on 'difference' than on universal standards or postulates. The enquiry into Aesthetics as Ethics in the sense of ethos concentrates on its empirical and social terms. Here the distinction can be made between post-structuralist ethics which follow up the ethics of difference (or of individuality) (M. Foucault), and sociological considerations emphasising the collective in the apparently individual or different (P. Bourdieu). The debate on 'the claim which aesthetics has on difference' versus 'the claim of aesthetics to universality'

19. This analogisation of aesthetically reflecting and morally reflecting judgements takes place in the neo-Aristotelian tradition in particular. This is continued (albeit mainly 'de-transcendentalised' via the 'pragmatic turn-around' right up to the discussion of communitarism in our own time. M. Walzer's casuistry is meant to exhibit the same formal structure as Kant's reflective judgements (Walzer 1990). See Reese-Schäfer 1994:166 ff. An important definition of this transfer of the structure of aesthetic judgment in the sphere of politics was provided by the deliberations of H. Arendt in her lectures on Kant's 'Critique of Judgement' held at the New School for Social Research in 1970 and 1971. On questions of 'casuistry' in Kant's works, see O. Höffe:1977:354-384, here p.366.

and to its accompanying suitability for ethics was taken up for educational science by Klaus Mollenhauer.[20] The 'Ethics of Difference' or the question of the 'educative' effect of works of art in connection with the question of the self-limitation of autopoietic educational processes via the representation of cruelty, adds contours to the discussion, as does the question posed in connection with the ecology debate in the field of environmental education, as to the meaning of sensuality and aesthetic experience for the good life or for a life in harmony with nature.[21]

References

Arendt, H. (1985), *Das Urteilen. Texte zu Kants politischer Philosophie*, München.

Baacke, D. and Schulze,T. (1993), *Aus Geschichten lernen*, Weinheim and München.

Baümler, A. (1967), *Das Irrationalitätsproblem in der Ästhetik und Logik des 18. Jahrhunderts bis zur Kritik der Urteilskraft*, Tübingen.

Beck, K. (1994), 'Das Leib-Seele-Problem und die Erziehungswissenschaft. Ein Orientierungsversuch', in H. Heid and G. Pollak (eds), *Von der Erziehungswissenschaft zur Pädagogik?* Weinheim.

Beck, U. (1988), *Gegengifte. Die organisierte Unverantwortlichkeit*, Frankfurt a. M.

Castoriadis, C.(1978), *Les carrefours du labyrinthe*, Paris.

Chadarevian, S. de (1990), *Zwischen den Diskursen. M. Merleau-Ponty und die Wissenschaften*, Würzburg.

Ehrenspeck, Y. (1996), 'Aisthesis und Aesthetik. Überlegungen zu einer problematischen Entdifferenzierung', in K. Mollenhauer and C. Wulf, *Aisthesis/ Ästhetik Zwischen Wahrnehmung und Bewußtsein*, Weinheim.

Feyerabend, P. (1984), *Wissenschaft als Kunst*, Frankfurt a. M.

Frank, M. (1980), *Das Sagbare und das Unsagbare. Studien zur neuesten französischen Texttheorie*, Frankfurt a. M.

Frank, M. (1989), *Einführung in die Frühromantische Ästhetik. Vorlesungen*, Frankfurt a. M.

Gadamer, H.-G. (1986), *Wahrheit und Methode*, Tübingen.

Gebauer, G. and Wulf., C. (1992), *Mimesis*, Reinbek bei Hamburg.

Hellekamps, S. (1994), 'Ästhetische Rezeption und moralische Sensibilisierung', in L. Koch, W. Marotzki and H. Peukert, *Pädagogik und Ästhetik*, Weinheim.

20. Mollenhauer 1993:673-678. Mollenhauer advocates 'claim to difference' thus employing a figure of thought from early Romanticism. On this topos see M. Frank 1989.

21. Exemplary for the discussion in the fields of educational science/pedagogics is Gerhard Schneider 1994.

Hellekamps, S. (1993), 'Ästhetisches und praktisches Subjekt. Zum Problem intersubjektiverDifferenzerfahrung', in. K. Meyer-Drawe, H. Peukert and J. Ruhloff (eds) *Pädagogik und Ethik. Beiträge zu einer zweiten Refelxion*, Weinheim.

Herbart, J. F. (1964), 'Über die ästhetische Darstellung der Welt als Hauptgeschäft der Erziehung (1804)', in *Sämtliche Werke*, Vol 1, eds K. Kehrbach and O. Flügel, Aalen.

Heyting, F. (1993), *Wissenschaft und Schrecken – einige Bemerkungen zur Grenze zwischen Wissenschaft und Ästhetik*, Mimeo.

Höffe, O. (1977), 'Kants Kategorischer Imperativ als Kriterium des Sittlichen', in *Zeitschrift für philosophische Forschung* 31.

Kokemohr, R. and Koller, H.-C. (1995), 'Die rhetorische Artikulation von Bildungsprozessen. Zur Methodologie erziehungswissenschaftlicher Biographieforschung', in H.-H. Krüger and W. Marotzki (eds), *Erziehungswissenschaftliche Biographieforschung. Studien zur Erziehungswissenschaft und Bildungsforschung* 6, Opladen.

Lenzen, D. (1994), 'Die erziehungswissenschaftliche Aktualität des Ästhetischen', in G. Selle, W. Zacharias and H.-P. Burmeister (eds), *Anstösse zum Ästhetischen Projekt. Eine neue Aktionsform kunst- oder kulturpädagogischer Praxis?* Unna.

Liebau, E. (1992), *Die Kultivierung des Alltags. Das pädagogische Interesse an Bildung, Kunst und Kultur*, Weinheim und München.

Lyotard, J.-F. (1989), 'Das Undarstellbare-wider das Vergessen. Ein Gespräch zwischen Jean-Francois Lyotard und Christine Pries', in Pries, C. (ed.), *Das Erhabene. Zwischen Grenzerfahrung und Größenwahn*, Weinheim.

Merleau-Ponty, M. (1994), 'Keime der Vernunft', *Vorlesungen an der Sorbonne 1949-1952*. Edited and with a foreword by B. Waldenfels, München.

Merleau-Ponty, M.(1966), *Phänomenologie der Wahrnehmung*, Berlin.

Miller-Kipp, G. (1992), *Wie ist Bildung möglich? Die Biologie des Geistes unter pädagogischem Aspekt*, Weinheim.

Mollenhauer, K.(1993), '"Anspruch der Differenz" und "Anspruch des Universellen" – eine Marginalie zur ästhetischen Bildung', in *Zeitschrift für Pädagogik* 39.

Mollenhauer, K. (1990), 'Ästhetische Bildung zwischen Kritik und Selbstgewißheit', in *Zeitschrift für Pädagogik* 36.

Mollenhauer, K. (1988), 'Ist ästhetische Bildung möglich?', in *Zeitschrift für Pädagogik* 34.

Mollenhauer, K. (1993), 'Über die bildende Wirkung ästhetischer Erfahrung', in D. Lenzen (ed.), *Verbindungen*. Weinheim.

Müller, H.-P. (1993), *Sozialstruktur und Lebenstile. Der neuere theoretische Diskurs über soziale Ungleichheit*, Frankfurt a. M.

Nibbrig, C. Hart (ed.) (1994), *Was ist Darstellung?* Frankfurt a. M.

'Pädobiologie' (1994), Themenheft der Zeitschrift 'Bildung und Erziehung', 4.

Pries, C. (ed.), *Das Erhabene. Zwischen Grenzerfahrung und Größenwahn*, Weinheim.

Recki, B. (1988), *Aura und Autonomie. Zur Subjektivität der Kunst bei Walter Benjamin und Th. W. Adorno*, Würzburg.

Reese-Schäfer, W. (1994), *Was ist Kommunitarismus?* Frankfurt a. M./NewYork.

Rorty, R. (1991), *Kontingenz, Ironie und Solidarität*, Frankfurt a. M.

Rumpf, H. (1987), *Belebungsversuche. Ausgrabungen gegen die Verödung von Lernkultur*, Weinheim und München.

Schneider, G. (1994), *Naturschönheit und Kritik. Zur Aktualität von Kants Kritik der Urteilskraft für die Umwelterziehung*, Würzburg.

Schönherr, H.-M. (1989), *Die Ökologie und das schwache Denken*, Wien.

Schumacher-Chilla, D. (1995), *Ästhetische Sozialisation und Erziehung. Zur Kritik an der Reduktion von Sinnlichkeit*, Berlin.

Simmel, G. (1908), *Kant und Goethe. Zur Geschichte der modernen Weltanschauung*, 4th edn, Leipzig.

Terhart, E. (1992), 'Reden über Erziehung. Umgangssprache, Berufssprache, Wissenschaftssprache', in *Neue Sammlung* 32, 2.

Waldenfels, B. (1985), 'Rationalisierung der Lebenswelt – ein Projekt. Kritische Überlegungen zu Habermas' Theorie des kommunikativen Handelns', in B. Waldenfels, *In den Netzen der Lebenswelt*, Frankfurt a. M.

Walzer, M. (1990), *Kritik und Gemeinsinn. Drei Wege der Gesellschaftskritik*, Berlin.

Welsch, W. (1990), *Ästhetisches Denken*, Stuttgart.

Welsch, W. (1993), 'Aesthet/hik. Ethische Implikationen und Konsequenzen der Ästhetik', in D. Lenzen (ed.), *Verbindungen. Vortrage anläßlich der Ehrenpromotion von Klaus Mollenhauer*, Weinheim.

Chapter 5

PROBLEMS AND PERSPECTIVES OF THE SOCIALISATION THEORY

Hermann Veith

Introduction

The concept of socialisation is one of those academic categories that has, as a result of a sudden surge of popularity, also found its way into the everyday language. While occurring very frequently in justificatory situations within social communication,[1] it is used in the context of scientific discussions either as a *descriptive category* to designate the lifelong process of the environmentally mediated development of the individual (Geulen 1977) or as a *conceptual generic term* under which various theoretical approaches to explanations are subsumed (Hurrelmann and Ulich 1980). If the semantic differentiations that characterise the scientific concept of socialisation are systematically faded out in everyday use, they threaten to blend into one another in international discussions on socialisation, as the communication-oriented use of common linguistic symbols veils the socio-historically and culturally determined semantic differences between the individual socialisation concepts and theories. Though elaborate communications processes assume a common linguistic code, mutual understanding is hardly possible without previous agreement on the meaning in each specific case. I should therefore like, in the following – taking as my starting point the fact documented in all relevant

1. By having recourse to the academic concept of socialisation in their everyday language, the actors often express that they can – and will – only partly be held responsible for their behaviour, as its course is influenced by non-intentional social influences.

manuals that the various sociological and psychological explanatory concepts relevant to international discussions on socialisation stand alongside one another as relatively unconnected terms, and that no general theory of socialisation has as yet been produced – to present some peculiarities of the discussion on socialisation in the Federal Republic of Germany, and to explain why it is here in particular that the project of a supra-conceptual integration of the theory seems to be of particular interest. As socialisation theories differ semantically in their dependence both on their socio-cultural origins and on the general theories from which they have separated off, the explanatory patterns in each case cannot be related to one another without difficulties.

I should like to propose the thesis that in all drafts relevant to socialisation theory – below the categoric level – ubiquitous social experience patterns reflect one another, permitting the shared historical relationships of the socialisation-theory form of reflection to be identified in a supra-conceptual way. With reference to the theme of the conference I shall illustrate, with the help of Georg Simmel's work (1908), how the modernisation process modifies the individual's foundations of social experience, particularly in the expanding urban industrial centres. Analysis of living conditions in metropolitan areas shows, prototypically, how the experience of the personal involvement – central to socialisation theory – of the individual in a society generated by social activity but functioning with a dynamism of its own determines everyday practice. Finally, in the awareness both of the socio-historical and cultural, of the object-perspective and methodological differences, I shall plead for a pluralisation of the socialisation theory discussion no longer aimed at the model of a general theory but at that of a widely varied discourse of differing disciplines and conceptions.

1. The Beginnings of Discussion on Socialisation in the Federal Republic of Germany

When the discussion on socialisation theory started up once more in West Germany in the 1960s, after a break of several decades,[2] its most significant impulses stemmed on the one hand from backward-looking, socio-psychological interests in distancing oneself from and coming to terms with the past and on the other from future-oriented economic and culture-policy demands for modernisation.

2. In the early 1930s, during the late stages of the Weimar Republic, the Frankfurt Institute for Social Research concerned itself systematically with questions of social integration and municipalisation. See in the context the work of Erich Fromm 1980a, 1980b and Max Horkheimer 1931.

Coming to terms with fascism

Coming to terms with fascism was effected both via social-philosophico-anthropological self-ascertainment and via moral-theory processing of the facts. Prototypically, the social-philosophico-anthropological efforts can be seen in Gerhard Wurzbacher's book entitled *Der Mensch als soziales und personales Wesen* published in 1963, which was the first attempt to document discussions on socialisation theory in West Germany. Wurzbacher criticises the fact that in the Anglo-American debate the concept of socialisation is one-sidedly overburdened with ideas concerning 'the mechanics of adaptation' (see Wurzbacher 1963:5), arguing that in most socially standardised situations outside of the pressure exerted by society to adapt, there are opportunities for personalisation in the sense of an autonomous 'self-shaping and self-guidance of one's own urge structures' (Ibid.:14) and of the active influencing of social groups and systems of cultural symbols and values. The postulate of the non-dissolubility of the individual in the social whole is one of the central motifs of Federal German socialisation discussion.[3] In the historical shadow of the mad National Socialist delusion of an Aryan community of peoples, which rapidly enveloped Europe in concentration camps and war, the decisive question of socialisation was, as Heinz Walter (1973) so succinctly put it '... no longer the question of the conditions under which the inclusion in and adaption to society could be carried out as unproblematically as possible' (1973:23). In a democratic Germany the question of how people become members of society in the course of ontogenesis had to be supplemented '... at least [...] by the question as to the development of a potential resistance to persuasion and social pressure' (Ibid.).

Pointing in a similar direction, but disproportionately more sharply polarised by the generation conflict between those born before and after 1930, the moral-biographically motivated attempts of the younger generation to understand, with the assistance of scientific theories, the often voluntary participation in the system exhibited by the 'hangers on' of the older generation, led to the practical resistance of the student movement and to the theoretical criticism of the younger social scientists towards all forms of repressive authority. Analysis of the mutual relationships between the individual and society was based not only on the early studies made in the 1930s at the Institute for Social Research founded in Frankfurt in 1923, but also on the more recent work of Herbert Marcuse on the repressive qualities of a mass culture that no longer calls for the renunciation of primitive urges (1955/1987).

3. Even before Gerhard Wurzbacher, Ralf Dahrendorf (1958), with reference to Kant, emphasised the unabolishable difference between the individual and society.

The modernisation of educational policy

Almost simultaneously with the social-philosophico-anthropological and moral-theory discussions of the National Socialist past, there developed a second context of discussion important from the socialisation theory standpoint. Although reconstruction in the Federal Republic of Germany had raised the material standard of living to the level of the early 1930s (see AG Bildungsbericht 1990:27) the country seemed uncompetitive on the international scene. As comparative studies showed, the Federal Republic was lagging behind in the field of education, which was playing an ever more important part in the modern technological world (Edding 1963 and Picht 1964). In the early 1960s educational policies adopting the direction of the pre-Fascist principle of class privilege in an authoritarian state were considered counter-productive. The necessary opening-up of the institutes of higher education and the universities to traditionally disadvantaged groups of the school population called for a radical rejection of received nativistic ideas of talent. Democratic educational policies which took seriously the right of the individual – enshrined in the country's Basic Law – to social equality of opportunity, could not be legitimised by recourse to biological inheritance. In consequence there was also a shift in the accents of academic discussions. The personality-formative functions formerly ascribed to the individual's genetic make up were now reserved for his/her social and material environment and restricted to the learning experiences accompanying ontogenesis.

For young West German academics, this constellation of interest in historico-biographical enlightenment, and attempts to modernise educational policies against the background of a change in socio-psychological mentality offered both an opportunity to establish tie-ins with traditional theories and a chance to re-orientate theoretical fundamentals.

2. Problems of Variety

While the theories of the Frankfurt School and psychoanalysis offered themselves as possible tie-ins in the context of the debate on authority, re-orientation in the scenario of the modernisation debate seemed possible via the reception of Anglo-American socialisation research. Both the attempt to compensate for the discontinuity by referring back to morally non-suspect theories and the attempt to close gaps in research and theory by importing methods and theories created a new series of problems. By borrowing concepts from psychoanalysis, the cognitive theory of development, behaviouristic learning research, Marxist social theory, role theory and symbolic interactionism it was impossible to produce a theory of socialisation that would structure the entire field of research '... from comprehensive points of view' (Krappmann, Oevermann and Kreppner 1976:258). Only against the background of this combination, typical of the period, of the various social, political and cultural currents and the research interests of the expanding social sciences, does it become clear why, since that time, the West German social-science debate has considered to be one of its most important tasks the development of a general theory of socialisation which would integrate the various approaches in a way not restricted to individual aspects.

As theories and cycles of theories cannot be understood in isolation from their socio-historical contexts of origin or reception, and as their relational-categorical structure forbids the eclectic separation of individual elements from the context as a whole, it is to be expected that the problem of integrating the various socialisation models at the level of the conceptually determined objective theory can hardly be dealt with. It is therefore a good idea to change the analysis level and then to ask whether, and if so which, relationships of social experience are shared by the various socialisation theories.

Historical origins

A historical review of the beginnings of modern socialisation theory shows that the theories indicating a development-relevant relationship of dependence between the individual and society were first propounded in the period between 1890 and 1930 (Durkheim 1977, Freud 1966, Mead 1965, see also Geulen 1980) – particularly in cases where changes in the reality of life caused by modernisation had the most dramatic effects e.g., in the expanding metropolises of modern industrial societies.[4] In the milieus of the big cities the experience of the existential dependence of the individual on superordinate social relationships crystallised and became part of everyday life. The same period saw a gathering in these urban centres of a wide range of productive competences, with the result that not only industrial mass-production but, increasingly, the academic production of user-related knowledge gained in importance. The changes within the academic world caused by the increasing relevance of scientific-technical individual disciplines to the disadvantage of philosophy, which Germany's educated middle-classes in particular revered as *the* integrating science pure and simple, created, in addition, an atmosphere in which it suddenly seemed possible for even the social and

4. As in Bordeaux and Paris (Durkheim 1977), in Berlin (Simmel 1908), in Vienna (Freud 1966) or in Chicago (Mead 1965, Watson).

human sciences to found independent theoretical perspectives. From the socialisation-theory standpoint it is precisely this connection between the everyday experience of social conditionality and the scientific differentiation of specialised theory programmes that is constitutive. As self-reflexive reference to the experience of socialisation was unavoidable, the theme of socialisation was treated simultaneously in several draft theories without any clear disciplinary attribution of the object becoming apparent.

Conceptuality

It cannot be over emphasised that the individual authors to whom today's discussions refer were at the time neither concerned exclusively with questions of socialisation theory, nor did they even take notice of each other with the intention of mutual discussion or understanding. The central socialisation question concerning the conditions for the socially transmitted genesis of personality was only dealt with *en passant* by Durkheim, Freud or Mead, to mention only three theoreticians. Socialisation theories are therefore not independent theories but integral components of superordinate theory systems which, for their part, grew up in different socio-cultural contexts and construct realities with the help of various methods and concepts.

The socio-historical contextualisation on the one hand and the relational categorical structure of these theories on the other, are linked to characteristic theory semantics to which individual concepts and segments of theory still remain connected even if they are separated from the overall theoretical framework. It is thus impossible to connect categories or theory building-blocks with one another along the lines of formal similarity or the fact that the themes supplement each other. If one nevertheless attempts to identify starting points for connecting up theories, it is a good idea to keep an eye open for precisely those shared socio-historical features from which the thinking behind socialisation theory received its principal impulses. These are anchored in the social conditions of social activity, and can thus be reconstructed for the facts of any given case as ubiquitous patterns of experience beyond all inter-conceptual terminological and methodological differences. In the following I would thus like to show, with the help of Simmel's analysis of life in a metropolis in 1903 those historical changes in the modalities of socialisation to which the earliest 'socialisation theoreticians'[5] reacted.

5. The italics are necessary in order to emphasise what was said at the beginning of this section.

3. Socialisation Theory and Urban Municipalisation

The works of Simmel, which by no means represent the majority opinion among the education-hungry bourgeoisie in Germany, are particularly suitable to the purpose of this discussion for two reasons: firstly, on the basis of the analysis of social interplay, they systematically relate social transformation processes to psychological changes; secondly – due not least to their essayistic form – they tend to have played a marginal role in discussions on socialisation theory, so that they do not offer themselves *per se* as an assimilation foil for attempts at integrating theories.

In contrast to the criticism of civilisation commonly levelled by the education-hungry bourgeoisie in Germany, Simmel saw, in the process of progressive urbanisation, not just the destructive potentials of a material consumerism borne by nameless masses and addressed to abstract customers and faceless spectators, but also the individual and intellectual gain of freedom which life in the big city brought with it. The difference between the modern and the 'estates of the realm' life-forms is doubly founded in the liberation of the individual '… from all historically-developed bonds with state and religion, morals and economy' (Simmel 1957:227) and in the acceptance of division-of-labour industrial production on the basis of monetary-economic relationships. Though there continue to be, even within urbanised societies, rural areas where 'people ruled by their hearts' are in personal contact with others, and who arrange their days in harmony with the rhythms of natural time-sequences, modern life is dominated by the metropolitan forms of rational organisation and by 'people ruled by their heads'[6] oriented towards artificial time divisions and abstract-objective standards of values. It is precisely in the pulsating bustle of the big city that the overwhelming force of a hypertrophied objective culture over the individual becomes clear. In the stream of urban dynamism, people experience their own existence in the setting of their individual existence against a society that is superordinate in all respects. The problems resulting from this situation and the corresponding attitudes and feelings can be sketched as follows:

(i) The economic dimension.

Modern economic activity and industrial production, which determine life particularly in the big cities, are 'almost completely' determined by market-shaped barter relationships. As the goods offered are produced '… for completely unknown customers who are never seen by the actual

6. The contrast between people ruled by their hearts and people ruled by their heads is in keeping with Tönnies dichotomy of community and society.

producer' (Simmel 1957:230) economic activity assumes '... a pitiless objectivity' (Ibid.:230). This is because '... money, with its colourlessness and indifference, sets itself up as the common denominator of all values, it becomes the most dreadful leveller' (Ibid.:233) of all contradictory interests. The '...de-coloration of things via their equivalence' (Ibid.) divests the particular of its aura of uniqueness, causing that generalised attitude of 'dullness' (1957:232) which is recognisable in the behaviour of the city-dweller as a blasé attitude.

(ii)The social dimension.

Modern society consists of a wide variety of social circles which are linked with each other via differentiated relationships of cooperation. The numerical growth of the population increases not only the size of the towns, but also the opportunities for individualisation. The more specialised and impersonal the social relationships between members of the society, the less effective the control mechanisms and the greater the free space for the development of personal special types. In its more critical form the modified social compulsion to individual peculiarisation is expressed both in the multifarious '... extravagances of apartness' (Simmel 1957:239) and in the desperate feelings of solitary loneliness. Mutual reserve, on the other hand, and aversively shaded indifference towards one's fellow men belong to the habitual standard forms which make daily symbiosis in the urban mass society possible. Only those who have learnt to react to superficial stimuli with indifference are in a position to show themselves to their best advantage in the fight for social recognition.

(iii)The cultural dimension.

Modern culture has prised itself loose from the embrace of religion and has devoted itself increasingly to the same rational principles which have proved their worth in the monetary economy. The cosmopolitan spirit of the big city has hereby concentrated the intellectual competences on the smallest possible space, so that, under the pressure of scientific findings, the traditional interpretation patterns have lost their sense-instilling obligatory nature. If life in the metropolis functions to the greatest possible extent without integrative collective ideas becoming lost in the chaos of mutually intertwining private interests, this is mainly because the people pursue their intentions objectively, orienting themselves along formal standards such as the value of money.

(iv)The psychological dimension.

In order to be psychologically suited to the alternation of physical and social stimuli that has become a permanent feature of the city environment, the modern individual must develop new ways of processing stimuli. He or she may neither respond directly to all stimuli nor react too emotionally to predominantly objective demands. In order for the individual to be in a position to distance him or herself to the necessary degree in every situation the superficial layers of understanding in the psyche must take over the control of behaviour and also repress, in particular, the impulses surging up from the deeper, affective levels of the soul. This control is effected in harmony with the cultural values and social standards imposed from outside and which have become integral components of the personality[7] in the shape of the social ego (see Simmel 1957:242ff).

Against the background of the changes in the forms of social activity described here as prototypical, the '… deepest problems of modern life' (Simmel 1957:227) which are of importance from the socialisation-theory standpoint can now be described. The functional differentiation of the monetary economy based on division of labour, the heterogenisation of the social environment and the rationalisation of cultural interpretation patterns are necessary conditions for the individualising municipalisation. Owing to the dynamism inherent in these processes, the totality of objective culture becomes involved in a conflict with the subjects' endeavours to autonomise. In their frontal opposition to 'the superior forces of society' (Ibid.) the individuals must not only shape a unique self, but also attempt to permanently assert their social identity in the difficult balancing act between invariant ego wishes and interiorised or anticipated social standards. The modern person experiences the determination of his/her character in the social sphere, understanding his/her existence as a socialised entity.

4. Conceptual Plurality

This historical experience of the dependence of the individual existence and personal biography on superordinated social institutions and cultural forms organised by their own dynamism is basic to socialisation theory. By analysing the influence of the socio-historically transmitted environment on the development of the individual and enquiring into the psychological structures which, as interiorised representatives of society, guarantee the social integration of the individual, this experience defines its object field diagonally to the directions of established disciplines. In order to

7. Simmel divides the personality into three parts. The personal ego contains all psychological content determinators which, in the course of socialisation, can only be shaped over by the social ego. The self, on the other hand, asserts itself in the balance between personal and social demands.

even get near to corresponding to the complexity of the questions raised, socialisation theory is obliged to make use of explanatory approaches which, from different perspectives and with different methods, emphasise and explain in a fragmentary way important aspects of the overall complex problem. To this extent, conceptual variety is necessary.

To summarise, it can be said that as empirical theories are to a great extent tied to authors and contexts of origin, they contain not only time-specific premises but also historically and culturally stamped semantics which, even where there is formal categorical agreement between different concepts, permit no connection. In order to avoid endless discussions on concepts it is therefore necessary to examine the individual theories against the background of the latest scientific findings, and to question their core assumptions critically. The project of formulating a theory of socialisation can only be realised in an appropriate way via polyphonic – and this also means international – discourse of the disciplines and conceptions relevant to socialisation theory. Only if the wide variety of theories is recognised and accepted as a necessary condition for sociological analysis, can the various facets of the experiences of socialised individuals be processed in a theoretically adequate way.

References

Arbeitsgruppe (AG) Bildungsbericht am Max-Planck-Institut für Bildungsforschung (1990), *Das Bildungswesen in der Bundesrepublik Deutschland*, Reinbek bei Hamburg.

Dahrendorf R. (1977), *Homo Sociologicus* (orig. 1958), Opladen.

Durkheim, E. (1977), Über *die Teilung der sozialen Arbeit* (orig. 1893), Frankfurt a. M.

Edding, F. (1963), *Ökonomie des Bildungswesens. Lehren und Lernen als Haushalt und als Investition*, Freiburg.

Freud, S. (1966), *Die 'kulturelle' Sexualmoral und die moderne Nervosität* (orig. 1908), in *Gesammelte Werke* Vol. VII. Frankfurt a. M.

Fromm, E. (1980a) *Arbeiter und Angestellte am Vorabend des Dritten Reiches* (orig. 1929), in W. Bonss (ed.) *Erich Fromm: Arbeiter und Angestellte am Vorabend des Dritten Reiches*, München.

Fromm, E. (1980b), 'Über Methode und Aufgabe einer Analytischen Sozialpsychologie', in *Zeitschrift für Sozialforschung* Vol.1 , Nos. 1/2, Leipzig.

Geulen, D. (1977), *Das vergesellschaftete Subjekt*, Frankfurt a. M.

Geulen, D. (1980), 'Die historische Entwicklung sozialisationstheoretischer Paradigmen', in K. Hurrelmann and D. Ulich (eds) *Handbuch der Sozialisationsforschung*, Weinheim/Basel.

Horkheimer, M. (1981), 'Die gegenwärtige Lage der Sozialphilosophie und die Aufgaben eines Instituts für Sozialforschung (1931)', in *Sozialphilosophische Studien*, Frankfurt a. M.

Hurrelmann K. and D. Ulich (eds) (1980), *Handbuch der Sozialisationsforschung*, Weinheim/Basel.

Krappmann, L., Oevermann, U. and K. Kreppner (1976), 'Was kommt nach der schichtspezifischen Sozialisationsforschung?', in M.R. Lepsius, *Zwischenbilanz der Soziologie*, Stuttgart.

Marcuse, H., (1987) *Triebstruktur und Gesellschaft*, Frankfurt a. M.

Mead, G. H., (1965), *Mind, self and society* (orig. 1934), Chicago.

Picht, G., (1964), *Die deutsche Bildungskatastrophe,* Olten/ Freiburg.

Simmel, G., (1957), 'Die Grosstädte und das Geistesleben' (orig.1903), in M. Landmann and M. Susman (eds), *Georg Simmel: Brücke und Tür*, Stuttgart.

Simmel, G. (1908) *Soziologie – Untersuchungen über die Formen der Vergesellschaftung*, Leipzig.

Tönnies, F. (1963), *Gemeinschaft und Gesellschaft – Grundbegriffe der reinen Soziologie* (orig. 1887). Darmstadt.

Walter, H. (1973), 'Einleitung oder Auf der Suche nach einem sozialisationstheoretischen Konzept', in H. Walter (ed.), *Sozialisationsforschung*, Vol. 1, Stuttgart.

Wurzbacher, G. (ed.) (1963), *Der Mensch als soziales und personales Wesen*, Stuttgart.

Chapter 6

THE PEDAGOGISATION OF SOCIAL CRISES

Considerations Taking the 'Ecological Crises' as an Example

Felicitas Thiel

'Increased burdens placed on the environment and the dangers involved [...] also represent challenges to educational policy', (Deutscher Bundestag 1990:10) to quote the concluding report, published on 5 September 1990, of the Commission of Inquiry set up by the German Parliament and entitled *Future Educational Policy – Education 2000.*

Under the heading 'Education is aimed at ecological responsibility', the Commission demanded that environmental education should generate a consciousness of the environment 'in the sense of a psychological processability (allowing the problem to approach one), ethical behaviour (responsibility for the future, for the consequences of one's own actions) and training the capacity to perceive (re-vitalisation of the senses)' (Ibid.:30ff).

Over the past twenty years the Environment has, in Germany, become a topic of education. This can be seen from countless recommendations, from the programming of the subject in the form of curricula and teaching material, and from the extremely involved flood of publications (see Thiel 1994).

The combatants in the conflict involving 'Environmental Education', 'Ecological Pedagogics' or 'Environment Teaching'- the descriptive terms certainly have a programmatic character – are arguing about questions of the positioning of nature's own right within educational and teaching theories, of the significance of aesthetic experience for a new understanding of nature, or the educational relevance of environmental ethics.

I shall not concern myself with these aspects in this chapter. My question will be far more modest: how does a crisis topic that starts off by applying pressure to the political system become an educational topic at all? In other words: what follows is a reconstruction of ecological communication in the Federal Republic of Germany (from the late 1960s to the late 1980s) with special reference to the transformation of a highly politicised theme into an educational topic.

In the following I shall work with the distinction between 'educational system' and 'environment of the educational system'. The theoretical construction of the inherent communicative logic of self-referential social functional systems (Luhmann 1987) serves as an instrument for reconstructing this 'ecological communication'. I shall, however, be concentrating on one partial environment of the educational system which has played a very special role since the start of the differentiation of the educational system and its reflective theory of pedagogics: the political system. I shall be observing the interference between the educational system and the political system.

My argumentation will be structured as follows:

a) firstly I shall clarify the concepts 'pedagogisation' and 'social crisis' which are basic to my analysis.
b) secondly I will show how the topic 'environment', which has enjoyed a high degree of public topicality since the beginning of the 1970s, has become a crisis topic, and how this crisis topic brings its demands to bear on the political system,
c) thirdly I shall investigate the possible impulse character of political communication for the pedagogisation of the topic,
d) and finally I shall consider the resonance capability of the educational system for social crisis topics.

1. The Pedagogisation of Social Crises

In the following I shall designate the translation of the experience of social crises into educational topics as pedagogisation. Pedagogisation is the attempt to process social crises with the instrument of education. The concept of pedagogisation is used here in a restricted way: we are concerned neither with the de-differentiation of the curriculum vitae and of the associated invalidation of significant differences between the life of a child and that of an adult, nor indeed with the possible consequences of pedagogisation in the sense that can be classified under the rubrics 'clientelisation', 'infantilisation' or 'Certification' (see Giesecke 1985, Kupffer 1980). This is to avoid, for the second time round, lamentations about the undesired side-effects of an expansion of education that Schelsky had already described in the earky 1960s, rather polemically, as 'a danger to civilisation' (Schelsky 1961). What will be discussed here are not the possible consequences of pedagogisation processes for the individual but, rather, the question of how the expansionist dynamic of pedagogics is itself stimulated under the special conditions of social crisis experience and how a pedagogisation process proceeds in detail.

Social crises may be designated as situations in which the institutions, techniques and regulations available to a society for processing insecurity cease to function, so that a dramatic situation of uncertainty arises (Rammstedt 1978) which provokes quick decisions. The result is a pressure to decide aimed primarily at the political system because, in modern societies, this is considered to be the most important control mechanism.

However, not every insecurity leads inevitably to a crisis. On the contrary: modern societies in particular, being to a high degree insecure societies already, have created and tried out regulatives and institutions for processing insecurity, which enable insecurities to be processed and accepted individually and socially. One example is the institution of insurance with its principle of 'precautionary after-care' (Beck 1993:535-558, Ewald 1993). If, of course, these proven regulatives and institutions permanently cease to function, we may talk of crises – of a crisis on the employment market, for instance, a crisis in the health system, or the ecology crisis.

Social crises, however, presuppose a 'consciousness' of the crisis nature of certain situations; or, rather, they assume communication. A happening only becomes a crisis when it is communicated. The question now becomes how the communication of such a crisis takes place and what role is attributed to educational processes in the context of this communication.

2. From the political issue of environmental pollution to the experience of the crisis

As a point of reference for the following observations I shall begin by selecting the political system.

How did the theme 'environment' become a crisis topic? As early as 1969, environmental pollution in the Federal Republic of Germany had already become a political theme. Within the context of the reform policies of the Socialist-Liberal coalition and in preparation for the first UN Environmental Conference (1972) a series of measures were undertaken, including the formation of a cabinet committee, the passing of a programme for immediate implementation and, finally, the presentation of the Federal Government's first comprehensive environmental programme in 1971. The passing of the environmental programme was followed by further measures for the institutionalisation of environmental policy making.

The establishment of environmental policy making was accompanied by a public discussion of the subject (Küppers 1978). As early as the summer of 1972 the theme 'protection of the environment' already occupied first place on the domestic policy list of priorities, having ousted the topic of 'social security', albeit only for a short period (INFAS Berlin 1973:4 ff).

In the early 1970s, however, the concept of environmental pollution was not as yet associated with the experience of a social crisis. While the protection of the environment was seen as an important political issue, the vast majority of the population remained at the same time convinced of the effectiveness of the well-tried technological regulatives to protect the environment. It is thus hardly surprising that there was at first a broad social consensus, ranging from the Federal Government to the Opposition and from the trade unions to the Confederation of German Industries, about the need for active environmental protection policies. For this reason Edda Müller designates the years from 1969 to 1973 as the 'phase of offensive "autonomous" environmental policies' (Müller 1986:51).

This phase saw the implementation of important environmental policy measures in the fields of air purification, water resources policy, waste disposal and noise abatement. While signs of a conflict of interests between environmental protection and economic growth were already appearing in many areas, it nevertheless proved possible to implement measures of public security policy in the environmental protection sector with relatively few problems (Wey 1982).

At the beginning of the 1970s, political decision-makers were still formulating problem diagnoses in a quite drastic way. The causes were generally attributed with the economy in mind. During this first phase, Federal German environmental policy was centred on the 'pay as you pollute' principle, clearly and unambiguously formulated in the 1971 Environment Programme: 'Everyone who pollutes or damages the environment shall meet the cost of such pollution or damage' (Environment Programme 1971:19). The right of the free development of economic activity, according to the state secretary responsible for environmental questions, reached its limits when the general public was adversely affected and was in need of corresponding state regulation (Hartkopf 1972:1).

After the downturn in the economic cycle caused by the so-called 'energy crisis' (1973-1974) the environmental consensus broke up. Representatives of industry and the trade unions forced a change of direction in environmental policy. This change of direction was expressed by the substitution of the 'pay as you pollute' principle by the 'general burdening principle' which cannot justify 'payment of damages and the duties of those responsible' (Environment Report 1976:88). The 'limits of environmental policy' were now defined in terms of the 'possibilities and limits of overall economic development' (Ibid.). This loosened up one core aspect of the first phase of environmental policy. From an offensive position, environmental policy saw itself forced into one of defence.

The conflicting aims of economic growth and environmental protection intensified, resulting in the almost total blocking off of environmental measures. The defensive position occupied by environmental policies from the mid 1970s onwards is characterised by the fact that between 1975 and 1978 it proved impossible to get a single item of environmental legislation through parliament (Müller 1986:106).

However, this blocking of environmental measures by the economy was in no way accompanied by a lessening of public interest in the topic of environmentalism. On the contrary: the downturn in the economic cycle produced a general mood of crisis which gradually consumed the utopian energy of the socio-technological planning and reform illusions. Suddenly the side-effects of industrial production, which had been able to conceal themselves while the economy was booming, came into the open.

The transformation of a political issue with a relatively high priority on the agenda of political problems into a crisis topic – this becomes clear from the increased use of crisis semantics: instead of 'environmental pollution', we now talk more about the 'environmental crisis' – was to a great extent due to the new social movements, particularly the ecology movement (Brand 1982, Kitschelt 1986:57-85). Employing dramatisation and scandalisation strategies first used for regional conflicts, they organised external pressure on the political system.

It was primarily the resistance to atomic technology which was to gain central importance for the formation and consolidation of the ecology movement (see Sieferle 1984; Touraine 1982; Evers and Nowotny 1987). Atomic technology became the strongest symbol for the dialectics of the policy of modernisation.

The topic 'ecological crisis' worked, so to speak, like a magnifying glass focussing the rays of criticism against modernisation. The concept 'ecological crisis', which gained a tremendous hold in the second half of the 1970s, offered an interpretation framework for the anti-modernist criticisms of the new social movements. This concept provided a common, popularisable denominator for side-effects of industrial modernisation which had hitherto been treated as individual items. However, 'ecology' is not only an analytical category, it is, at the same time, a programmatical one. Perhaps the topos was and is so persuasive and successful because it unites a new – scientifically supported – thinking with a new 'practical, life-oriented behaviour' (see Brand et al. 1984:96) and a new social design principle. 'Ecology' is the expression of a holistic philosophy of life combining the community with nature in a social utopia of decentralised autonomous, yet integrated units. This philosophy of life, having the threat of the apocalypse as its negative point of reference, forces on its followers a strong moralistic tone both in political activity and in individual lifestyle.

The formation of the ecological movement in the Federal Republic of Germany can thus be understood as an effect of and, at the same time, a concentration of social self-disconcertion – or, as Luhmann puts it, 'self-alarming' (1986) – which led to the shaking of the technico-industrial paradigm of progress and its socio-political legitimation – the distribution of the profits of growth. The proportion of the population who began increasingly to question the promises of the modernisers that all was safe was constantly on the increase. A general mood of crisis spread.

A topic which had been placed as a political issue by politics itself – albeit under quite different circumstances – in the late 1960s developed a dynamism of its own under the conditions of the recession and now rebounded on the political system in the form of pressure to act.

How did the political system react to this strong expectationary pressure in a situation in which the normal techniques of political intervention had been blocked?

3. Impulses of Pedagogisation

My argument is as follows: the political system reacts to such 'blockage' situations probably by making a change in the focus of its crisis diagnoses which permits the alleviation of calls for political intervention. As an analytical investigation of the contents of the most important materials and documents on Federal German environmental policy has shown (Thiel 1994), the blocking of political activities in the field of environmental protection from the mid 1970s onwards, already described above, corresponded to a shift in the diagnosis of crises. Since the mid 1970s an increased focus on individual behaviour has been observable. In contrast to the system's own set of environmental-policy instruments, particular attention was now focused on the attitudes and behaviour of the citisens.

As a typical example of this, allow me to quote the 1976 Environmental Report of the Federal Government, apostrophised as an extrapolation of the 1971 Environment Programme but clearly placing different emphases. This report states that:

> ... protection of the environment, however, is not just a matter for politics and industry. Environmental protection is a challenge for every one of us – at school, at work, at home and during our leisure time. Without active collaboration and a fundamental change of attitude in every individual, environmental policies cannot be implemented. [...] The majority of citizens, however, still expect an improvement to be achieved solely or mainly by governmental measures. A shift in thinking towards the critical examination of one's own behaviour and a conscious turning towards environmentally-justified actions would, however, be both desirable and necessary. (Environmental Report 1976:22 ff.)

This shift of burdens from a politically-enforced environmental policy to one of public enlightenment can be clearly followed by analysing the corresponding material (Thiel 1994). In line with this shift in crisis diagnosis, environmental policy in the second half of the 1970s was increasingly staged as an 'all-together-now' campaign. Projects to tidy up woods, recycling campaigns, consumer education, information campaigns on ecology in the home, or the annual implementation of an 'Environment Day' achieved a high degree of political attention.

How, then, can this focussing on individual behaviour in crisis diagnosis since the mid 1970s be explained? Social crises – according to the above considerations – generate an expectationary pressure on the political system because the structural conditions of political communication in modern societies force a reaction to highly political topics. Or, to put it more clearly: the political system must react to a publicly communicated topic if this can be decoded by means of the system-specific code of Government/Opposition. A topic produces an echo in the political system whenever, in discussions about the topic in question, '"public opinion" as the real sovereign suggests differential chances of re-election' (Luhmann 1986:175). In the case of the topic 'environmental pollution' this has been the situation since at least the mid 1970s.

Basically, the political system has several possible ways of reacting to the scandalisation of a highly political topic (see Stölting 1990):

1. By playing the situation down or by presenting a plausible de-dramatising diagnosis.
2. By weighing up the risks against possibly even greater disadvantages. Here the expected damage is apostrophised as side-effects which have to be accepted.
3. By a demonstration of vigorous activity aimed at overcoming the crisis. This apparently so obvious reaction is often not as easy as it

> would seem, as the opportunities for the government and the administration to actually intervene and control matters are limited in all directions.

In the case described, the political processing strategies outlined above only functioned, paradoxically, for as long as the topic 'environment' had not been communicated as a *critical* topic, i.e., during the first, 'offensive' phase of environmental policy making.

Scandalisation and dramatisation of the environmental topic gave rise to a critical awareness that prevented the successful processing of the subject with the help of strategies 1 (plausibilisation of a de-dramatising diagnosis) or 2 (weighing up the risks against greater disadvantages).

For now non-intended side-effects of industrial production appeared. Booking large-scale global risks – of atomic energy, for instance – as necessarily acceptable side-effects of progress thus suddenly became just as unacceptable to a relevant sector of society as the offer of compensation for these risks in the form of greater prosperity. Simultaneously the third strategy (the demonstration of vigorous activity) was rendered impossible by the exaggerated conflict of ecological and economic interests.

However, the strong pressure to do something, which had been maintained at a constant level over the years by the scandalisation strategies of new social movements, now also prevented a relegation of the topic of the environment to the lower level of the domestic-policy agenda. Political decision makers reacted to external pressure to act by focusing on individual behaviour and by staging environmental policy as an 'all-together-now' campaign, thus obtaining the effects of a (temporary) respite.

This shift in crisis diagnosis is a decisive feature in the process of the pedagogisation of a social experience of crisis, since individualising crisis diagnoses guaranteed that educational programmes could be attached to social crises. Only a generally plausible attribution construction aimed at individual cognitive, moral or motivational deficits provokes processes such as education – and in modern societies, these deficits are primarily matters for the educational system. Individualising crisis diagnoses communicated in the environment of the educational system are thus the decisive impulses for the pedagogisation of crisis topics.

4. The Ability of the Educational System to Produce a Resonance

I shall now change my system of reference, and observe the educational system: the individualising crisis diagnoses which at times have dominated environmental policy communication since the mid 1970s were interpreted within the educational system as a demand for educational programmes, and this demand was accordingly met.

During the second half of the 1970s, environmental education became a subject of educational communication. This can be seen, on the one hand, from educational policy recommendations and, on the other, by the incorporation of the subject into the curricula, by the development of teaching materials, learning materials and teaching units. Then, in the late 1970s, came specialised publications addressing their suggestions and hints to members of the teaching professions in schools and further education (Thiel 1994).

In 1980 the Conference of State Ministers of Education in Germany finally published its conclusions entitled 'The Environment and Teaching' enshrining environmental education as an all-subject teaching principle. This decision underlined, as it were, the existing programmes and activities with an educational policy statement of intent.

According to the Ministers of Education, it was one of the 'tasks of schooling to generate in young people an awareness for environmental questions, to promote readiness to act responsibly towards the environment and to teach them environmentally conscious behaviour patterns which will continue to be effective even when they have left school.' (The Environment and Teaching 1980)

'The Environment and Teaching' was followed by countless educational policy recommendations, comments, the implementation of model experiments and, finally, the setting up of special roles and specific installations such as posts for experts on environmental education, institutes for the development of curricula, teaching units and further education measures (e.g., the Central Agency for Environmental Education at the University of Essen, or the Centre for Environmental Education at the Federal Institute of Vocational Training). These specialists in environmental education have ensured, to this day, that the topic continues to be positioned within the context of educational policy communication.

How though, is it possible to explain the capacity of the education system to echo these crisis diagnoses? Here, too, it seems a sensible idea to start from the structural conditions of pedagogical communication. My *thesis* is as follows: the educational system has a structural openness for reform generated by an educational establishment which, in its turn, makes use of a semantic apparatus the core of which is the educational aspiration to 'bring up individuals as human-beings in the face of a deficient reality' (Oelkers 1989).

The concept of the educational establishment is defined by Luhmann and Schorr as a set of roles for specialists in the educational system who are not directly occupied with education and/or teaching but with the administration, training individuals for the teaching profession, developing curricula, advising on policy, representing the educational professions (Luhmann and Schorr 1988:343 ff.). This educational establishment takes care of the reflexion theory of the educational system, so to speak. Here problems are defined, desiderata characterised, new programmatics, concepts and topics developed. The fact that functional systems can theoreticise themselves, i.e., develop a theory about themselves which guarantees the self presentation – or the unity – of the system is described by Schorr as 'a problem following on from the functional differentiation of society' (Schorr 1979:885). The organisational basis of this 'theory of itself' can be designated as 'establishment'. The educational establishment sets itself apart from concrete teaching, obtaining its standpoint by discussing the latter. Or, rather, its activities are basically aimed at improving actual teaching.

Why? According to Schorr, an inherent dynamism arises in the face of concrete teaching simply because the educational establishment does not just generate any old theory of the educational system. It has, at the same time, to ensure its own permanence (Schorr 1979:888). This is done via a theory of reflexion aimed the need and capacity for reform exhibited by educational practice. The descriptions of the deficits in actual teaching are contrasted with the pedagogical aspiration of 'educating individuals ... in the face of a deficient reality' (Oelkers 1989), which has a long tradition. Educational aspirations function along the pattern of contrasting a deficient present with the potentials of education and training. This contrast produces a utopian surplus. Educational aspiration thus provides, so to speak, the semantic background for the pedagogical programming of new reform topics.

Social crises thus produce such a strong echo in the educational establishment, and are so suitable for the ever new concretisation of its structural openness to reform because their public thematicisation in the form of individualising crisis diagnoses can be interpreted as a challenge to the latter's pedagogical processing. The continually new processing of social crises concretises and consolidates the claim to reform made by the educational establishment, thus ensuring its own permanence.

The pedagogisation of social crises is usually aimed in the first instance at reforming the themes rather than reforming the structures. Themes are easier to alter than structures. This may be a second reason why this form of concretising the reforming intentions of the educational establishment has appeared particularly attractive over the past few years – especially after all the problems experienced with *structural* reforms within the educational system in the 1960s and 1970s!

The reconstruction of 'ecological communication' sketched out, with special reference to the transformation of a politicised crisis theme into an educational theme, showed the following development: publicly circulated crisis diagnoses directed at individual cognitive, motivational or moral deficits are particularly widely spread in political communication if the more limited arsenal of political crisis-processing strategies is blocked. These individualising crisis diagnoses generate within the educational system – and here primarily within the educational establishment – an echo, and are transformed into educational programmes, generally at the level of firmly establishing new topics in the curricula.

There are signs that the pattern of transforming political into pedagogical themes demonstrated by the example of 'ecological crisis' communication can also be transferred to other crisis themes.

5. Final Comments on the Risks of this Form of Generation of Educational Topics

Under the conditions of constantly declining reliability of political intervention as a controlling and checking mechanism, educational action is being recommended more frequently as an instrument for 'risk management' (see in this context Heyting 1994).

The pedagogisation of social crises only functions against the background of a potentially *successful* processing of these crises by means of education. This assumption will probably prove unrealistic in extensive areas, as 'educational action remains bound to the conditions of the […] educational system' (Herrmann 1984:38).

The educational programmatics often take the form of moral appeals; they bring educational aspirations up to date without possessing any corresponding technology to realise them; they operate more or less without empirical cover.

Pedagogisation programmes, however, need to do more than just grapple with the problem of the successful control of educational action which Eduard Spranger discussed at a very early juncture under the title 'undesired side-effects' (Spranger 1962). They must, in addition, come to terms with the problem of translating individual changes of consciousness – should these actually take place – into corrections in the courses taken by social systems.

In both cases the self-referentiality of the relevant system context must be taken into account. Psychological systems arrange their self reproduction exclusively through consciousness. This means that changes in the operations of a psychological system can only be made by the system itself, they are not effects of inputs from outside. In the case of society the system-specific dynamics of the functional differentiated systems (for example the economic system or political system) must also be taken into account. Thus pedagogisation programmes, measured in terms of actual problem-solution potentials, are fraught with considerable risk of disappointment.

With the pedagogisation of the ecological crisis the educational profession is burdened for a second time with responsibility for processing a social crisis topic which it cannot, for structural reasons, undertake: for as has already been said, the question of how teaching in a school class or a measure of further training can stimulate effects capable of altering the control of component systems of society such as the economy or science has still to be answered. In this respect pedagogisation cannot help producing disappointment 'so that the only surprising thing is how disappointment never fails to inspire new hope' (Oelkers 1990:6).

References

Beck, U. (1993), 'Risikogesellschaft und Vorsorgestaat', in F. Ewald (ed.) *Der Vorsorgestaat*, Frankfurt a.M.

Brand, K. W. et al. (1984), *Neue soziale Bewegungen in der Bundesrepublik Deutschland*, Frankfurt a.M.

Brand, K. W. (1982), *Neue soziale Bewegungen. Entstehung, Funktion und Perspektive neuer Prostestpotentiale. Eine Zwischenbilanz*, Opladen.

Der Deutsche Bundestag 6 (1971), Wahlperiode: Umweltprogramm der Bundesregierung, 14 October, Bundestagsdrucksache 6/2710.

Der Deutsche Bundestag (ed.) (1990), Schlußbericht der Enquete-Kommission 'Zukünftige Bildungspolitik – Bildung 2000', 5 September, Bundestagsdrucksache 11/ 7820.

Environment and Teaching. Resolution of the Konerenz der Kultusminister der Länder, 17 Oct. 1980. In *Informationen zur politischer Bildung*, 1990, 219,47.

Evers, A. and Nowotny, H. (1987), *Über den Umgang mit Unsicherheit. Die Entdeckung der Gestaltbarkeit von Gesellschaft*, Frankfurt a.M.

Ewald, F. (ed.) (1993), *Der Vorsorgestaat*, Frankfurt a.M.

Giesecke, H. (1985), *Das Ende der Erziehung. Neue Chancen für Familie und Schule*, Stuttgart.

Hartkopf, G. and Bohne, E. (1983), *Umweltpolitik*, vol.1, *Grundlagen, Analysen und Perspektiven*, Opladen.

Herrmann, U. (1984), 'Pädagogisierung sozialer Probleme. Entwicklungen und Folgeprobleme des Einfusses sozialer Probleme auf erziehungs-wissenschaftliche Theoriebildung und pädagogische Praxis', in H. Heid and W.Klafki (ed.), *Arbeit – Bildung – Arbeitslosigkeit. 19. Beiheft der Z.f.Päd*, Weinheim/ Basel.

Heyting, F. (1994), 'Pluralisierungstendenzen in der Gesellschaft und pädagogische Risikobeherrschung', in D. Benner and D. Lenzen (ed.), *Bildung und Erziehung in Europa. 32. Beiheft der Zeitschrift für Pädagogik*, Weinheim/ Basel.

INFAS-Berlin (1973), *Umweltpolitisches Bewußtsein 1972*, Berlin.

Kitschelt, H. P. (1986), 'Political Opportunity Structures and Political Protest: Anti-Nuclear-Movements in Four Democracies', in *British Journal of Political Sciences* 16.

Kupffer, H. (1980), *Erziehung als Angriff auf die Freiheit. Essays gegen eine Pädagogik, die den Lebensweg des Menschen mit Hinweisschildern umstellt*, Weinheim/ Basel.

Küppers, G. et al. (1978), *Umweltforschung – die gesteuerte Wissenschaft? Eine empirische Untersuchung zum Verhältnis von Wissenschaftsentwicklung und Wissenschaftspolitik*, Frankfurt a.M.

Luhmann, N. and Schorr, K.-E. (1988), *Reflexionsprobleme im Erziehungssystem*, Frankfurt a.M.

Luhmann, N.(1986), *Ökologische Kommunikation. Kann die moderne Gesellschaft sich auf ökologische Gefährdungen einstellen?* Opladen.

Luhmann, N. (1987), *Soziale Systeme. Grundriß einer allgemeinen Theorie*, Frankfurt a.M.

Müller, E. (1986), *Innenwelt der Umweltpolitik. Sozial-liberale Umweltpolitik – (Ohn-) Macht durch Organsisation?*, Opladen.

Oelkers, J. (1989), *Die große Aspiration. Zur Herausbildung der Erziehungswissenschaft im 19. Jahrhundert*, Darmstadt.

Oelkers, J. (1990), 'Utopie und Wirklichkeit. Ein Essay über Pädagogik und Erziehungswissenschaft', in *Zeitschrift für Pädagogik* 36,1.

Pollack, G.(1991), 'Der Begriff der "Pädagogisierung" in der erziehungswissenschaftlichen Diskussion. Vorbereitende Untersuchungen zur Bilanz der Erziehungswissenschaft', in D. Hoffman and H.Heid (eds), *Bilanzierungen erziehungswissenschaftlicher Theoriebildung. Erfolgskontrolle durch Wissenschaftsforschung*, Weinheim.

Radtke, F.-O. (1991), 'Die Rolle der Pädagogik in der Minderheitenforschung. Bemerkungen aus wissenschaftssoziologischer Sicht', in *Soziale Welt* 42, .

Rammstedt, O.(1978) *Soziale Bewegung*, Frankfurt a.M.

Schelsky, H. (1961), *Anpassung oder Widerstand? Soziologische Bedenken zur Schulreform*, Heidelberg.

Schorr, K.-E.(1979), 'Wissenschaftstheorie und Reflexion im Erziehungssystem' in *Z.f.Päd.* 25,6.

Sieferle, R. P. (1984), *Fortschrittsfeinde? Opposition gegen Technik und Industrie von der Romantik bis zur Gegenwart*, München.

Spranger, E. (1962), *Das Gesetz der ungewollten Nebenwirkungen in der Erziehung*, Heidelberg.

Stölting, E. (1990), 'Zeit, Kompetenz und Ressort. Bürokratische Probleme bei der Bewältigung von Umweltkrisen', in H.-P. Dreitzel and H. Stenger, (eds), *Ungewollte Selbstzerstörung. Reflexionen über den Umgang mit katastrophalen Entwicklungen*, Frankfurt a.M.

Thiel, F. (1994), 'Die "ökologische Krise" als pädagogisches Thema. Überlegungen zum Prozeß der Pädagogisierung einer gesellschaftlichen Krisenerfahrung', Dissertation Freie Universität Berlin.

Touraine, A. et al. (1982), *Die antinukleare Prophetie. Zukunftsentwürfe einer sozialen Bewegung*, Frankfurt a.M.

Umwelt und Unterricht (1990), 'Beschluß der Konferenz der Kultusminister der Länder vom 17 October1980'. In: *Informationen zur politischen Bildung* 219, 47

Umweltbericht'76 (1976), *Fortschreibung des Umweltprogramms der Bundesregierung vom 14 July 1976*. With an introduction by W. Maihofer, Stuttgart.

Wey, K.-G. (1982), *Umweltpolitik in Deutschland. Geschichte des Umweltschutzes in Deutschland seit 1900*, Opladen.

Chapter 7

THE NON-DECEPTION OF VIOLENCE

A Challenge to Education

Christoph Wulf

To the same extent that sex begins to lose its fascination, violence becomes more attractive. Now that sexuality has lost its taboo character, violence and monstrosity has begun to appear to be particularly fascinating. This fascination also appears in the realm of the imagination. Films which show acts of violence, contain scenes with atrocities, and present invasions of the monstrous have become box-office hits. Videos with similar contents have introduced horror into one's 'leisure time'. Violence and horror confront one's everyday reality, which has become boring, and its ritualised monotony with new forms of 'intensity'. Crime fascinates; it promises moments of a more exciting life. The order and safety of the middle-class everyday life requires the addition of something that has been excluded in order to be able to constitute it in this form. In order to dissolve the rigidity of everyday life and liberate new energy and intensity, at least in the imagination, it was necessary to extend the non-available, the arbitrary, and the destructive. The image of man that these films and videos stage is an anti-picture; it expresses another kind of anthropology than politics and economics, law and public administration, education and science would like to admit to. The aesthetisation of the monstrous and the horrible appears to have become a widespread form of dealing with violence.

What happens with violence in film productions, television and video? On the one hand the portrayals of violence usually show the unusual, which produces tension, intensity and fascination. They refer to the horror and cruelty of violence, but this reference is only in the world of the imaginary. Through the representation of horror, violence and terror, a de-tabooing process takes place. At the same time violence is minimised in these productions. The production itself of horrible cruel deeds remains in one's mind without any consequences, and the viewer of these atrocities thinks in his/her mind that this is only a question of images and arrangements of the images. Nevertheless, the observer becomes fascinated through the reference of the images to real acts of violence and cruelty. There is some plausibility in the fear that a continued encounter with images of violence gradually makes one immune to the acts of violence and thereby reduces the inhibition threshold for violent action. The fact that most of the time the 'hero' is not a victim of violence also supports such an assumption. He survives; for he is not vulnerable and is immune to the transitory. Therefore, these productions always contain myths and dreams of invulnerability and survival under inhuman conditions. Violence concerns only someone else, makes him a victim, but the 'hero' and the viewer identifying with him never succumb to it.

The difference between the antisceptic electronic world and the world outside is considerable. Sign worlds (simulcra) have been constructed in the electronic world. In these violence becomes a play of signs in which the difference between victim and culprit disappears. In addition, the identification of the viewer is directed toward both participants. Pain and suffering, which represent the real difference between the culprit and the victim, are minimised in the production. The culprit and victim become signs for action and suffering – for the energy of violence. In their game almost everything is allowed. Sign games without consequences in 'reality'. Do these image-orgies of violence support the anaesthesia of the viewer, who becomes accustomed to horror as an evening entertainment programme. This probably occurs largely because the difference between the images of horror in news broadcasts in which the relation to reality is mediated through corresponding commentary, and the images of horror in films on the level of the images is often not perceptible.

How strongly the presentations of violence sensitise one to the suffering of the victim and thereby protect against acts of violence, or how much an imitation of violence leads to promoting readiness for violence has been disputed since Plato and Aristotle's different view of the effects of models, and in spite of extensive recent empirical research, has not been explained. It is probable that the effects of the presentations of violence depend essentially on *how* the violence is presented and which possibilities of treatment exist for the presentations of violence. Plato emphasised the inevitability of the mimetic effect of a presentation. In his view, mimesis has such tremendous power that one cannot avoid it, even when one is conscious of its effects and defends himself against it. Therefore, one must avoid presentations of violence which, through the mimetic processes, lead inevitably to negative effects. On the other hand, Aristotle referred to the necessity of a confrontation with negative behavior. It is not the ignoring of violence that protects one from it, but only dealing with it directly. Only in this way can an immunisation against violence and cruelty take place. These different evaluations of the effect of negative 'models' have still not been solved. This applies especially to the presentations of violence in 'virtual worlds' produced in the media, which offer new possibilities for presentation and effects to the polymorphous character of violence.

Violence was not only a theme of enormous magnitude in films and videos.It is also evident in ethno-social wars, to which we are witnesses in the former Yugoslavia, in Rwanda and other places, leading to a lasting confrontation with violence. Racist violence and hostility to foreigners have shown their horrible faces in Germany and other places. Actually these are only the conspicuous manifestations of violence. The comprehensive discussion of violence in research on peace and conflict had already contributed considerably to the broadening of the concept of violence. Along with their manifest striking forms there are forms of violence that can be identified which are not obvious at first glance. They appear in gender- and generation relationships, in hierarchies of social institutions, in the ritualisation of social life. That which respectively can be viewed as violence depends on the values, ideas, concepts, therefore, on the reference points of the observer. These introduce social and cultural norms into the evaluation, which allow some social phenomena to appear as violent, others as free of violence. The historically and culturally specific character of this evaluation is obvious.

In terms of language 'violence' is a collective term, with whose help different phenomena can be characterised. The evaluation of social phenomena in regard to their violent character is not certain; they can change. Actions which as individual activities appear free of violence can reveal their violent character as collective activities. Thus, driving a car is not very violent as an individual act, however, it can become destructive as collective action. The destructive character of many social phenomena is often not obvious at first, but appears massive later on. In turn, social actions at first considered destructive can later be evaluated as innovations. In such cases violence creates positively evaluated social change; it appears as a 'violence fondatrice', as creative violence. In the confrontation between the younger and older generation it is mainly this destructive side of violence which manifests itself.

The socialisation of man is violent. Schopenhauer, Nietzsche and Freud have already pointed this out. Culture is connected with renunciation of drives and desires, with asceticism and discipline, with violence against another and oneself. The capability for violence probably makes possible above all the preservation of the human species. Biologists speak of 'genetic self-interest', of human action, whose moral judgment they consider to be a question of cultural value. In extreme cases the morally negative evaluated acts of violence in the middle- or long-term can ensure the preservation of the species or particular societies and cultures. Individual altruistic acts themselves can serve a genetic, or rather species-specific egoism. From this perspective violence as a destructive force can hardly be distinguished from violence as a constructive force. An evaluation of its different forms is possible only in terms of context.

Also from a systematic perspective, it is difficult to avoid forces which endanger the preservation of the system. They appear as 'surprising behavior', as surprises for the system. In order that the negative forces do not lead to the destruction of the system, the system reacts with an intensification of its controls. This strengthening of efforts to exclude 'bad surprises' once again lead to an increase in the forces endangering the system. The stronger the controls are that are directed to the preservation of the system, the greater are the forces aimed at its change and reshaping. Herein lies a paradoxical situation, whose consequences require further attention for the understanding of power and systemic organisation.

Neither living beings nor systems are 'selfless'; rather, with their wish for self-preservation, they produce related 'egoistic' violence and antiviolence. From one perspective, which refers the concept of violence not only to manifest forms of violence, but also in the violent aspect of life, systematic organisation, gender- and generation relationships, the human relationship to nature and to oneself, the concept of violence gains a new anthropological complexity. If one sets up the foundation of this type of a broadened understanding of violence, then the concept indeed loses its simple clarity which it had in its sole application to manifest forms of violence. Nevertheless, the broadening of its meaning is inevitable, since otherwise many forms of its appearance which are designated with concepts like 'structural violence' (Galtung), 'foundation violence' (Girard), 'symbolic violence' (Bourdieu) cannot be understood as forms of violence.

Violence is articulated as 'will to power' (Nietzsche), as a 'force of destruction', as 'the death drive' (Freud). It becomes evident in the denial of minimal living conditions. It appears in socially tolerated forms as ambition, competition and rivalry. Violence becomes manifest conspicuously in damage to the human body, in its mutilation and its annihilation. It occurs arbitrarily, unforeseen, accidentally and without calculation. In war, in crowds, in dreams, reason and individual control of one's actions cease to be in force. Violence mingles with a desire for risk, for the uncertain, for the sudden. It attracts and repulses; it is fascinating like horror and fright. Violence is a condition of human life and human socialisation and is as such undeceivable.

The broadening of the concept of violence leads to scepticism in regard to any hope for overcoming violence. This scepticism does not include denial of political and social action. It is inadequate to understand violence only as 'undesired social behavior' and to create a reductionist concept of violence as the starting point of an opposition strategy. In order to be able to work out the given potential for violence with biological equipment and the socialisation of man, a comprehensive understanding of violence is required. Due to the threat proceeding from the current racist acts of violence and acts directed against foreigners, the demand for rash political and social action is understandable and politically sensible: as an expression of resolute action, they create for politics an urgently needed legitimation and develop models of engaged social relations. Thus, at the time it is difficult to foresee which effects this social and pedagogical intervention in the struggle against racism, hostility to foreigners and violence may have.

If people, because of their different outlook, their belonging to a different ethnic group or religion, through no fault of their own become victims of violence, then the understanding of such events pushes one to a limit with which one cannot come to terms, but which also cannot be overstepped. The attempts to understand the acts of violence from individual life histories of the culprits explain some things, but still shed little light on the puzzling nature of the deed. What is striking in many acts of violence of young people is the lack of insight into the consequences of the deed. Breakdown of inhibitions and brutalisation rarely are followed by sympathy for the victim. Instead one observes an upsetting inability for the perception of the victim's pain and suffering, an anasthesia for which there is insufficient explanation.

Many acts of violence are carried out as group action. In order to be able to make the object of violence the scapegoat, a social crisis is required, which can arise through unemployment, social and cultural identity crises, lack of perspective, and which is seen as the cause and blame, which is different and which, therefore, presents itself as the object of projections of blame and exoneration. As an object of exclusion and ascribing of guilt, someone becomes a victim and makes possible a lack of feeling and violence. The scapegoat is percived not in his similarity but in his differentness and supposed culpability and is made a victim. Since the blame for social crises are ascribed to him, the group suffering in the crisis is 'authorised' to mistreat the respected person as guilty. Since the group situation reduces the individual competence and responsibility for the act of violence, it is no longer the single individual who commits the act of violence, but the 'mob'. In mimetic processes the differences between the single members of the group are annulled, so that an anonymous 'mass subject' arises, which commits the act of violence. Since the deed is not the action of a single but a 'mass subject', the individuals usually manifests no consiousness of wrongdoing. The projection of unsolved problems of life and violence onto a scapegoat and the delegation of the act of violence to a 'mass subject' are mechanisms which allow such acts of violence to arise, which, however, in order to be effective may not be thoroughly understood by the persons involved.

Many people feel pleasure when harm and mutilation of victims occurs. With gladiator fights in the Roman stadiums during the times of the emperors, the ritual sacrificing of prisoners among the Aztecs, the feeling of omnipotence of an Indian despot who allows people to be executed in order to please his survivors, there is likewise a pleasure in the suffering and dying of other persons. War films and catastrophe films promise similar experiences, so that films such *Apocalypse Now* and *Jurassic Park* become great hits. Below the feeling of horror at willful and cruel acts of violence lies a layer on which such outbreaks of violence attract people against their will. The fascination with violence, war and catastrophe is the expression of attraction and repulsion simultaneously.

In view of this situation the development of Christian morals can be understood as an attempt, through a reevaluation of archiac and pre-Christian values, to control the side of man which feels the desire for destruction. The difficulties to which the attempts to contain power lead have been proven all too clearly by European history. Indeed, the inadequacy of this attempt is not an objection to it. One can – like Girard – see a hope in the Christian religion to breaking the cycle of violence, which has arisen through the idea that every act of violence, in order to avenge the victim, must be followed by another. When it is possible to forgive the enemy's act of violence, then this cycle of violence can perhaps be broken.

If violence fascinates, because it is connected with great fantasies, with situational self-enhancement, with the hope of freeing oneself from suffering due to violence through acts of violence, then it becomes clear how difficult it is for explanations, argumentation and insight to stand against it or can even be accepted. If violence is the formless power of destruction, which calls into question the contextually different connections and can be expressed in many phenomena, it is difficult and often hopeless to protect oneself against its amalgamation. In spite of many attemps by theology, philosophy and science to understand the processes of the origin of violence, recognition is pushed continually to the limit. All attempts at clarification are somewhat provisional, so that the puzzling nature of the amalgamation of violence is not capable of being resolved. Since violence as an energetic force cannot be differentiated basically from other types of human energy, but results in a transformation of formless energy into specific situations and constellations, the explanation of its origin is particularly difficult. Violence is a possibility of human action and a virtual component of the human world, which can be actualised time and again.

Those who suffer violence or become witnesses of violence acts experience the vulnerability and frailty of human life. The democratic societies of the West have been invested to control and channel the economic, political and socially determined potentials for violence. The decisive role belongs to the state, with whom the monopoly of violence lies. If its monopoly on violence is called into question, an irritation arises in the political order. If rituals of social interaction occur without force, this leads to an outbreak of violence, in the course of which particular persons or groups are made responsible. If in such situations the mechanism of the regulation of violence is no longer understood, the relative lack of violence in everyday life is destroyed.

Situations of open violence constantly leave doubt as to the success of human development. Uncontained wars with horrible cruelty and tremendous violence against nature strengthen the perception of the great vulnerability and endangering of human life. A sensibility to the destructive side of human development arising out of such observations can lead to confronting the social and individual potential for violence, if the hope for controlling it once and for all has disappeared. Possibly this insight into the limits of controlling violence is a prerequisite for individually and socially productive relations with it.

References

Arendt, H. (1970), *On Violence*. New York: Harcourt.

Arendt, H. (1994) *The Human Condition*. Chicago.

Bourdieu, P. (1993), *La Misère du Monde*. Paris.

Bourdieu, P. and J.-C. Passeron (1970) *La Réproduction*. Paris.

Canetti, E. (1976), *Macht und Masse*. München.

Colpe, C. and W. Schmidt-Biggemann (1993), *Das Böse. Eine historische Phänomenolgie des Bösen*. Frankfurt.

Diekmann, B. and Wulf, C., Wimmer, M. (eds) (1997), *Violence. Nationalism. Racism. Xenophobia*, Münster/New York.

Galtung, J.(1969), 'Violence, Peace and Peace Research', *Journal of Peace Research*, 6, 167-191.

Gebauer, G. and C.Wulf (1995), *Mimesis. Culture – Art – Society*. Berkeley/ Los Angeles/London..

Gebauer, G. and C. Wulf (eds)(1993), *Praxis und Ästhetik*. Frankfurt.

Girard, R. (1988), *La Violence et le Sacré*. Paris.

McKenna, A. (1992), *Violence and Difference*. Urbana/Chicago.

Schuller, A. and W. von Rahden (eds) (1993), *Die andere Kraft. Zur Renaissance des Bösen*. Berlin.

Wulf, C. (ed.) (1995), *Education in Europe: An Intercultural Task*. Münster/ New York.

Chapter 8

DOMAINS OF DECISION MAKING IN EDUCATIONAL ORGANISATIONS

The Case of Colleges for Secondary Vocational Education

Pieter L.J. Boerman

Introduction

Decentralisation is a critical issue in organisational research (Pugh et al. 1968:65-105, Mintzberg 1979, Kochen and Deutsch 1980). It is considered to be one of the main determinants of organisational structure and a key factor for organisational effectiveness.

The majority of studies on decentralisation have focused on defining the construct itself (Mintzberg 1979, Veen 1980). Only a few studies have subjected the concept to empirical investigation (Pugh et al. 1968, Hoeksema 1995), or examined the effect of varying degrees of decentralisation on organisational outcomes. In the present study an attempt is being made to develop a questionnaire for key persons in educational organisations and to examine the empirical structure of the concept.

During the 1980s the Dutch government started a policy of deregulation and increasing autonomy for schools. This policy aimed at reinforcing the management and increasing the effectiveness of schools (in terms of pupil outcomes, i.e., more certification and less dropout).

Within the Dutch education system, secondary vocational education (Dutch: MBO) represents a major sector (see Ax et al. 1993). It has the highest percentage of pupils aged between sixteen and nineteen following full-time education. In addition, secondary vocational education offers many opportunities for young people and adults to follow part-time courses. At present, there are about 140 colleges with between 500 and over 20,000 pupils. These large colleges face practical problems of organisational design. What is the most effective organisational structure? What degree of centralisation is desirable?

Besides these practical questions, there is the academic question of how to investigate the concept of centralisation within school organisations. The main question is which domains of decision making can be distinguished in schools? Our research focuses on the relationship between the degree of decentralisation within Dutch colleges for secondary vocational education and its effects on several dimensions of organisational effectiveness. This chapter will discuss the empirical structure of the independent variables: the degree of decentralisation within school organisations.

First, I will introduce our research, and then present the results of a explorative factor analysis. Finally, I will discuss our findings.

Decentralisation as a Characteristic of Organisational Structure

Pugh et al. (1968) define *centralisation* as the degree to which the authority to make decisions is located at the top of the management hierarchy. According to this definition, the degree of centralisation is a feature of organisational structure (The structure of an organisation is defined as the sum total of the ways in which its labour is divided into distinct tasks and then these tasks are coordinated (Mintzberg 1979). In a typical highly centralised organisation top management is closely involved in a whole range of decisions (Butler 1991:80). There is little structuring of activities in this type of organisation except for a tendency to standardise recruitment policies, demonstrating a concern to ensure that people are carefully selected. A highly decentralised organisation is one in which the responsibility for the outcomes of the decision-making process lies entirely at low organisational levels.

Kochen and Deutsch (1980) argue that there is no single index for the degree of decentralisation in large and complex organisations. The reason is that there are different *areas or domains of decision-making*. Depending on the area of decision-making, the degree of decentralisation will vary. Moch et al. (1983) make similar comments.

Notwithstanding the frequent call for a distinction to be made between different domains of decision making, there appears to be no generally agreed taxonomy of organisational decision making. For example, Moch et al. (1983) distinguish between decisions about work, resource allocation and coordination of activities while others like Bacharach et al. (1990), Sleegers (1991) or Hanson (1985) respectively distinguish four, two or three domains. For example, Hanson suggested a three-domain classification of administrative and educational decision-making, plus a contested zone.

In the following paragraphs I briefly discuss two of these approaches. Firstly, I will focus on the multi-domain approach of Bacharach et al. and secondly, will discuss the two-domain approach in the literature on professional bureaucracies.

Bacharach et al. (1990) suggest that decisions in educational organisations may vary according to whether they directly affect only individuals or the organisation as a whole. While some strategic decisions may have a direct organisational impact (e.g., a budgetary decision), others may primarily affect individuals (e.g., a long-term career assignment). Similarly, operational decisions may affect the organisation as a whole (e.g., development and evaluation of tasks and professional-client relations); alternatively, they may primarily affect individuals (e.g., implementation of work assignments). Bacharach et al. combine these two dimensions of decision-making (strategic versus operational and individual versus organisational) to generate four decision domains (i.e., strategic-organisational, strategic-individual, operational-organisational, operational-individual). In their article they provide empirical evidence to demonstrate the validity of this four-domain framework, as well as the value of the multi-domain approach when operationalised in terms of these four domains.

According to Mintzberg schools can be described as professional bureaucracies with a dichotomy of decision domains (Mintzberg 1979; Sleegers 1991; Witziers 1992). These two domains are the administrator/bureaucratic domain and the teacher/professional domain. Both domains or zones are clearly distinguished from each other. The organisational type of the professional bureaucracy is related to three characteristics. Firstly, executives have a rather independent position. In school organisations teachers are the executives; they are the professionals at the heart of the organisation. Secondly, the relationship between management and professionals is characteristic. Owing to their expertise the professionals do not accept interference from the management. A third characteristic is the way in which the professionals use a fixed repertoire of procedures and skills. Mintzberg calls this process 'pigeon-holing'.

In the remainder of this chapter I will focus on the domains of decision making, and will empirically examine the different frameworks of decision-making domains within school organisations.

Method

Population and response

A questionnaire assessing decentralisation in decision-making was administered to key persons (i.e., educational coordinators) in Colleges for Secondary Vocational Education in the Netherlands. All key persons from colleges with a technical and/or economics department were asked to respond to the questionnaire, resulting in 481 educational coordinators from exactly 100 schools. The study encompassed the total population of schools.

The response amounted to 62 percent (299 completed and usable questionnaires) of the key persons covering 87 percent of the schools in the population. Questionnaires with more than ten missing items were left out of the analysis.

Measures

In total sixty items were developed to measure the degree of decentralisation in fifteen areas of decision making. Some items were adopted from scales developed by Pelkmans and de Vries (1992), Bacharach (1990), and Ax et al. (1993). Descriptions of these items are found in appendix A. The fifteen areas used to measure decentralisation were:

1. teaching methods/aids
2. student tracking
3. student assessment
4. scheduling courses
5. modularisation
6. organisation of work experience
7. organisation of teaching process
8. operational staff management
9. staff performance evaluation
10. monitoring of students
11. monitoring of teachers
12. external relations
13. policy on public relations
14. strategic policy and control
15. operational control

The items consisted of short statements each describing an issue that requires a decision, for example:

Figure 8.1 Example of a Questionnaire Item

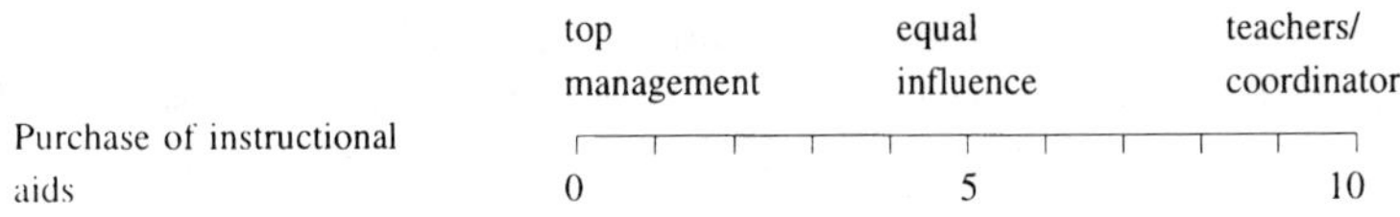

Respondents were asked to indicate the organisational level at which decisions on the issue are made. The answers on the sixty items could be indicated on a straight line ranging from '0' (decision made totally by top management) to '10' (decision are made by teachers+coordinator).

Analyses and Results

The first step in the analysis was to look at the reliability of the sixty items on the fifteen scales. Homogeneity scores of the scales are presented in table 8.1. An acceptable criterion for Cronbach's alpha is 0.70 or higher.

Table 8.1 Homogeneity of Items in Different Areas of Decision Making (Cronbach's Alpha; n = 299)

Scales	α	# items
1. instructional methods/aids	0.72	6
2. student tracking	0.77	4
3. student assessment	0.75	3
4. scheduling courses	0.80	3
5. modularisation	0.85	3
6. organisation of work experience	0.82	3
7. organisation of teaching proces	0.80	4
8. operational staff management	0.84	3
9. staff performance evaluation	0.83	4
10. monitoring of students	0.80	3
11. monitoring of teachers	0.84	3
12. external relations	0.85	2
13. policy on public relation	0.75	2
14. strategic policy and control	0.76	6
15. operational control	0.83	4

Since the homogeneities of the scales are high, sum scores are made for each of the respondents.

In the following table the means and the standard deviation of the sum scores are presented (table 8.2). A score of 10 indicates decision making has been at a low organisational level, which means that the degree of decentralisation within that domain is very high. A score of 0 means that decision-making is highly centralised. A score of about 5 implies that both high and low organisational levels have an influence on the decision making.

Table 8.2 Mean Sum Scores and Standard Deviations of the Scales (n=299)

decision making domain	mean	st.dev
1. instructional methods/aids	9.07	0.82
2. student tracking	5.67	2.01
3. student assessment	7.68	2.02
4. scheduling courses	5.50	2.68
5. modularisation	7.09	2.23
6. organisation of work experience	7.07	2.41
7. organisation of teaching proces	4.98	2.40
8. operational staff management	4.28	2.17
9. staff performance evaluation	2.90	2.15
10. monitoring of students	7.07	2.31
11. monitoring of teachers	3.11	2.48
12. external relations	4.57	2.65
13. policy on public relation	3.56	2.17
14. strategic policy and control	2.16	1.38
15. operational control	3.79	2.09

The analysis shows that the degree of centralisation differs across domains. For example, decisions on teaching matters are made at a lower level (9.07) than decisions on organisational control (resp. 1.11 and 3.79). A t-test confirmed the differences in means ($p < 0.01$).

In figure 8.2 we present a ranking order of the means of the composed variables. Note that a '0' on the vertical axis means that decision making is totally centralised, a '10' implies totally decentralised decision making and a '5' means that both the top level and bottom level have an influence on decision making.

We used an explorative factor analysis (i.e., principal component analysis) to determine whether the variables measuring decentralisation in decision-making domains would factor into the dimensions of the conceptual framework. A three-factor solution (PCA-extraction) was the result of the analysis (the correlation matrix is found in appendix B). The varimax-rotated loadings are presented in table 8.3. The three factors accounted for 64.4 percent of the common variance of the composed variables.

Figure 8.2 Ranked Means of the Fifteen Composed Variables

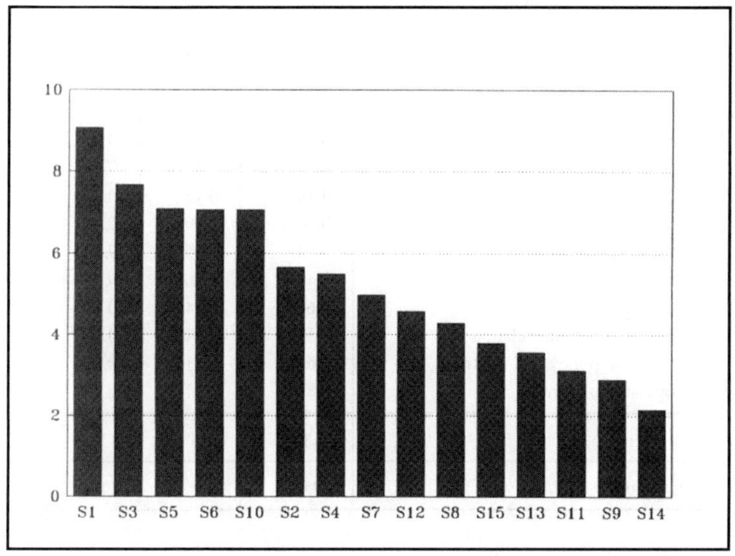

Key to numbers (hor.axis)

s1. instructional methods/aids
s2. student tracking
s3. student assessment
s4. scheduling courses
s5. modularization
s6. org. of work experience
s7. organization of teaching proces
s8. operational staff management
s9. staff performance evaluation
s10. monitoring of students
s11. monitoring of teachers
s12. external relations
s13. policy on public relation
s14. strategic policy and control
s15. operational control

The factor analysis presents a picture of segmentation in the areas of decision making within colleges for vocational education. Factor loadings marked in bold in table 8.3 indicate variables that are most heavily weighted in the interpretation of the factors. Factor loadings in italics indicate variables that are theoretically assumed to belong to the factor, but also have a high loading on another factor.

Factor 1 reflects decision making on issues concerning budgets and organisational goal setting and includes variables 8, 12, and 15. Issues concerning staff management, strategic management, strategic control

Table 8.3 Factor Loadings of Decision Domains (PCA, Varimax Rotation)

Variable	Factor 1	Factor 2	Factor 3
1. instructional methods/aids	0.09	**0.75**	-0.18
2. student tracking	0.57	***0.51***	0.26
3. student assessment	0.11	**0.75**	0.17
4. scheduling courses	0.47	***0.57***	0.48
5. modularisation	0.29	**0.73**	0.23
6. organisation of work experience	0.42	0.32	0.29
7. organisation of teaching proces	0.62	0.41	0.43
8. operational staff management	**0.76**	0.17	0.29
9. staff performance evaluation	0.56	0.09	***0.63***
10. monitoring of students	-0.04	0.55	***0.61***
11. monitoring of teachers	0.41	0.20	***0.73***
12. external relations	**0.62**	0.24	0.24
13. policy on public relation	0.12	-0.01	**0.72**
14. strategic policy and control	***0.66***	0.11	0.52
15. operational control	**0.81**	0.01	-0.10
% of variance	46.3	10.5	7.5
Eigenvalues	6.95	1.58	1.12

and operational control belong to this factor. The core issue addressed by this first factor concerns organisational control, including items like budgetary allocation, accommodation and equipment. Though item 14 also loads on the third factor, it is placed in the first factor because of its content. This factor is labelled the *administrative factor*.

Factor 2 reflects decision making on teaching matters in an educational 'zone'. Three items load on this factor: 1. teaching methods, 3. student assessment and 4. modularisation. These are typical issues concerning curriculum issues within the school and with that the core activities of a school organisation. The factor is labelled the *educational factor*. Besides the three high-loading items mentioned, the variables student tracking, scheduling courses, and monitoring of students show substantial correlations with this factor. These issues are also concerned with activities in the educational zone. It can be stated that decisions about the organisation of the primary processes or activities are made at a low organisational level (bottom of the organisation).

Factor 3 reflects decision issues concerning variables related to the flow of information between the top and bottom level of the school organisation. Both organisational levels are involved with these issues, so that both levels have a certain interest in keeping informed about these issues. The issue of public relations – item 13 – shows a high loading on this factor. With respect to their content items 9, 10, and 11 are attributed to the third factor. Item 10 – monitoring of students – also loads high on the teaching factor, which means that it correlates highly with the issues of the primary processes in the school. It can be stated that these issues also reflect some kind of information exchange and negotiation. This is called the *contested zone*.

Conclusion and Discussion

This chapter began by stating that a central challenge in education is to face problems of organisational design. One of the design issues concerns the degree of centralisation within an organisation. It was suggested that the degree of centralisation cannot be represented by a single index. It has to be conceptualised and measured in relation to a certain area of decision-making. This paper examined the conceptual advantages of a multi-domain approach to examining decision-making domains in an educational setting.

Our findings in the present study suggest that a multi-dimensional approach is likely to prove a generally useful tool for researchers. The delineation of three decision domains in school organisations supports and extends the multi-dimensional approach suggested by earlier studies of the school as a professional bureaucracy (Mintzberg 1979). The two domains of teachers versus administrators were confirmed. The third domain of information flow can be interpreted as a linking domain through which information between the two organisational levels (bottom vs. top) flows.

A second finding is concerned with the combination of the three factors and the ranking order of the means of the single variables (see figure 8.2). The factors are set up as variables next to one another (only variable 14 is an exception). That means that certain decision domains belong to certain organisational levels in a fixed way. This finding corresponds with Mintzberg's typology of the dichotomy of professional organisations and Witziers' observations (1992) that schools are bureaucratic organisations in essence, because of the fixed rules and regulations.

With both findings in mind, researchers may want to examine, for example, the impact of domain-specific decision-making efforts on overall effectiveness.

References

Ax, J., Bosma, Y. and Wieringen, A.M.L., van, (1993), *Funding and Policy-making in Colleges for Vocational Education*, Amsterdam. (report no. 346).

Bacharach, S.B., Bamberger, P., Conley, S.C. and Bauer, S. (1990), 'The Dimensionality of Decision Participation in Educational Organisation: the Value of a Multi Domain Evaluative Approach', *Educational Administration Quarterly*, Vol. 26 no. 2.

Butler, R. (1991), *Designing Organisations. A Decision Making Perspective*, London.

Kochen, M. and Deutsch, K.W., (1980), *Decentralization. Sketches Toward a Rational Theory*, Cambridge, mass.

Hanson, E. (1985), *Educational Administration and Organisational Behavior*, Boston. (first edition 1979).

Hoeksema, L.H. (1995), *Learning Strategy as a Guide to Career Success in Organisations*, Leiden.

Mintzberg, H. (1979), *The Structuring of Organisations. A Synthesis of the Research*, Englewood Cliffs.

Moch, M., Cammann, C., and Cooke, R.A., (1983), 'Organizational Structure: Measuring the Distribution of Influence'. In Seashore, S.E., Lawler, E.E., Mirris, P.H. and Cammann C., (eds) *Assessing Organizational Change. A Guide to Methods, Measures, and Practices*, New York.

Pelkmans, A., and Vries, B. de, (1992), *De V van SVM; inventarisatie van vernieuwingen in onderwijs en organisatie in de SVM-instellingen voor middelbaar beroepsonderwijs (1990-1991)*. Nijmegen.

Pugh, D., Hickson, D., Hinnings, C. and Turner, C. (1968), 'Dimensions of Organisation Structure', *Administrative Science Quarterly*, Vol. 12 no.1.

Sleegers, P. (1991), *School en beleidsvoering*, Nijmegen.

Veen, P. (1980), 'Kenmerken van organisaties', in Drenth, P.J.D. et al. (eds), *Handboek Arbeids- en Organisatiepsychologie*, Deventer, pp.Afl.2, 4.1: 1-37.

Witziers, B. (1992), *Coördinatie binnen scholen voor voortgezet onderwijs*, Enschede.

Appendix A. Description of Composed Variables

1. *Teaching methods/aids*
   This variable measures decisions about micro-instructional issues such as teaching aids, what to teach, how to teach, the contents of tests and the amount of homework.
2. *Student tracking*
   This variable measures decisions about students' options and is concerned with different tracks and changes in learning tracks.
3. *Student assessment*
   This variable measures decisions about the organisation of testing and evaluation of student achievement.
4. *Scheduling courses*
   This variable measures decisions about timetables, courses and lessons.
5. *Modularisation*
   This variable measures decisions about the number of curriculum units and the time devoted to them.
6. *Organisation of work experience*
   This variable measures decisions about the organisation of practical training. It measures the division of tasks between teachers and coordination of contacts.
7. *Organisation of teaching process*
   This variable measures decisions about individual supervision and coaching of students, timetables, and student assignment to classes.
8. *Operational staff management*
   This variable measures decisions about training and development of staff and task specialisation.
9. *Staff performance evaluation*
   This variable measures decisions about the functioning of staff: initiatives and design of interviews.
10. *Monitoring of students*
    This variable measures decisions about recording student achievement and absenteeism.
11. *Monitoring of teachers*
    This variable measures decisions about teachers' work load/stress, recording absenteeism caused by illness.
12. *External relations*
    This variable measures decisions about external relations esp. relations with related colleges and national curriculum committees.
13. *Policy on public relations*
    This variable measures decisions about pr and recruiting students.
14. *Strategic policy and control*
    This variable measures decisions about the allocation of the budget to units and accommodation.
15. *Operational control*
    This variable measures decisions about the equipment in the school.

Appendix B. Correlation Table S1 to S15

	S1	S2	S3	S4	S5	S6
S1	1.00					
S2	.34**	1.00				
S3	.37**	.40**	1.00			
S4	.25**	.69**	.56**	1.00		
S5	.41**	.58**	.56**	.66**	1.00	
S6	.26**	.43**	.19**	.53**	.35**	1.00
S7	.21**	.65**	.46**	.76**	.53**	.50**
S8	.17*	.55**	.28**	.58**	.39**	.41**
S9	.09	.49**	.28**	.56**	.37**	.36**
S10	.34**	.38**	.41**	.53**	.43**	.37**
S11	.10	.53**	.32**	.64**	.40**	.38**
S12	.16*	.56**	.29**	.53**	.42**	.38**
S13	.03	.24**	.13	.34**	.23**	.32**
S14	.07	.58**	.27**	.58**	.43**	.35**
S15	.16*	.33**	.11	.29*	.19**	.32**

	S9	S10	S11	S12	S13	S14
S1						
S2						
S3						
S4						
S5						
S6						
S7						
S8						
S9	1.00					
S10	.38**	1.00				
S11	.74**	.51**	1.00			
S12	.43**	.24**	.40**	1.00		
S13	.40**	.35**	.42**	.33**	1.00	
S14	.70**	.36**	.63**	.59**	.41**	1.00
S15	.36**	.08	.27**	.37**	.16*	.44**

N of cases: 298   1-tailed Signif: * - .01   ** - .001

Key to abbrevations:

S1. instructional methods/aids
S2. student tracking
S3. student assessment
S4. scheduling courses
S5. modularization
S6. organization of work experience
S7. organization of teaching proces
S8. operational staff management
S9. staff performance evaluation
S10. monitoring of students
S11. monitoring of teachers
S12. external relations
S13. policy on public relation
S14. strategic policy and control
S15. operational control

Chapter 9

EFFECTS OF CULTURAL CAPITAL IN PERIODS OF SOCIAL CHANGE

The Election of School Tracks as a Taken Opportunity

Hans Merkens and *Karen Dohle*

1. Introduction

As Wilensky (1965:xxix) has stated, edcucation 'is often the only distinction that matters when the "classes" are compared'. One of the new challenges for people in the so-called 'new countries' of the FRG, the former GDR, is to choose one of the school streams in the education system. In Germany the choice of a school stream is a matter of societal selection. The Gymnasium and comprehensive schools open the opportunity to go to universities, Hauptschule and Realschule give only the opportunity to continue education at the level of vocational education. The choice of the different school streams at secondary school is made, in Berlin and Brandenburg, between grades six and seven.

During the time of the former GDR a selection process of this kind was unknown. All pupils had to go to the so-called polytechnical high school, and had to stay at the polytechnical high school up to grade ten. Only a small percentage – 9 percent – had the opportunity to continue their education at the so-called extended high school. These students were selected in relation to their school performances, their class status, and their societal actvities. Another five percent reached this goal in combination with a vocational education. The selection of students was made by the school in combination with the Party and the youth organisation of the Party. There was no direct influence of the parents in this process of selection. They could only contribute to the process in an indirect way, by supporting school performances and motivating their children to participate in the youth organisations of the SED. Therefore parents are not experienced in processes of selecting school streams. This statement is important because the parents themselves, during their school days, joined a very similar education system.

The ideological approach of the former GDR was that education had to contribute to the transformation of society. The society was defined as socialistic on the way to communistic. To advance this process, it was the aim of education that children whose parents were workers should have better opportunities for getting higher examination results than children with parents of other classes. As we now know this approach did not work as was claimed by the SED, the Communist Party in the GDR.

Theoretical Considerations

Choices of school streams can be studied from the point of different perspectives. Meulemann (1990:100) found for the transition from primary school to the different streams of secondary school, that if school performances were controlled, the social status of the father operationalised by profession was a relevant factor for the final placement. Bolder (1983:246) and Hansen, Rösner, and Weissbach (1986:70-101) found a very similar relationship between social status of parents and placement in the education system. In addition the latter authors noticed that the Gymnasium and the Realschule increased in attractiveness in contrast to a decrease in attractiveness of the Hauptschule. In the case of France, Bourdieu (1982) confirmed the tendency that parental social status will be reproduced for the children by the education system.

After aspirations of parents, a pupil's primary school performance influences the choice of school track. Results from primary school will be interpreted by parents with a low social status as important information about the future expectations of their children (Fauser 1981:81-96, Alamdar-Niemann, Herwartz-Emden, and Merkens 1987).

At the end of grade six primary schools give their recommendation as to which final examination the pupils should attempt. That recommendation covariates by similar school performances of the pupils with the social status of the parents (Fauser 1984). In countries of the FRG with a comprehensive school as an alternative to the different school streams parents who are not satisfied with the recommendation of the primary school tend to choose the comprehensive school. Ditton (1992) has differentiated this picture: in the case of a father with high social status the educational aspirations of the parents will be determined by the father, whereas in the case of a father with low status the mother is the important factor for the choice of the school stream.

There are several different theoretical approaches which can give a base for the study of the choice of school streams.

- In the tradition of Bronfenbrenner (1976, 1989) it is possible to control effects of the exosystem, that is, for example, the school administration of the education system, and the mesosystem between family and primary schools.
- In the tradition of the egaliterian approach it is possible to control influences which are in a sense at work that produce inequality in the education system (Rolff 1988).
- In the tradition of Bourdieu (1982) the question is of how social positions in a society will be transformed from one generation to the next.
- In the tradition of the theory of rational choice, the ways in which people structure and define their own surroundings, which then influence the choice of school stream is interesting (Ditton 1992).

In our study we decided to work within the approach of Bourdieu (1982). He differentiates several types of capital, which can be accumulated by individual human beings:

Types of Capital (Bourdieu)

Cultural capital

Incorporated cultural capital. This is cultural capital which is gained and accumulated in everyday life, including cultural habits and abilities, e.g., taste for books, paintings and music.

Objectivated cultural capital. This is materialised cultural capital such as books, musical instruments or paintings which are owned by the family.

Institutionalised cultural capital. These are for example the final examinations of the education system which the parents have reached or the marks achieved by children.

Social capital

This is the professional status of the parents and their social relations.

Economical capital

This is the monthly family wages.

During the period of the former GDR economical capital was not important. In many cases the family wages were higher than the costs of living. Often, demand in the market place was higher than the supply. The system did not reward the accumulation of social capital with higher monthly wages, in fact in many cases the opposite occured. The lower wages of workers were rewarded by low taxes. Clerks, who earned more money had to pay high taxes. In this way they had lower net wages compared to workers with lower gross wages. The status of the worker was rewarded by the system. Nevertheless, the old bourgeois elite survived in the former GDR and a new socialist elite grew up. Members of this new elite had leading positions in the Party, the government, the economy, and in science. They had accumulated much social and cultural capital.

Since the unification of Germany many members of this new elite have lost their positions. Many of them are unemployed or are now in lower positions in the public or industrial sector. The main question of our study is how these people try to give their children a good starting position in the new society of Germany. The main assumption is that they attempt this by activating their accumulated cultural capital and by choosing the best school stream for their children.

The difficulty is that there was not a differentiated social system in the former GDR. In official GDR statistics there was only one social class which consisted of the workers. Therefore the first challenge for our study is the reconstruction of a differentiated social status of the population in the former GDR. In the next step it is possible to prove our main hypothesis by computing a correlation beween social status and cultural capital. After that we can try to evaluate the process of activating cultural capital by the parents.

Design of the Research

Processes such as activating cultural capital can only be explored in a study with a longitudinal design. We have produced a four-step design:

- At grade four parents will be asked for details of their cultural, social, and economical capital. This will be done within dimensions described by Bourdieu. In the case of social capital we differentiate between social capital in the former GDR and social capital in the new FRG. The parents will also be asked for the first time about their aspirations in relation which final examination their children should obtain in the education system. At grade five the pupils will be asked for details of their cultural and social capital.

This will be done using questions in the tradition of Bourdieu and by standardised tests.

- At grade six the parents will be asked for a second time about their aspirations in relation to their childrens' final examination. The teachers will also be asked for their recommendations in relation to the final examination.
- At grade seven the pupils will be asked for a last time. They will now be at secondary school and will have a place in one of the streams.

This research was to be carried out in the eastern part of Berlin and two cities in Brandenburg: Frankfurt/Oder and Cottbus. Two years later the research would be started for a second time.

In 1994 we finished the first questioning of parents with pupils in the fourth grade.

Results

Table 9.1 gives a description of the sample size.

Table 9.1 Description of the Sample Size

Berlin	329
Cottbus	173
Frankfurt/Oder	209
N	711

We had planned to question 300 parents in East Berlin, 150 in Cottbus, and 150 in Frankfurt, but because we expected sample mortality, we were not unhappy about the higher than expected numbers in all cities.

Table 9.2 Desired Final Examination

	N	%
Hauptschul examination	50	7.0
Realschul examination	122	17.2
Abitur	431	60.6
Not clear at this time	108	15.2

Table 9.2 gives information about the desired final examination. Only 15 percent of the parents were not able, at the time of questioning, to give a precise answer. Of the remainder, 60.6 percent of them desire the Abitur as the final examination. Only 7.1 percent designate the Hauptschul examination. The percentage of parents with high aspirations

is a little higher than has been reported up to now for the old Länder, but it confirms a trend which was noticed for the old Länder of the FRG: the attractiveness of the Abitur as the final examination is increasing. One of the reasons for the higher percentage of parents in our sample who want the Abitur as their children's final examination may be that they interpret the longer period of schooling up to the Abitur as a kind of moratorium. It provides an opportunity to make a decision at a later point in their children's school career as to whether they should have the opportunity to study at a university or continue their education with a vocational education. Another reason may be the fact that not all parents agreed to participate in our study. Parents with an increased interest in the school careers of their children may be over represented. Nevertheless, this will not falsify our numbers significantly, the figures for the last two years, of pupils who want to transfer to the Gymnasium system support our result.

As there is no Hauptschule in Brandenburg, only a Realschule, a comprehensive school, and a Gymnasium, it is not meaningful to compare the desired type of school in Berlin and the two other cities. However, in Cottbus and Frankfurt, as well as in Berlin, Hauptschul examination is noticed by parents.

In the first step of our study we have tried to construct an index of social status of fathers and mothers which give the opportunity to differentiate further than was possible in the official statistics of the former GDR. We have done this on the basis of information obtained from parents, asking them about their own final school examinations and their professions during the time of the GDR. For this purpose we have combined the social and the institutionalised cultural capital of fathers and mothers.

***Table* 9.3** Social Status of the Parents

	Father		Mother	
	N	%	N	%
1. Workers with skilled worker examination	173	31.2	67	10.0
2. Clerks with skilled worker examination	77	13.9	210	31.3
3. Intelligence and bureaucracy with skilled worker examination	27	4.9	12	1.8
4. Clerks and workers with technical college examination	38	6.8	141	21.0
5. Bureaucracy with technical college examination	28	5.1	13	1.9
6. Intelligence* with technical college examination	27	4.9	80	11.9
7. Clerks and workers with university examination	40	7.2	44	6.5
8. Bureaucracy with university examination	38	6.9	8	1.2
9. Intelligence with university examination	106	19.1	97	14.5
	554		672	

* This is a label of social class in the former GDR.

The distributions which we obtained are very similar to an U-shape. This is particularly so in the case of the fathers with the extreme categories including the highest percentages of cases. This distribution gives, in our opinion, a better information about the division of social status in the former GDR than the official statistics of the government. Surprisingly, only twice did the parents give us information that one of them had worked for the Party, the government, or the Stasi. This is surprising because our study in Berlin was carried out in Lichtenberg, where under the former GDR large numbers of people were employed by the Stasi or the Party. Another interesting point is shown in table 9.3. As reported in our opening remarks only 14 percent of the population of the former GDR had the opportunity to study at a university in a direct way. Now though, one third of the fathers and a little more than one fifth of the mothers have a university examination. This discrepancy is not an error in the study, but has its roots in the fact that in the former GDR many opportunities were given to adults to continue education, for instance through study by correspondence course. This led to the opportunity to obtain a university examination.

For the families, social status was computed using the addition of the father's and mother's social status. This permits the inclusion of remarks by Ditton (1992), who found a stronger effect of fathers where the father had high social status and of mothers where the father had low social status. In table 9.4 the results of an analysis of variance about the attractiveness of school streams in relation to the social status of families is represented.

Table 9.4 Attractiveness of School Examinations in Relation to the Social Status of Families

Arithmetic means

Hauptschul examination	5.8
Realschul examination	6.0
Abitur	10.0

Analysis of Variance

Source	df	Sum of Squares	Mean Squares	F Ratio	F Prob.
Between Groups	2	1.514	757	34.0	0.00
Within Groups	440	9.793	22		

The results give an impressive picture. There is a significant influence of the social status of the family in relation to the desired final examination in the education system. This strong effect works only through the differentiation between the Abitur and the other examinations. A small difference also exists between the Hauptschul examination and Realschul examination. The propabiblity of the F-ratio is lower than 1 percent. This means that the propability that the differences were obtained by chance is lower than 1 percent.

If the main hypothesis of our study is correct then there must be a significant correlation between the social status of a family and the cultural capital which is accumulated by the family. At present final proof cannot be presented. However, there are some indicators which demonstrate that this assumption can be confirmed in our study. Up until now we have only very weak indicators as measuring instruments for objectivated and incorporated cultural capital:

- Objectivated cultural capital: number of books at home
- Incorporated cultural capital: attitude towards art and number of books recognised out of a list of ten books

***Table* 9.5** Correlation Matrix of Cultural Capital and Social Status

Cultural Capital		**Social status**	
	Father	**Mother**	**Family**
Attitude to paintings	0.31	0.31	0.34
Number of books at home	0.41	0.41	0.47
Number of known books	0.36	0.40	0.44

As table 9.5 shows there is a strong relation between the different types of cultural capital and the indices of social status for fathers, mothers and the family. The highest correlation exists between the family index and the three indices of cultural capital. This confirms our index construction a second time.

A final proof of our main hypothesis is shown by an analysis of variance. Here we compared the parents' desired school examination for their child with the familiarity of books on our list. A low mean signifies that the parents are familiar with many of the books.

***Table* 9.6** Attractiveness of Desired School Examination in Relation to the Books

	Arithmetic means
Hauptschul examination	18.8
Realschul examination	18.2
Abitur	17.4

The hypothesis is confirmed by this analysis. The propability of the F-ratio is lower than 0.01. In this case the differentiation between parents who aspire to the Hauptschul examination and those who aspire Realschul examination works, as well as the differentiation to the parents who aspire Abitur as the final examination in the education system.

Conclusion

In a first analysis of data resulting from the questioning of parents in three cities of the new Länder the hypothesis could be confirmed that different types of cultural capital are at work in the process of choosing school streams. However, another result which is evident must be looked at carefully with great attention: the results which were obtained using a newly constructed index for the measurement of social status reveal that there was only a very small middle class in the former GDR. This is indicated by the U-distribution. The interesting question is who among the former upper classes will decrease to the middle class and who among the former working class will increase. Perhaps this research along with other analyses can provide a preliminary answer to this question.

References

Alamdar-Niemann, M., Herwartz-Emden, L., and Merkens, H. (1987), *Schulverlauf deutscher und türkischer Schüler im Berliner Schulsystem. Gutachten für die Senatsverwaltung für Schule, Berufsbildung und Sport*, Berlin.

Bolder, A. (1983), *Ausbildung und Arbeitswelt. Eine Längsschnittstudie zu Resultaten von Bildungsentscheidungen*, Frankfurt.

Bourdieu, P. (1982), *Die feinen Unterschiede. Kritik der gesellschaftlichen Urteilskraft*, Frankfurt.

Bronfenbrenner, U. (1976), *Ökologische Sozialisationsforschung*, Stuttgart.

Bronfenbrenner, U. (1989), *Die Ökologie der menschlichen Entwicklung*, Frankfurt.

Ditton, H. (1992), *Ungleichheit und Mobilität durch Bildung*, Weinheim.

Fauser, R. (1981), 'Bildungsentscheidungen für Kinder, Bildungswünsche und Beschäftigungssituation von Eltern', in R. Fauser, and N. Schreiber (eds), *Bildung und Arbeitsfeld*, Konstanz.

Fauser, R. (1984), *Der Übergang auf weiterführende Schulen. Projekt: Bildungsverläufe in Arbeiterfamilien. Abschlußbericht 1*, Konstanz.

Hansen, R., Rösner, E., and Weissbach, B.(1986), 'Der Übergang in die Sekundarstufe', in H.-G. Rolff, and K. Klemm (eds), *Jahrbuch der Schulentwicklung*, vol.4, Weinheim.

Meulemann, H. (1990), 'Schullaufbahnen, Ausbildung, Karrieren und die Folgen im Lebensverlauf. Der Beitrag der Lebenslaufforschung zur Bildungssoziologie', in *KZSS*, Sonderheft 31.

Rolff, H.-G.(1988), *Ansätze zu einer Theorie der Schulentwicklung*, IFS-Werkheft 28, Dortmund.

Wilensky, H.L. (1965), 'Introduction: The Problems and Prospects of the Welfare State', in H.L. Wilensky and C.N. Lebeaux (eds): *Industrial Society and Social Welfare*, New York.

Chapter 10

CONSIDERATIONS OF A VOCATION-PREPARATION PROJECT FROM THE STANDPOINT OF ORGANISATIONAL THEORY

Harm Kuper

In this chapter I shall describe the results of a case study carried out at the Institute für Allgemeine Pädagogik Arbeitsbereich Empirische Erziehungswissenschaft, at the Freie Universität Berlin from September 1993 to March 1994 in a project with a pedagogical objective.

I should like to start with a brief description of the context in which it originated, its targets and the organisational structure of the project. In the second section I will outline a theoretical framework which clarifies the questions we pursued during the course of the study. In the third section I shall describe the course of the first half year of the project under the aspects previously obtained. Finally two theses will be formulated from this section which may indicate the usefulness of a case study for possible subsequent projects.

In 1992 the Berlin city parliament authorised finance amounting to DM 126 million for a special Youth Care Programme. The background to this decision was the political pressure caused by increasing unemployment among young people and public anxiety about the increasing readiness of young people to resort to violence. The intention of the city parliament was thus to finance educational measures to integrate young people into work contexts and to promote individual life perspectives. It was hoped that this would result in a reduction of the readiness to resort to violence.

A so-called steering group was set up in Berlin's state administration to put this project into practice. This originally consisted of representatives of three different administration bodies of the Senate, those responsible for:

- labour and women,
- youth affairs,
- municipal development and environmental protection.

This steering group was entrusted by the political body (the city parliament) with the following primary tasks: firstly, to find suitable sponsors for corresponding educational projects; secondly, to discuss with potential sponsors the programme, structure and financing of the projects and, thirdly, to oversee the progress and success of the projects. The steering group thus had to make sure that the financial funds were used in ways which suited the purpose.

This offer from the political system to finance the establishment of educational projects was taken up by one sponsor that had already gathered experience with measures to integrate and give further training to the unemployed. This sponsor hoped to extend its field of activities and safeguard jobs via the financing of one further project. Two of the sponsor's employees (later in charge of the project) became permanent negotiation partners in the steering group in order to coordinate conceptional and organisational conditions for the setting-up and promotion of a concrete project. That programmatic coordination of the contents of the project's aims proved difficult even on the political level was shown by the withdrawal of one of the Senate administrations – that responsible for youth affairs – from the steering group. The aims finally decided upon clearly bear the stamp of the influences exerted by the two remaining Senate administrations: a combination of vocation-preparatory and environment-educational components was considered pedagogically suitable.

Young people who were disadvantaged on the labour market were selected as the target group for the project. This group included young people without a school-leaving certificate or with one from the lowest level of secondary education (Hauptschule) where the grade awarded was below 'satisfactory', young people who had broken off a course of vocational training, and young people whose backgrounds or social situations precluded them from starting a course of training leading to a vocational qualification. This definition of 'disadvantagement' was based on Paragraph 40c of the Promotion of Labour Act (AFG).

The young people were to be prepared for their vocations by a one-year practical course. For this purpose the young people were to be placed with employers in both the public and private sectors. The employers had to undertake to guarantee for the young people training and activity in the work sector concerned. There was no expense involved for the firms as both wages and the cost of social insurance for the young people, as well as any other material costs incurred, were to be borne by the Senate's programme.This strategy promised not only to enable the young people to enter the world of work but also to ensure that some of them would, at the end of the year, be taken on as trainees or given a job at the work place concerned.

The acquisition of suitable work places, the recruitment of interested young people and mediation between these two groups of actors thus became the primary task of the project.

Alongside the work-oriented component, the project was to ensure opportunities for learning and obtaining qualifications above and beyond those required for the job concerned. These comprised, firstly, the socio-pedagogical care of the young people. The intention here was to give the clientele of disadvantaged young people support for the period of transition into the world of work, and assistance in formulating their interests and in developing personal job perspectives; it was also intended to make use of social pedagogues in possible cases of conflict between the young people and their work place. Secondly, a programme of seminars was planned. Five weeks of seminars on subjects related to environmental protection, practical fields of work and general vocational information were planned for each participant.

As a concept, the environmental protection component was taken into account not only by the seminar programme. The workplaces were to be selected according to criteria which took into account not only the aim of vocational preparation but also that of environmental education. The steering group did not, however, carry out any specification of possible workplace criteria for these two categories. In this respect those employed on the project were allowed a certain freedom of interpretation and action.

There were, nevertheless, formal stipulations formulated in the steering group. These fixed, among other things, the size, allocation scheme and schedule of the project. After six months the project was to have provided workplaces for 390 young people. To regulate the time sequence a plan was produced which provided for the creation of groups of fifteen young people at fortnightly intervals. With an allocation scheme of one social pedagogue for every thirty young people, the employment of further social pedagogues was linked to the fact that those already employed must have provided work placements, on fixed dates, for two 'complete' groups of fifteen young people each. Only when the actions of the staff already employed had been successful was the project able to expand. In addition to the thirteen posts for social pedagogues, which could only be occupied in succession, posts for two project leaders and two coordinators were established.

The financial support of the project depended on another criterion, which seemed important to the steering group. They attempted to safeguard the fulfilment of the criterion by formalisation: a minimum quota of disadvantaged young people entering the project amounting to 75 percent. This criterion, which could be examined at an early stage, was joined by a second: the quota of those young people taken on into permanent employment after participating in the project or who had otherwise found jobs or training opportunities through participation in the project was to be a measure of its success. Though this quota was not formally specified owing to a lack of quantifiable expectation values, as high a proportion as possible of successfully placed young people was nevertheless clearly formulated as the criterion for success.

So far I have described some of the important framework conditions under which the project under investigation developed. We monitored this development process for six months. During this time we carried out guideline interviews of, on average, 1.5 hours, with all those employed in running this project. In addition, we arranged a group discussion with members of the steering group. These methods permitted us to express the views of those interviewed on the following question complexes:

- What experiences are gained during everyday work?
- What organisational structure does the project have, and what are the consequences for the activities?
- What pedagogical aims are pursued in the project and what is the methodological procedure?

Our considerations in obtaining and evaluating the data follow systems-theory models:

A systems-theory perspective following Luhmann (1986) raised the following question with reference to the project: how was the project differentiated as a system from its environment and which system-internal perceptions of the environment took place? This framework implies the question of which sections of the environment were perceived as system-internally relevant, how the links between the project and its environment were communicated internally and what actions resulted.

These questions meet in the interest of understanding how structures form within the project. We are assuming, here, that the challenge facing the project was to construct an internal structure that would permit the execution of the pedagogical commission. For this the demands made on the project from environmental circles had to be considered and the environment had to be structured within prescribed tolerances. In doing so, incongruent interests of the environmental actors had to be coordinated with the project's own interests.

This was then carried out on the basis of a concept of the neo-institutionalist theory of organisation that could be integrated into the systems-theory.

In an essay dated 1977 and entitled 'Institutionalised Organisations: Formal Structure as Myth and Ceremony', Meyer and Rowan placed the environmental relationships of organisations with pedagogical aims at the centre of their considerations. Their treatment concentrates on the function of the formal structure of such organisations. According to Meyer and Rowan, the formalisation of structural elements in organisations in which activities cannot be standardised has a symbolic function. It makes communication with institutions from the organisation's environment possible. The authors designate this formalisation as 'vocabularies of structure' via which, for instance, a form of professional work is signalled or via which the exchange of financial funds is regulated. This is of particular significance to one type of non-profit-making organisation to which the project belonged. These organisations are dependent on external financing by other organisations. Through the implementation of formal elements a non-profit-making organisation can negotiate with its financier based on the success or failure of its work and stimulate confidence in the professionalism of its activities; this is independent of what actually goes on within the organisation. The formalisation is thus directly linked to the legitimation obligation which a non-profit-making organisation must fulfil towards its financier. The presentation of success and professionality via formal structural elements guarantees, according to Meyer and Rowan, the legitimacy of an organisation. Thus an environmental connection is regulated by means of formalisation.

By contrast to Meyer and Rowan, who assume that action in organisations remains to the greatest extent unaffected by formalisation, the effects which formalised contact with the environment had on the internal project-structure formation was followed up in our investigation.

In addition, we did not just enquire into the legitimacy requirements which have to be fulfilled towards the financier – represented here by the steering group. We also dealt with the fields of application and disadvantaged young people as environments which the project had to incorporate into its concept of action. Legitimacy requirements had to be negotiated not just with one environment – the steering group: there was a pluralistically structured environment which made divergent claims on the project.

The structure-formation process may be understood as a process in which, within the project, the perceived claims made by the environments are coordinated with the pedagogical aims and in which an attempt is made to integrate the incongruent project environments into the action concept.

The action strategy worked out in the steering group saw the project as having mainly a mediatory function, i.e., finding disadvantaged young people work placements. The year-long activity at these work places was considered to be of educational value with regard to job preparation and environmental education. The fulfilment of this mediatory function called for comprehensive preparatory work in two directions by those project members concerned.

First a base of workplaces satisfying the criteria of job preparation and environmental education had to be established, and young people had to be recruited who were both disadvantaged and also interested in a one-year course of practical work in the 'ecological'job sector.

As already mentioned, the timetable produced by the steering group put considerable deadline pressure on the project. Those in charge of the project used this to justify their strict supervision of rapid procedure in acquiring work places and placing participants. Here, use was made of bureaucratic means which dominated the work of all those involved during the start-up phase of the project and provoked a negative attitude among the educationalists. The setting up of a system of filing whereby the number of already-placed young people was monitored affronted the educationalists, who saw their task not so much in the achievement of 'target figures' on paper, but in personal contact with the young people. The bureaucratisation of contact between pedagogues and young people becomes dramatically clear in the following quotation from one of the educationalists 'The young people arrive in the shape of an application form. I then look to see if we have a workplace which I think might interest the individual concerned.'

In order to integrate work place and young person as environments in the project's action concept, project staff had to take the initiative. This meant, initially, drafting suitable strategies to attract the target group of disadvantaged young people and formulating suitable selection criteria to make a selection from the unstructured environment of potential workplaces which further the aims of the project. Selection and acquisition of the work placements was an activity which – with the exception of the project leaders – was borne by all members of staff. This, too, was due to shortage of time. It was possible to carry out negotiations in the workplaces with the project making the offers: after all, one or more young workers were being placed for the duration of one whole year, free of charge! In return work was expected where the young people would not be exploited but given an insight into possible environmentally related fields of work and training. The high value placed by those interviewed on the 'ecology' aspect as a criterion for selecting work places was particularly striking. The stress laid on this aspect enabled the project leaders to profile the project in such a way as to distinguish it from other job-preparation measures. For the vast majority of other staff the 'ecology' aspect was linked to ideas of ecological urban remodelling or information campaigns opposing the environmentally damaging effects of industry. Throughout, the ecological direction was conceded to have a motivating effect which would help to integrate young people into the world of work. In addition, it was believed that coming to terms with the concept of 'ecology' might offer a favourable entry into the world of work, because this topic could be used not only to illustrate the contradictions of working life, but also to provide practice in 'networked thinking' that would benefit disadvantaged young people when considering their social position. These idealisations of the 'ecology' aspect were extremely important for the strategies used in selecting the work places. They concentrated attention primarily on sectors of an ecologically oriented niche economy, i.e., trade involving ecologically produced goods, or activities which could be associated with the re-establishment of nature or the addition of greenery. Work places in the industrial sector were systematically excluded, and places in traditional craft, trade or technical sectors were only given marginal consideration. The four hundred or so workplaces offered by 150 employers six months after the project had begun shows the direction taken by the search (table 10.1).

Table 10.1 Distribution of Workplaces in Percentages (February 1994):

Trade sectors 50 %	Wholefood shops etc.	17.5%
	Nurseries and market gardens	11%
	Planning/Counselling	7.5%
	Cycle shops	6%
	Handicraft trades	2%
	Others	6%
Greenery production (children's day centres / landscape protection)		35 %
Environmental-protection associations		15 %

This selection of work places was legitimised by the understanding of ecology circulating within the project. From the job-preparation point of view, however, it was considered problematic. This can be explained by the fact that only a few of the work places selected offered activities which could be classified as preparation for a job requiring formal vocational training. In cases where the employers might have been expected to prepare young people for jobs involving vocational training, the job requirements often did not correspond to the training needs of the disadvantaged young people (e.g., environmental-protection associations and planning offices expected young people with a grammar-school education), or the young people were shown how to do jobs of little importance in an urban context (almost half of all the young people – 46 percent -worked in nurseries, market gardens or on greenery-creation projects, a proportion which cannot be justified by Berlin's requirement for gardeners). Additionally, the size and financial means of many employers offering work placements did not permit them to make the young people a firm offer of a training place after participation in the project. The large greenery-creation projects had, in fact, been set up to take on participants in the project. They depended for their existence on the project from which they drew their manpower. Thus these sectors could not offer young people a vocational start.

The heavy emphasis on the ecological aspect in selecting work places and the lack – due to shortage of time – of preliminary conceptual deliberation with regard to the relationship between job preparation and ecology led to a selection of work places which did justice to a cliché-ridden concept of ecology without keeping the target dimension of job training in view. This problem was communicated as a dilemma between ecology and job training; staff perceived that it was possible to choose either ecology or job training, but not both.

Above and beyond the strategy for selecting work places, this dilemma gained extensive significance in the need for the project to justify its activities to the steering group. Insofar as the success of the project was to be judged by the quota of young people consequently taken on as full-time trainees or employees, neglecting this aspect might lead to a reduction in, or even cancellation of, financial support.

The project leaders developed a counter-strategy in reaction to this problem. It provided for a classification of fields of employment into 'hard' and 'soft' types. 'Softer' types were fields of employment where the ecological aspect was uppermost. These sectors were considered to be removed from the economic necessity of striving for success, thus permitting the young people a 'soft' entry into the world of work. 'Hard' was the term used to designate fields of employment which neglected the aspect of ecology in favour of that of job preparation. These would be in economically stable sectors where more would be expected of the young people but where, at the same time, the chances of being employed would be higher.

Within the project, the young people involved were to first go through a 'soft' phase, followed by a 'hard' phase, in order to do justice to the two target dimensions of ecology and job training one after the other, and formally demonstrate the success of the placement quota. The implementation of this strategy of action, however, involved an increase in bureaucratic coordination work. Information on the work places had to be compiled schematically and standardised. A card index which was to contain, in brief, all relevant information on the work places formed the principal means for putting the strategy into practice. Setting up this index involved the educationalists in activities which contradicted their own conception of their role – they were to process the information on workplacements with the help of prepared forms. Thus the obligation to do justice to a formal criterion was passed on from the project leadership right down to the activity level of the educationalists.

The educationalists dealt with the dilemma differently. On the whole, they considered it their job to inform the young people about the problems involved in the relationship between ecology and job preparation and then to present them with a choice between several work placements, allowing the young people to effectively make their choice according to their own interests. The pedagogical staff considered the young people to be subjects capable of making their own decisions whose individual interests should be given greater importance than orientation towards the achievement of as high a quota as possible of young people actually placed. The educationalists considered the evaluation of the individual case to be a measure of the success of the project, not some formal criterion. This indicates that the differences in environmental contact between the various members of staff engaged on the project resulted in incongruent directions of action. The standards of the opposing position in each case were thus considered obstacles to the implementation of one's own intention.

The recruitment of disadvantaged young people laboured, right from the start, under a heavier burden than the acquisition of work placements. There was uncertainty about whether the publicity campaigns in youth centres, the underground railways and job centres would reach the desired target group. It did not, in fact, prove possible to recruit the required quota of 75 percent disadvantaged young people. After six months only 57 percent of young people participating fulfilled this criterion. The considerable proportion of grammar school and polytechnical school pupils was attributed by project staff members to an increased interest in ecological topics among young people of higher educational standard. Compared with them, young people disadvantaged by a lower standard of education were said to be less interested in ecology than in obtaining a 'leg up' into the world of work. Despite all of the interest in ecology, staff soon realised that, in combining environmental education with job preparation, they would not only have to unite two contradictory aims but would also 'miss' the target group originally aimed at. Even this point of conflict triggered different reactions between the project leadership and the educational staff. Once again the project leaders reacted by demanding supervision of the formal criterion of disadvantagement in order to achieve composition of the group of participants in keeping with the definitions of the steering group. The educational staff took this as an affront to their pedagogical intentions, which were incompatible with such 'pigeon-hole thinking'. On the spot they declared the formal criterion of disadvantagement to be invalid, substituting it with a concept of disadvantagement oriented, in its turn, towards the individuality of each young person. Often precisely those individuals who were not 'disadvantaged' as understood by Paragraph 40 c of the Promotion of Labour Act (AFG) were, due to their personal situation or lack of perspective, considered to be disadvantaged – thus the educationalists could justify the participation of grammar school pupils in the project. This corresponded to the evaluation that many formally disadvantaged young people had shown themselves to be highly imaginative and thus capable of both seeing vocational perspectives and implementing opportunities for their realisation.

Here, too, a pattern of a collision of directions between the various functionaries within the project was once again seen. The differences in directions described was mainly attributable to the incongruence of the environments with which contact had to be maintained – and towards which different justification requirements had to be fulfilled. The fact that it was at first impossible to mediate between the divergent requirements was mainly due to the pressure of time which, via the sequence schedule, dominated internal project activities. Pressure to act prevented conceptual work which, for example, might have permitted a correction in the selection strategies for work places. Instead of reflection on the aims of the project, the correct implementation strategies and the work experience gained so far, an apparatus of bureaucratic supervision corresponding in the main to the justification requirements of the steering group was able to assert itself.

The course of the project as described above suggests two fundamental requirements which must be taken into account if planned projects, due to the involvement of several environmental actors, are forced to move within a complex field of action – i.e., one that is fraught with uncertainty. These are mentioned here as concluding theses:

Firstly, in setting up measures with educational aims, a run-in period should be guaranteed during which detailed conceptual considerations reveal and minimise possible differences of interests in order to enable considerations of content to be set above the structural compulsion to make decisions.

Secondly, no concept can be so perfect that it can anticipate all imponderables. It should thus always be possible to suggest improvements to the concept which take account of both the formalised framework of categories and the experience gained during the work.

References

Luhmann, N., (1986), *Soziale Systeme. Grundriss einer allgemeinen theorie,* Frankfurt a. M.

Meyer, J. and Rowan, B. (1997), 'Institutuonalised Organisations: Formal Structure as Myth and Ceremony' in: *American Journal of Sociology,* 349-363.

Chapter 11

SCHOOL PRINCIPALS IN 'OWN-GENDER' AND 'OPPOSITE-GENDER' SCHOOL CULTURES

Meta Krüger

Introduction

Are there any differences in female and male principalship? Do female and male principals have different portfolios, ways of allocating time, leadership styles and targets? As very little research has been done on this topic, a nation-wide empirical study into the leadership of female and male school principals was conducted recently in the Netherlands (Krüger 1994). A 'matching' method was devised to generate pairs of compatible schools, the 'only' difference being that one school was managed by a female and the other by a male principal. Ninety-eight principals, 673 of their teachers and 858 students were requested to complete a questionnaire. The results demonstrate that the 'gender' variable has significant effects on leadership performance. Moreover, the results vary with the different cultural settings in which leadership is being exercised. The results show that it makes a difference whether leadership is exercised in an 'own-gender' or in a 'opposite-gender' culture. In this chapter the research results will be presented and discussed in the light of differences in school culture.

Problem Definition and Research Questions

In the last decade, there has been much discussion about and literature dedicated to the position of women in school management. The emphasis has often been on the small number of female principals. This is not surprising because in many countries the proportion of female principals is quite low. In this respect the Netherlands seem to beat the lot. In spite of various government interventions and initiatives in the field, the percentage of female principals in Dutch general secondary education has only increased from a mere four to six percent in recent years. The arguments for increasing the number of women in school management were usually confined to the principle of equal opportunities. Scant reference has been made to the specific contributions that women could make to school management. We are still confronted with a lack of knowledge upon which such an argumentation could be founded. It was not until the 1970s that the gender variable started to be included in school management research (Meskin 1974; Meskin 1979; Gross and Trask 1976; Fishel and Potker 1977; Frasher and Frasher 1979). In the Netherlands this kind of research is even more recent. The first empirical studies in this field started in the second half of the 1980s (Bonhof et al. 1986; Ruijs et al. 1986; Ruijs 1990). This kind of research focused particularly on career patterns of female school managers and was not really concerned with questions related to gender differences in the way school leadership is exercised. Moreover, the few international studies in this domain have focused on managerial styles and often showed methodological weaknesses (Adkinson 1981; Jones 1990). The results of various studies proved to be inconsistent and sometimes even conflicting. Until now the gender of the principal has never been included as a variable in school-effectiveness research. The lack of scientific knowledge has inevitably resulted in a public debate concerning the position of women in school management. This debate which has mainly been based on prejudices and stereotypes regarding the characteristics and qualities of female as well as male principals. Are there actually any reasons to think in terms of gender-specific differences in principalship? The development of a theory in this domain would appear to be needed.

In view of these considerations it was decided to conduct a literature study into the practice of school principalship and into gender differences in this domain. This resulted in the following problem definition:

Are there any differences and if so, what are the differences between female and male principals in secondary education in the Netherlands with respect to

- their tasks,
- their management styles,
- their orientations,
- their perceptions of their own leadership position and
- the effects on the school organisation and culture.

Research Set Up

An empirical comparative study was set up among school principals in secondary education to investigate the problem defined above. Twenty-two specific hypotheses were formulated. Using a 'matching' procedure (the 'guaranteed variable caliper matching' of Althauser and Rubin 1970) pairs of compatible schools were formed, the 'only' difference being that one school was managed by a female and the other by a male principal. All female principals in the Netherlands that could be traced were requested to participate in this research. More than eighty percent of these women reacted positively to the request. Subsequently, by means of a computer programme, schools managed by male principals were chosen for each of the schools managed by female principals. 'Matching' was based on characteristics such as school type, school size, denomination and urbanization, principal's age, duration of principalship, and the composition of the management team, the teacher population and the student population. Following the withdrawal of some principals, mainly due to school mergers, the final population consisted of 98 principals: 49 school pairs, each of them containing a female and a male principal.

At the time the research population was being built up, the instruments were mostly constructed in the form of Likert-scales. Existing useable instruments formed the basis for the construction of the instruments for this research. All these instruments had to be adapted to the Dutch situation, to secondary education and/or to the research goal. At some places self-developed Likert-scales were added. All instruments were subjected to factor analyses and reliability measurements.

Each school was visited by a postgraduate student in educational sciences. Apart from the questionnaires presented to the principals, the students also presented questionnaires to 10 randomly selected pupils and 9 randomly selected teachers at each school. Ninety-four percent of the pupils and eighty percent of the teachers filled in their questionnaires. The data were analyzed by means of paired multivariate analyses.

The 'matching' method enabled adjustment for context variables, which were expected to have an influence on principals' functioning. In this way the 'net effect' of the 'gender' variable could be determined.

Besides, 'matching' proved to be a suitable method given the proportion of female and male principals in secondary education in the Netherlands. The small number of female principals made it easy to find a well-matching male school for each female school.

Even before the 'matching' procedure was started school principals were divided into three groups: AVO (general secondary education), MBO (vocational secondary education for 16+) and adult education. There were 52 principals in general secondary education, 26 principals in secondary vocational education and 20 in adult education; that is 26, 13 and 10 paired cases, respectively.

Research Results

Many hypotheses had to be rejected, not because there were no gender differences, but because the gender differences varied by school type, while the hypotheses were formulated for all school types together. Three different pictures clearly emerged, as the results will show.

Portfolios and time allocation

Women appear to be significantly more oriented towards the instructional task than their male counterparts, judging from the importance they attach to this task (table 11.1), the fact that they keep this task in their portfolio more often (table 11.2), and the amount of time they spend on it (table 11.3). Male principals keep the 'administrative tasks' portfolio in their own hands more often than women, and they spend more time on this portfolio, as well as on external contacts. No gender differences were found in the other portfolios or in the allocation of time to other tasks.

Only 'instructional matters' showed a school type effect on portfolios as well as on time allocation. Although women in all three school types attach more importance to instructional matters than their male counterparts (table 11.1), table 11.4 shows, that this is only true for general secondary education and adult education. In vocational secondary education for 16+ no gender differences were found.

Further research into instructional tasks was done by asking the principals as well as their teachers how often they performed 52 instructional activities. Again, women come out as stronger instructional leaders than men, as table 11.5 shows. This gender difference shows up even more strongly from the teacher data than from the data gathered from the principals themselves. It is remarkable that again in vocational secondary education no gender differences in instructional activities were found at all.

Table 11.1 Importance attached to Instructional and Administrative Tasks (1 = of no importance; 6 = most important)

	F	M	p gender difference
Instructional tasks	4.1	3.6	0.000**
Administrative tasks	3.1	3.0	ns
p task difference	0.000**	0.000**	

Table 11. 2 Portfolio (1 = self; 2 = self + delegated; 3 = delegated)

	F	M	p
Organisational development	1.20	1.12	ns
Internal communication	1.53	1.63	ns
Instructional matters	1.67	2.22	gender effect 0.002** schooltype effect 0.002** interaction effect gender and schooltype ns
Personnel management	1.20	1.27	ns
Counselling	2.74	2.92	0.05* ----> cov. school size 0.07; gender difference ns
Administrative matters	1.94	1.55	0.04* ----> cov. culture at entry 0.02; gender difference ns
External contacts	1.18	1.29	ns
Marketing	1.80	2.00	ns

Table 11. 3 Time Allocation (1 = less time; 8 = most time)

	F	M	p
Organisational development	6.4	6.0	ns
Internal communication	5.4	4.6	0.04* ---> cov. student gender 0.03; gender diff 0.21 ---> cov. teacher gender 0.04; gender diff 0.13
Instructional matters	5.5	4.6	gender effect 0.06* school type effect 0.008** interaction effect gender and schooltype ns
Personnel management	5.6	5.0	ns
Counselling	2.1	2.0	ns
Administrative matters	3.5	4.5	0.007**
External contacts	4.6	5.8	0.001**
Marketing	3.0	3.5	ns

Table 11.4 Portfolio 'Instructional Matters' and Time Spent on this Portfolio Divided into School Types

	Portfolio (1=self; 2=self/delegated; 3=delegated)			**Time spent** (1 = least time; 8 = most time)		
	F	M	p	F	M	p
GSE	1.46	1.92	0.05*	6.3	4.8	0.02*
VSE	2.23	2.54	ns	4.1	3.9	ns
Ad.Ed.	1.50	2.60	0.02*	5.5	4.9	ns
all	1.67	2.22	0.002**	5.5	4.6	0.05*

Table 11.5 Principals' Instructional Activities Divided into School Types

	All schools		GSE		Adult Educ.		VSE
Mission	P*	T**	P*	T*		T**	
Culture	P*	T*	P*		P*	T**	no
Classroom		T*		T**		T**	significant
Teacher reward	P**	T**	P**	T**	P+	T**	gender
Professional development	P**	T**	P*	T**	P+	T**	differences
Orderly task oriented climate						T**	

P : according to principals women are more instructional oriented than men
T : according to teachers women are more instructional oriented than men
** : $p = \leq 0.01$
* : $p = \leq 0.05$
+ : p = trend (>0.05 en <0.08)

In summary, women are more oriented towards primary processes, towards instructional goals in their schools than their male counterparts. Some international studies in this domain had already pointed this out (Gross and Trask 1976; Charters and Jovick 1981; Pitner 1981; Shakeshaft 1987; Brubaker and Simon 1987; Hallinger and Murphy 1985; Hallinger et al. 1990). Some evidence for this more frequent performance of instructional activities by women had also been found in Dutch primary education (Van de Grift and Kurek-Vriesema, 1990). For secondary education these results appear to be even more evident. Earlier research results (Gousha 1986; Leithwood et al. 1990), showing that principals are mainly occupied with administrative tasks in practice, while they would prefer to spend more time on instructional matters, are only confirmed here for male principals. Amongst female principals this separation into real and preferred practice was hardly noticeable.

Consideration and initiation of structure: involvement with others

The stereotype that in leadership women are more personally or relationship-oriented (consideration) than men was only confirmed for adult education where women appear to be not only more relationship-oriented but also more task-oriented (initiating structure) than their male colleagues. In general and vocational secondary education women are neither more relationship-oriented nor more task-oriented than men. Table 11.6 shows the styles of conflict management of women and men.

Table 11.6 Styles of Conflict Management (0 = not at all; 6 = strong)

Styles	school type and number of cases	F	M	p gender differences adjusted for covariates	
Competition:	*all schools (47)*	*1.96*	*2.79*	*effect gender:*	*0.02**
				effect school type:	*0.01***
	GSE (26)	1.73	2.42	*int-effect school type / gender:*	*ns*
	VSE (12)	1.83	3.25		
	Ad.Ed.(9)	2.78	3.22		
Adaptation:	*all schools (45)*	*3.38*	*3.04*	*effect school type:*	*ns*
				cov. culture at entrance:	*0.000***
	GSE (25)	3.40	3.12	*gender difference:*	*0.03**
	VSE (12)	3.83	3.17		
	Ad.Ed.(8)	2.63	2.63		
Collaboration:	*all schools (49)*	*3.61*	*3.51*	*cov. yes/no children:*	*0.003***
				effect gender:	*ns*
	GSE (26)	3.89	3.69	*effect school type:*	*0.03**
	VSE (13)	3.23	3.54	*int.-effect school type / gender:*	*ns*
	Ad.Ed(10)	3.40	3.00		
Avoidance:	*all schools (44)*	*3.11*	*2.66*	*effect school type:*	*ns*
				gender difference:	*ns*
	GSE (24)	3.00	2.79		
	VSE (12)	3.25	2.08		
	Ad.Ed.(8)	3.25	3.13		

No gender differences were found with respect to the degree to which female and male principals use *collaboration strategies*. The stereotype that men are more *competitive* than women was confirmed. Men strive to solve conflicts more often than women, whereas women tend to use adaptation strategies. In vocational general education women try to *avoid* conflicts significantly more often. Female principals appear to have tasks such as *internal communication* and *personnel management* in their portfolios as often as their male counterparts (table 11.2). Moreover, women and men appear to spend the same amount of time on these tasks (table 11.3). An initial view of table 11.3 shows that women spend more time on internal communication than men. However, this is explained by the significant covariate 'student gender'. Women are appointed to schools which count more girls among their students. When men have more girls among their students they also spend more time on internal communication. Finally, women appear to include others in *decision-making processes* to the same degree as men do. Both sexes, it turned out, use relatively democratic styles.

Teachers do not show any differences with respect to the orientation to relations in the leadership styles used by female and male principals. Generally, female teachers are more positive than their male colleagues toward the style used by female principals, and male teachers seem to be more positive with respect to the style used by male principals than their female colleagues. The student data did not show any differences with respect to the relation orientation of female and male principals.

Although women's strong involvement with others is constantly emphasised in discussions on gender differences in leadership, no general evidence could be found in this respect, in spite of the fact that involvement was tested with various instruments.

Self-perception of leadership position: self-confidence, power and 'token' positions

Table 11.7 Principals' Self-Perceptions (1 = low; 6 = high)

self-perception	school type and number of cases	F	M	p	gender differences adjusted for covariates	
'token'	GSE	3.9	4.0	ns	effect school type:	ns
	VSE	4.1	3.8	ns	interaction-effect	
	Ad.Ed.	3.8	4.1	ns	school type / gender:	ns
					covs. student gender. and	
	all	3.9	3.9	ns	vice-principal gender:	0.006**
self-confidence	GSE	5.4	5.3	ns	effect school type:	ns
	VSE	5.4	5.1	0.06	interaction-effect	
	Ad.Ed.	5.6	5.0	0.06	school type / gender:	ns
					covs. first principal elsewhere; first	
	all	5.4	5.1	0.009**	vice-princ.; living conditions:	0.016*
power	GSE	3.7	4.2	0.04*	effect school type:	ns
	VSE	4.0	3.9	ns	interaction-effect	
	Ad.Ed.	4.8	3.4	0.02*	school type / gender:	0.004**
					cov. urbanisation:	0.05*
	all	4.0	3.9	ns		

effect gender: p = 0.05*
effect school type: p = ns
interaction-effect
school type / gender: p = 0.04*

Starting from the socialisation theory one could state that women are dependent and passive. They do not see themselves as potential power figures, because they have learned that power has negative connotations. Furthermore, according to this theory, women lack self-confidence whereas men are self-confident (Chodorow 1980). None of these statements seems to apply to school principals. Female principals hardly differ from their male colleagues in the way they experience power. Besides, women appear to be even more self-confident with respect to their leadership position than men. Further analyses of covariates showed that, unlike their male counterparts, they seem to build their self-confidence, among other things, upon the fact that before being appointed to their present position they had already worked as principals somewhere else, and instead of reaching their actual position via deputy functions they were directly appointed as principals. It is interesting to note that women who broke through the 'glass ceiling' relatively abruptly appear to show more self-confidence as leaders than women who moved up slowly.

Due to the fact that they are strongly outnumbered, it might be expected that female principals, unlike their male counterparts, would end up in isolated, so-called 'token' positions (Kanter 1977). A 'token' woman is not only seen as an exception but also as an example to her gender. Therefore she will always be the centre of attention and her mistakes will always be noticed. The results showed that it is not true that women experience a 'token' position and men do not. Both recognise and experience this 'token' position. Women in vocational secondary education experience it more strongly than their male colleagues, and men in adult education experience it more strongly than their female colleagues.

Orientations towards innovation

It is often stated that women are more often oriented towards innovation than men. In the Netherlands, this statement has been confirmed by earlier research (Ruijs 1990). However, the situation seems to be more varied. Women are, indeed, more open to innovation in adult education, but men in turn are more so in vocational secondary education. In general secondary education women are more oriented towards emancipatory activities in their schools.

Leadership effects according to teachers' and students' perceptions

The first international studies indicated that women principals are more effective than men (Gross and Trask 1976; Charters and Jovick 1981). Others were more hesitant (Adkinson 1981; Krüger 1989). The results of this research are more varied on this point, at least when measured in terms of the way teachers and students perceive the school environment. Teachers in adult education experience the school environment as being better under female principals, whereas the opposite occurs in vocational secondary education, as is evident from table 11.8. Male teachers generally seem to have a less positive perception of the school environment under female leadership than under male leadership.

Students have a slightly more positive perception of the environment in schools with male principals (table 11.9). In general secondary education they are more positive about male school culture and in vocational secondary education about male school organisation. Remarkably, female students prefer the male principals' school environments above female ones, except in adult education where they like the female culture more. Male students do not report a difference.

Table 11.8 Teacher Perceptions of School Environment (1 = negative; 6 = positive)

school type and number of cases	F	M	p
GSE (25)	4.32	4.45	ns
VSE (13)	3.93	4.40	0.005**
Ad.Ed.(10)	4.69	4.26	0.007**
all school types (48)	4.29	4.40	

effect school type:	0.05*
interaction-effect school type / gender:	0.005**
cov. organisational stage at this moment:	0.02*
effect gender:	ns

Table 11.9 Student Perceptions of School Environment (1 = negative; 4 = positive)

Student-perceptions	**school type and number of cases**	**F**	**M**		**p gender difference**	
Culture:	*all schools (47)*	*2.08*	*2.18*		*effect school type:*	*0.000***
					effect gender:	*ns*
	GSE (24)	2.00	2.16	0.008**	*int.-effect school type/gender: 0.012*	
	VSE (13)	2.02	2.18	ns		
	Ad.Ed.(10)	2.42	2.26	ns		
Organization:	*all schools (47)*	*1.92*	*2.00*		*effect school type:*	*0.000***
					effect gender:	*ns*
	GSE (24)	1.84	1.94	ns	*int.-effect school type/gender: 0.05**	
	VSE (13)	1.66	1.86	0.04*		
	Ad.Ed.(10)	2.48	2.32	ns		

Discussion

Have we found gender differences or cultural differences in this research? It appears that differences in leadership between men and women are determined by *gender in combination with school culture*. Gender roles and the resulting expectations for the leadership of women and men seem to be prescribed by the organisational culture. More specifically: it seems to make a difference whether one is running an organisation in which the rules of conduct, norms and values are established by one's own gender or in which these rules etc., are established by the opposite gender. In other words, it seems important to make a difference between *own-gender* and *opposite-gender* cultures. So, an important result obtained in the present study is that in researching gender differences in school leadership a distinction has to be made about the degree to which the culture in which this leadership is taking place is 'female' or 'male'. One can judge this on the basis of the number of women and men that occupy managerial positions and work and learn in the organisation, in combination with the historical development of the school culture.

In this study the culture of adult education can be seen as a 'female' culture. This type of education stems from special education for women, the so-called 'moedermavo' (general secondary education for mothers). In this sector women find themselves in an 'own-gender' culture, whereas men experience it as an 'opposite-gender' culture. Vocational secondary education is a type of education in which one can talk about a 'male' culture. It incorporates many technical and economical subjects and from way back it has been controlled by men. In general secondary education also, there have always been significantly more male than female principals. Thus, originally, general secondary education was a 'male' culture, even though the difference between this type of education and vocational secondary education is that the former is geared to general education and the latter to professional training with an emphasis on technical subjects. In general and vocational education women find themselves in an 'opposite-gender' culture, whereas men experience it as an 'own-gender' culture. In these school-types, the assumption that women could be at a disadvantage in relation to men because they are 'female in a male culture' (Shakeshaft 1987) seems to be confirmed by the results of this study. In adult education, on the other hand, the dominating culture was originally 'female', which for women means an 'own-gender' culture. Given the results of this research men appear to be at a disadvantage here as 'males in a female culture'. Owing to its 'male' culture, secondary education seems to lead to a situation in which women cannot use their good leadership skills which are so apparent in adult education. In a 'female' culture, such as adult education, men are not able to use their leadership capacities optimally, whereas women function better here than in other school types and are also more efficient, judging from teachers' and students' perceptions of the school environment. Adult education is clearly the only school type in which women have a stronger feeling of power, and feel less 'token' than men. We cannot say that a female principal is expected to be 'twice as competent as a man' *in general*. However, this must be the case in an opposite-gender culture such as general secondary education and, even more so, in vocational secondary education. 'Having to be twice as good' makes it difficult for women to be more effective than men. The 'male' school culture combined with gender-role socialisation of women seems to have a negative influence on the effectiveness of women's leadership.

At this point it would be interesting to refer to the meta-analyses of Eagly and Johnson (1990) and Eagly et al. (1992). They made a distinction between field studies and laboratory studies. They found no gender differences with respect to relationship- and task-orientation in field studies but they did find some differences in laboratory studies. They explain this by the fact that selection criteria and socialization mechanisms in organizations reduce the tendency of managers to exercise their authority in a stereotypical manner. Organization roles seem to dominate gender roles. From this we can conclude that the stereotypes which have developed in daily life might not be unreal after all. It is possible that women do indeed show more consideration and involvement with others than men, but possibly they cannot demonstrate this in actual leadership practice where they are still confronted with many 'male' cultural characteristics. Gender interferes with social stereotypes of good leadership. This stereotyping is different in 'female' and 'male' cultures and even evokes gender differences in leadership. Therefore, based on these results one must argue in favour of mixed-gender school management. This would enable the strong points of both genders to be exploited, and justice could be done to the pedagogical function of education. In the coming years emphasis should be on transforming schools into 'female-male' cultures. In order to be able to achieve this, we will have to search for ways to change certain factors in school organizations, in order to remould schools into organizations in which both women and men can feel at home. Appointing more women as principals and underlining their qualities as school leaders, qualities which have been demonstrated by this research, could have a positive influence on the image of women principals, and could finally lead to a reduction in gender stereotypes.

REFERENCES

Adkinson, J.A. (1981), 'Women in School Administration: A Review of the Research', *Review of Educational Research*, Vol.51, No.3, 311-343.

Althauser, R.P. and D. Rubin (1970), 'The computerized construction of a matched sample', *American Journal of Sociology*, 76, 325-346.

Bonhof, G., P. de Greeuw, M. Pollemans and E. Vogelaar (1986), *De laatste directrices*, Reeks.

Brubaker, D.L. and L.H.Simon (1987), 'How do principals view themselves and others?', *National Association of Secondary School Principals Bulletin*, Vol.71, No.495, 72-82.

Charters, W.W. Jr. and T.D. Jovick (1981), 'The gender of principals and principal-teacher relations in elementary schools', in P.A. Schmuck, W.W. Charters Jr. and R.O. Carlson (eds), *Educational Policy and management: Sex differentials*, New York.

Chodorow, N. (1980), *Waarom vrouwen moederen*, Amsterdam.

Eagly, A.H. and B.T. Johnson (1990), 'Gender and Leadership Style: A Meta-Analysis', *Psychological Bulletin*, Vol.108, No.2, 233-256.

Eagly, A.H., S.J. Karau and B.T. Johnson (1992), 'Gender and Leadership Style Among School Principals: A Meta-Analysis', *Educational Administration Quarterly*, Vol.28, No. 1, 76-102.

Fishel, A. and J. Pottker (1977), 'Performance of women principals: A review of behavioral and attitudinal studies', in J. Pottker and A. Fishel (eds), *Sex bias in the schools: The research evidence*. Cranbury, N.J., 289-299.

Frasher, J. and R.S. Frasher (1979), 'Educational administration: A feminine profession', *Educational Administration Quarterly*, 15(2),1-13.

Gousha, R.P. (1986), *The Indiana School Principalship: The role of the Indiana principal as defined by the principal*, Bloomington, Indiana.

Grift, W. van de and C. Kurek-Vriesema (1990), *Schoolleidingen in de basisschool*. Forum 1, Amsterdam / Lisse..

Gross, N., and A.E. Trask (1976), *The Sex Factor and the Management of Schools*, New York.

Hallinger, P. and J. Murphy (1985), 'Assessing the Instructional Management Behavior of Principals', *The Elementary School Journal*, Vol. 86, No. 2, 217-247.

Hallinger, P., L. Bickman and K. Davis (1990), 'Modeling the Effects of Principal Leadership on Student Achievement', *Paper presented at the International Congress for School Effectiveness*, Jerusalem.

Jones, B.K. (1990), 'The gender difference hypothesis: A synthesis of research findings', *Educational Administration Quarterly*, Vol.26, No.1, 5-37.

Kanter, R.M. (1977), *Men and Women of the corporation*. New York.

Krüger, M.L. (1989), 'Female and male school leadership and school effectiveness in secondary education', in J.T.Voorbach and L.G.M.Prick (eds), *Teacher Education 5*, 's Gravenhage, 125-139.

Krüger, M.L. (1994), 'Sekseverschillen in schoolleiderschap', Alphen aan den Rijn, (Dissertation).

Leithwood, K.A., P.T. Begley and J.B. Cousins (1990), 'The Nature, Causes and Consequences of Principals' Practices: An Agenda for Future Research', *Journal of Educational Administration*, Vol. 28, No.4, 5-31.

Meskin, J.D. (1974), 'The performance of women school administrators: A review of the literature', *Administrators Notebook*, 23 (1), 1-4.

Meskin, J.D. (1979), 'Women as principals: Their performance as educational administrators', in D. Erickson and T.L. Reller (eds), *The Principal in Metropolitan Schools*, Berkeley.

Pitner, N.J. (1981), 'Hormones and harems: are the activities of superintending different for a woman?', in P.A. Schmuck, W.W. Charters Jr., and R.O. Carlson (eds), *Educational Policy and Management: Sex Differentials*, New York, 221-234.

Ruijs, A., A. Mens, C. Baggen and B. Jansen (1986), *Schoolmanagement: een mannenzaak?*, Nijmegen.

Ruijs, A. (1990), *Vrouwen en schoolmanagement*. Amsterdam / Lisse.

Shakeshaft, C. (1987), *Women in Educational Administration*, Beverly Hills.

Chapter 12

SCHOOL QUALITY IN THE PROCESS OF REUNIFICATION

Four Former East Berlin Schools and Their Transformation (1991-1993)

Axel Gehrmann

Introduction

The fall of the Berlin Wall on 9 November 1989 put all of Berlin's social subsystems under enormous pressure for change without the participants being able to anticipate the future speed of the processes of that change. Perhaps this was felt so strongly in Berlin because the interface between East and West was, as it were, 'just over the road', and the primary goal of the politicians very soon became the production of equal levels in living conditions in order to discourage commuting between East and West. The school system was not unaffected by this development.

As the initial reform euphoria of the 'Round Table' was increasingly replaced, even in the education system, by the consolidation of parliamentary democracy, a pragmatism in educational policy established itself in Berlin. The aim of this was to apply to the eastern half of the city the West Berlin school legislation and the types of school enshrined within it by 1 August 1991, less than one year after reunification or two years after the fall of the Wall. From October 1990 to the summer of 1991 the preconditions were created. In the eastern half of the city 136 schools (55 comprehensive schools, 48 grammar schools, 25 secondary-technical and 8 secondary-modern schools) were set up almost from scratch in the secondary sector alone.

Work on setting up these schools was urged forward by the centralised State Ministry for Schools, Vocational Education and Sports, which assisted the individual East Berlin administrative districts in their search for and selection of sites, and which advised them in assembling staff. It soon became clear that the establishment of local district administration and policies was accompanied by independent district options which while provided for in the school legislation, nevertheless showed a clear degree of inherent dynamism towards the requirements in respect of the overall development of schools in Berlin. It was thus impossible to establish a centralised school network plan which, scientifically monitored, for instance, might have been able to show that circumstances would not stabilise of their own accord, once a site had been chosen and the decision made as to which type of school should be built. Nor was a permanent advisory body consisting of academics, teachers and civil servants set up within the Ministry to accompany the transformation.

Research into the establishment of comprehensive schools, particularly in the Federal Republic of Germany, has, however, clearly demonstrated the problems facing comprehensive schools, for example, if they have to compete with the three-school system in a large-town market model. This critical evaluation with reference to the transformation process of the overall school system was unable to assert itself. Instead every district, tried to set up its new school structure on the basis of its knowledge of the conditions prevalent in its own area, more or less ably assisted by its 'twin district' in the West. Generally this procedure led first to the securing of the primary sector – primary schools close to the homes of the children – and then to the restructuring of the secondary sector. Here questionnaires about the types of schools which parents wanted for their children were intended to support the district administrations. This was the pattern for the school network established in the administrative districts of East Berlin on 1 August 1991.

At the beginning of the first school year in reunited Berlin, 49.6 percent of seventh-grade children attended comprehensive schools in the eastern part of the city, 36.2 percent grammar schools, 11.9 percent a secondary-technical school and 2.3 percent a secondary-modern school. At the beginning of the third school year in the reunited city (1993/1994) only 30.94 percent of seventh-graders attended comprehensive school, 40.94 percent grammar schools, 23.59 percent a secondary-technical school and 4.53 percent a secondary-modern school. So in these two years, comprehensive schools in the eastern part of Berlin had lost 37.7 percent of their pupil potential by comparison with the first school year in the reunited city, whereby secondary-technical schools (+98.3 percent) and grammar schools (+13.0 percent) in particular profited (see Table 12.1).

The Project

Immediately after the fall of the Wall, educational scientists at the Institute for the Sociology of Education at the Free University of Berlin showed interest in the reorganisation of East Berlin schools. Intensive contacts during school year 1990/1991 resulted, among other possibilities, in links with the East Berlin district of Treptow and its association with a project entitled 'Radical changes in Berlin's schools'. A study was carried out, aimed primarily at following up the transformation process at the four newly founded Treptow comprehensive schools and investigating, during the first two school years involving the reunited Berlin (1991-1993), the following questions: How do the individual comprehensive schools in the Berlin district of Treptow develop against the background of their market position, in competition with the non-comprehensive three-school system and in competition with each other? Which factors capable of holding up or furthering a school ethos newly constituting itself are affecting the school? Which indicators for this are 'home-made' and which have been forced on the school 'from outside' by the district or by the centralised school administration? How do individual teachers and head teachers handle the overall process of social change at the individual schools?[1]

The longitudinal section investigation planned as a study of individual cases comprised of an interview at the beginning of the first common school year after the reunification of Berlin (during October and November 1991), at the end of the first school year (in May and June 1992) and at the end of the second school year involving the whole of Berlin, in February and March 1993.[2]

1. Gehrmann A. (1996), *Schule in der Transformation. Eine empirisch-vergleichende Untersuchung an vier Gesamtschulen im Berliner Bezirk Treptow (1991-1993)*, Frankfurt.

2. Teachers of German and Work Theory at the individual schools were visited while they taught during one week each over the two years and subsequently interviewed. Polytechnical teaching/Work Theory and German were selected as examples because it could be assumed that teaching in these subjects would have to make the greatest changes in contents (Work Theory) or, while retaining the contents, have to make the greatest didactical changes (German) without any change in staff.

A total of 24 interview reports, 30 half-hour tape-recordings and 30 quantitative questionnaires were evaluated. There were also four one-hour interviews with school heads and four one-hour interviews with the body administrating the school (school inspector, town councillor, senior inspector of schools in the State Ministry for Schools, Vocational Education and Sport).

The transcribed interview material ran to approx. 800 pages, 80 hours of teaching were observed and reported during the three phases of the survey.

At the beginning of the investigation a total of 22 teachers of the subjects concerned had volunteered. Approx. three from each subject and school were required. During the

The project attempted to enquire into the qualitative character of everyday school life, the 'ethos' at the newly founded comprehensive schools and thus to describe how former Polytechnical High Schools of the GDR changed into comprehensive schools as understood by the old West Berlin school legislation. The main concern was not with quantitative data on school attendance, pupils' behaviour, learning success or delinquency (Rutter 1980) but with the evaluation of qualitative interviews with teachers and with the administration accompanying them on the basis of the Federal German discussion on the quality of schooling and what has, in Germany, been referred to since the 1980s as 'the good school'.

Federal German Discussions on the Quality of Schooling and 'The Good School'

Investigations into the implementation of comprehensive schools, the extension of the traditional non-comprehensive, three-school, vertically organised school system in the Federal Republic to a four-school system consisting of *Hauptschule* (secondary-modern school), *Realschule* (secondary-technical school), *Gymnasium* (grammar school) and integrated *Gesamtschule* (comprehensive school) encouraged discussions in the 1980s on 'school quality' and 'the good school'. Fend not only pointed out the possibilities offered by the comprehensive school but also drew attention to an 'unenlightened remainder' when he emphasised:

> The system question, the evaluation of the importance of comprehensive schools in comparison with the traditional education system can, in my opinion and as far as such a thing is possible at all, be considered as relatively easy to deal with conclusively here. It will however be clear that we would be well advised to devote ourselves to the question of how any particular comprehensive school could best be designed. The question we are really asking, however, is – if we generalise the direction of the question – nothing more *than the question of the quality of individual schools*. (Fend 1982: 487)

---

course of the investigation illness, transfers or subsequent refusal to collaborate meant that 19 teachers were prepared to have their teaching observed and to discuss it afterwards during Phase 1 of the survey, 19 during Phase 2 and 15 during Phase 3.

The guided interviews recorded on tape were evaluated with the help of a computer. For this purpose the data-base system MAX, developed by Udo Kuckartz of the Department for Educational and Teaching Science at the Free University of Berlin was used (1992). This software program is able to evaluate qualitative research material such as guided interviews, observation reports and group discussions. Here it was, for instance, possible to immediately compare on the screen all the answers given by teachers at all schools to a certain question. It was thus possible to filter out in each case anchor examples from the individual schools which represented the individual situation most clearly.

These findings helped to fire the discussion on the 'quality of the individual school' in empirical educational research in the Federal Republic of Germany because the large school-comparison studies had shown just how varied the quality of individual schools may be – with regard, for instance, to the scholastic performance of their pupils.

The debate concerning the external reform of the school system, macro observation, turned into the debate on internal school reform, micro observation, although 'the results of research into comprehensive schools in the Federal Republic of Germany and Great Britain (have) … shown that simple and empirical criteria for school quality shared by all are not available' (Rolff 1991:877). For what the individual observer understands by 'school quality' depends, after all, on his or her standpoint and research design. He or she may be concerned with the school atmosphere, equality of opportunity, the pupils' performance etc., terms which themselves 'sparkle' of their own accord. So Rolff can conclude his evaluation with the statement that educational science: 'can expect no definitive answers concerning the 'quality of schooling' from empirical studies. The nature of empiricism is descriptive, the question of the 'quality of schooling' is normative' (878).

Discussions on 'school quality' and 'good schools' have, however, still not come to an end in the Federal Republic of Germany. They can be found in the relevant literature such as Steffens and Bargel 1987, Tillmann 1989, Aurin 1990, Steffens and Bargel 1993 and Aurin 1993.

In contrast to countries in the Anglo-American tradition, Germany has never brought itself to ask about 'effective schools', i.e., schools 'in which the pupils perform better than could have been expected on the basis of their prerequisites' (Mortimore 1994:118). Federal German discussions on 'good schooling' and its quality have, rather, led to a conception of the individual school as a 'pedagogical activity unit' (Fend 1986:275) the quality of which is not just visible in 'good scholastic performance'. The 'good quality of the individual school' is, rather, attributable to 'a complex network of cause-and-effect connections and processes' about 'the interplay between which very little knowledge so far exists' (Steffens and Bargel 1993:128). The perspective has changed, as it were, from perception of the variance between scholastic performances at individual schools in the 1970s to the differentiation of quality criteria as well as the internal and external variables in conditions at 'good schools'.

Internal variables in conditions at 'good schools' in the Federal Republic may be taken as: (a) the atmosphere and ethos of the individual school, (b) the school administration, (c) co-operation and communication among the staff and the commitment of the individual teacher. External variables in conditions may be taken to be: (d) the school inspectorate and (e) the 'market situation' of the individual school in competition with the three-school system (as in the case of comprehensive schools).

At this point some cursory notes on the research results concerning the above may be made. These are, additionally, focussed on conditions in Berlin.

a) Research into school atmosphere is based, in particular, on the work of Fend and Rutter, who came to similar conclusions: 'a certain canon of basic convictions among the staff' (Fend 1977:221), a 'certain measure of jointly accepted standards at the school' (ibid.) emphatically stamp the atmosphere of each individual school. External background conditions, supposedly the most visible indicators of variance between schools – things like buildings, distribution of the sexes, internal forms of school organisation – are of virtually no significance. The central indicator for the variance of individual schools, if not placed on its own in the school context, is the efficiency of the individual pupil at the beginning of his or her secondary-school career. This efficiency, however, does not cancel out the overall inter-relationships. Schools with less efficient pupils can still, in the eyes of their pupils and teachers, be schools where more is achieved than in other schools (see Rutter et al. 1980:123).
b) School heads are particularly 'successful' if their style of leadership emphasises neither authoritarian nor laissez-faire elements, if they commit themselves to the development of 'their' schools, take teachers, parents and pupils seriously, allow them the right to participate, generally accomplish the most varied tasks with calmness and composure, reach decisions quickly and act 'justly'. They must know the legal limits of their opportunities to influence things, yet should administer their schools with 'tact and sensitivity' rather than by insisting on their rights. Finally they must have the development of their schools 'at heart': 'running a school', just 'getting by' in the everyday school scenario without setting positive examples is counter-productive (see Baumert and Leschinsky 1986; Lenz 1991).
c) The more systematic observation of cooperation and communication in groups of staff at ten examples of secondary-modern and comprehensive schools in Berlin forced Roeder and Schümer (1986) to the conclusion that, in particular, minimal fluctuations in staff composition, a shared consensus on the tasks and objectives of the school, and a mutual liking for one another that goes beyond everyday teaching matters are decisive factors for good

cooperation between teachers. The comment here on the commitment of the individual teacher reads: 'In general the teacher's work is hardly conceivable without affective commitment which colours relationships with his or her pupils and ensures an individualisation of the teacher's style of handling matters' (Roeder and Schümer 1986:3).

d) Even the first discussions in the Federal Republic of Germany about the 'goodness' and 'quality' of individual schools pointed out that 'flanking measures of support from the schools' inspectorates' should be accepted as an indicator for the development of 'good' schools (see Steffens 1986:299). What was meant, in particular, was that attention should be given to the extent to which the state schools' inspectorates in the Federal Republic of Germany granted individual schools the right to make autonomous decisions, thus allowing – or not allowing – them some scope in decision making with regard to regional conditions, and whether the schools' inspectorate itself actually supports and advises the individual schools in their development. In the context of the Federal Republic this meant, in particular, balancing the relationship between the 'autonomy of the individual school' versus 'administered schooling' without any decision making competence.

   In Berlin 'flanking measures of support from the schools' inspectorates' have been traditionally more forthcoming from the individual education offices than from the State Ministry for Schools, Vocational Education and Sports, which only uses its legal powers to intervene or take the initiative if the local education authorities make no decision or go astray on some legal point. Advice to individual schools about their quality and possibilities is not institutionalised in Berlin, nor does the city possess, to date, any comparative investigations or institutions which devote themselves to this subject. Though district school inspectors could be the strongest force in the institutionalisation of 'advice', they only actually do this to a limited extent, as they have special responsibility for staff matters and thus possess only limited resources of time. There is thus a gap here in Berlin's educational policies across which the individual school has to find its own way between the interests of the district and those of the centralised administration.

e) There is a clear overall tendency in Berlin in connection with the establishment of comprehensive schools: the comprehensive school has been accepted in the city for twenty years, though its acceptance in individual districts varies considerably. The 'market position' of the comprehensive school shows its 'degree of acceptance' more clearly. Its quality corresponds to its reputation, which may attract or put off the more efficient pupils, and to the support given by the intermediate instance of the local district authority, because the centralised administration at State level plainly furthers the development of comprehensive schools. The so-called 'creaming off' of the most gifted pupils is observable to different degrees over a wide range. On average only 5.7 percent of pupils recommended for grammar-school attendance went to comprehensive schools in the year before reunification (compared with 43.6 percent of those recommended for secondary-modern schools and 45 percent of those recommended for secondary-technical schools). There were, however, comprehensive schools with a share of pupils recommended for grammar schools of 42 percent (Schöneberg). In comments on the district-to-district and school-to-school variance in the acceptance of the comprehensive school it has already been said that 'the decision for an individual school [can be] more important than the selection of a type of school' (Baumert 1986:101; see also Raschert 1992).

Individual Results

The investigation brought to light a compendium of reasons for the difficulty in establishing comprehensive schools in the Berlin district of Treptow. Its contents were drawn from the context of decisions taken by the district council regarding the restructuring of schools prior to the introduction of the West Berlin school system in August 1991, as well as decisions made during the first two years during which Berlin's schools were united, and the arrangements made by individual schools. These were nourished by the regional integration of the individual school in the overall school structure in Treptow, by material and objective conditions at the beginning of the first school year in reunited Berlin, by the way it broke with the old GDR structures and by a consensus on regulations and standards at the individual schools established in the course of the first two years of schooling in the reunified city. This consensus was clearly stamped by the commitment of the individual teachers and their head teachers to accelerate the progress of reunification at the level of the individual school. These processes were not emphatically influenced by the inspectorate of schools in the district, nor by the State Ministry for Schools, Vocational Education and Sports. It appeared that during the transformation process the schools were left, instead, to themselves to carry out their duties as pedagogical action units, as it were, being forced for the time being to process their originatory problems as subsidiary matters, something that was accomplished more or less successfully by the individual school.

Every single one of the four comprehensive schools, their heads and their teaching staffs had to deal with the vacuum – breaking with the old without knowing the deficits of the new – and to find their own path. The 'West' only provided the corset that was held together by the new legal prescriptions of the western system and its support to improve the material conditions at the individual schools in the form of new teaching equipment (e.g., computers or books) or in the form of spatial additions or renewals (e.g., equipment for special rooms, making rooms and playgrounds more pleasant). The realisation that these could only stabilise the teaching process itself to a relative extent, that laws must be applied flexibly and that improved material conditions can only combat to a certain extent the anomalous tensions at individual schools took a while to gradually establish itself at the individual school sites.

It also became clear that, during the first two school years in the reunited city of Berlin, the individual comprehensive schools had developed very different styles. Though there was, according to almost all those involved no unified profile, visible to outsiders, at the individual schools, it was nevertheless plain that each separate comprehensive school had dealt very differently with identical problems at each of the four sites. Right at the start the individual schools were all jointly concerned with anomalous tensions, deficits in equipment and further training measures, as well as unclarified questions on how to come to terms with the past. These problems were then dealt with successively and in very different ways at the individual schools. During the course of this the style of the individual comprehensive schools could be seen taking shape.

The central interface for processing problems was the introduction of and subsequent adherence to the newly self-imposed regulations at the schools. This was the clearest indicator of whether the individual school had found its way to and also implemented a new consensus shared by all, or whether this had only been accepted by acclamation without being realised in actual teaching practice. In the latter case the atmosphere at the individual schools suffered considerably in the opinion of those involved.

The newly negotiated and implemented style at the individual comprehensive schools also confirmed the thesis, repeatedly proposed in Western investigations, that the atmosphere at an individual school need not coincide with the performance of its pupils. The differing levels of performance in the individual Treptow comprehensive schools prove this.

The 80 percent of comprehensive-school pupils starting seventh grade at Treptow Comprehensive School No. 1, which took no pupils recommended for grammar-school entry, and the 30 percent share of secondary-technical school and 20 percent share of grammar-school recommended pupils at Treptow Comprehensive School No. 4 at the start of the 1991/1992 school year did not create a considerably more complicated atmosphere at Comprehensive School No. 1 (cf. the differing entry conditions and variations between individual schools in Figs. 12.2 and 12.3). This example proved, instead, that after two years a more stable atmosphere had, indeed, established itself here than at Comprehensive Schools Nos. 3 and 4.

It was thus also shown that the improved spatial, material or regional preconditions at the other comprehensive schools in the district at the beginning of the first school year in the reunited city of Berlin had not necessarily led to more stable school conditions as perceived by the teachers themselves two years later.

The investigation also proved that democratic school conditions during the transformation could only be established via the day-to-day 'face-to-face' relationships between teachers, pupils, head teachers and the administration, exactly as Fend would have intended, an essential condition being that 'each will act for the welfare of the other' (1980:256). Within the framework of this investigation the commitment of the individual teacher, in the form of the desire to actually overcome the problems arising from the transformation, to renew old competences and to shape new ones, became the central indicator.

Finally, the investigation was also able to demonstrate that there had obviously been problems in controlling the development of schools in the eastern part of Berlin during the first two school years after the reunification of the city, both for the district administrations accompanying the schools through the transformation and for the centralised State Ministry for Schools, Vocational Education and Sports. The problem of sharing competence for external educational matters (for which the individual district is responsible) and for internal educational matters (for which the central administration is responsible), a legally imprecise division of labour even under the conditions prevalent in pre-reunification West Berlin, became aggravated within the framework of the transformation in the eastern part of the city. Taking Treptow as an example it was possible to show that it was not possible to separate these two aspects under the conditions of transformation, as the one is inseparable from the other.

The withdrawal of centralised administration associated with the introduction of the validity of West Berlin's school legislation on 1 August 1991 was, in the final instance, linked with the complete transfer to the district authorities of the development of individual schools without the latter having been given an accompanying instance which might have been able to show how the newly won freedom could have been used on the basis of the experience gained by school developments in the western part of the city. The result was a very varied acceptance of comprehensive schools, which may negatively influence the development of this school type in the eastern part of the city, for the reputation gained can only be altered in the individual districts within an extremely lengthy time frame.

Conclusion

The investigation entitled 'Radical changes in Berlin's schools' was able to demonstrate, in the final analysis, that it was perfectly possible to use the criteria for evaluating the quality of individual schools worked out so far during the transformation phase. This three-year research process did, however, show that the transformation itself constantly created new problems in the individual schools, each of which had to be dealt with individually without there being any set solution patterns. Thus many an individual could still go astray against the background of discussions on school quality. In the East Berlin district of Treptow, the variance of the individual school within the same system was amplified to a far greater extent than in the western part of Berlin.

Problems concerning overall school development which now also arose in the eastern part of Berlin (e.g., comprehensive schools with or without senior grades at grammar-school level, competition with the three-school type system, varying acceptance by parents of the various types of school) cannot, however, be argued out on the back of individual schools and the question of school quality. They must also be dealt with structurally, i.e., by posing, among other things, the question of what an individual comprehensive school may and should, in future, actually look like, and what perspective of educational policy is discussed in public with reference to the relationships between the individual members of the system.

Table 12.1 Data on School Development in West Berlin / East Berlin / Treptow

Districts in Comparison

Percentage share of Grade 7 at comprehensive school by comparison with percentages in three-school-type system

1st School Year of Reunified Berlin (1991/92)

	Gesamtschule	Gymnasium	Realschule	Hauptschule
West Berlin	28.1	40.0	19.8	12.1
East Berlin	49.6	36.2	11.9	2.3
Berlin Treptow	47.2	32.7	17.0	3.1

2nd School Year of Reunified Berlin (1992/93)

	Gesamtschule	Gymnasium	Realschule	Hauptschule
West Berlin	27.5	41.7	19.2	11.6
East Berlin	33.7	40.5	21.5	4.3
Berlin Treptow	26.7	38.9	31.1	3.2

3rd School Year of Reunified Berlin
Gains and losses after two years in percent (rounded out)

	Gesamtschule	Gymnasium	Realschule	Hauptschule
West Berlin	26.9 (-6.9)	41.1 (+2.8)	19.9 (+0.5)	12.1 (0)
East Berlin	30.94 (-37.7)	40.9 (+13)	23.6 (+98.3)	4.5 (+95.7)
Berlin Treptow	21.2 (-55.1)	44 (+34.6)	31.8 (+87.1)	3 (-3.2)

Source: Seiring 1993 and own calculations.

Table 12.2 The Four Treptow Comprehensive Schools in Comparison

Name	GS 1	GS 2	GS 3	GS 4
Formerly	O 24 Erich Lodemann	O 10	–	O 27 Michael W. Frunse
Precinct	Plänterwald	Adlershof	Altglienicke	Baumschulenweg
Near to grammar school	no	no	yes	no
Senior grades at grammar-school level	no	no	no	yes
Location	Mixed residential area 1960s high-rise flats	Mixed residential area 1900s, 1960s detached houses	New estates, high-rise flats of prefabr. sections	Mixed residential area 1900s, 1960s detached houses
School founded	1974	1898	10.8.1991	1900/1911/1912
Profile	Music/Art	Work Theory	Science/Sport	Languages
Staff at present	33	38	25	54
Of whom				
old	14	17	–	34
new	19	21	25	20
Female	26	27	19	42
Male	7	11	6	12
Young teachers born post 1955	17	17	13	27
Old teachers born pre 1955	16	21	12	27
German teachers	9	9	5	12
Work theory teachers	4	4	3	4

Source: Treptow Education Office: 6/1991

Table 12.3 Variance Between Individual Schools – May/June 1992 – May 1993

School	GS 1	GS 2	GS 3	GS 4	Σ
Pupils 91/92	270	395	193	600	1458
Pupils 92/93	254	421	225	550	1450
Teachers	30	36	26	53	145
Female	21 (70%)	25 (70%)	21 (80%)	40 (79%)	117 (78%)
Male	9 (30%)	11 (30%)	5 (20%)	11 (31%)	36 (22%)
Streams (91/92)					
Grade 7	3	4	3	5	15
Grade 8	4	4	3	5	6
Grade 9	3	3	3	5	14
Grade 10	2	4	5 (3 x 11)	11	
# Grades	22.5	26.3	21.3	26	
# Grade 7	67.5	105.2	63.9	130	366.6
Enrollments	GS 1	GS 2	GS 3	GS 4	Σ
May 92	45 (-33%)	71 (-33%)	52 (-19%)	47 (-64%)	215 (-28%/-37%)
Start of school year 92/93	50 (-17.5) -26%	76 (-29.2) -28%	52 (-11.9) -19%	61 (-69) -46%	239 (-127.6) -24%/-30%
Enrolments May 93	13 (-37)	108 (+32)	–	37 (-24)	158 (-82)
Drop v. previous year	-74%	+40%	–	-40%	-34%
Drop over two years	-80%	+2%	–	-71%	57%
Recommen-dations 1991/92 %	GS 1 80H/20R/0G*	GS 2 42H/55R/5G	GS 3 48H/44R/2G	GS 4 50H/30R/20G	
Recommen-dations 1992/93 %	80H/20R/0G	56H/42R/1.5G	67H/31R/2G	40H/60R/00G	
Leavers Grade 10 1992 %	26H/65R/9G	30H/36R/34G	30H/40R/30G		
Catchment primary schools	3	7	3	2	

Source: Details given by individual schools and own calculations*
H = *Hauptschule*, R = *Realschule*, G = *Gymnasium*

References

Aurin, K. (ed.) (1990), *Gute Schulen – worauf beruht ihre Wirksamkeit?*, Bad Heilbrunn.

Aurin, K. (ed.) (1993), *Auffassungen von Schule und pädagogischer Konsens. Fallstudien bei Lehrerkollegien, Eltern- und Schülerschaft von fünf Gymnasien*, Stuttgart.

Baumert, J. (1986), 'Auf dem Weg zur neuen Dreigliedrigkeit? – Zur Differenzierung des Sekundarschulangebots in Berlin (West)', in Hessisches Institut Für Bildunsplanung und Schulentwicklung (eds) *Sekundarschulen unter Konkurrenzdruck – Fallstudien aus dem viergliedrigen Schulsystem*, Wiesbaden, 79-102.

Baumert, J. and Leschinsky, A. (1986), 'Berufliches Selbstverständnis und Einflußmöglichkeiten von Schulleitern. Ergebnisse einer Schulleiterbefragung', in *Zeitschrift für Pädagogik* 32, 2, 247-266.

Fend, H. (1977), *Schulklima: Soziale Einflußprozesse in der Schule. Soziologie der Schule III*, Weinheim.

Fend, H. (1980), *Theorie der Schule*, München, Wien, Baltimore.

Fend, H. (1982), *Gesamtschule im Vergleich. Bilanz der Ergebnisse des Gesamtschulversuchs*, Weinheim, Basel.

Fend, H. (1986), '"Gute Schule – schlechte Schule". Die einzelne Schule als pädagogische Handlungseinheit, in *Die Deutsche Schule* 3, 275-293.

Gehrmann, A. (1996), *Schule in der Transformation. Eine empirisch-vergleichende Untersuchung an vier Gesamtschulen im Berliner Bezirk Treptow (1991-1993)*, Frankfurt.

Kuckartz, U. (1992), *Textanalysesysteme für die Sozialwissenschaften. Einführung in MAX und TEXTBASE ALPHA*, Stuttgart, Jena, New York.

Lenz, J. (1991), *Die Effective School Forschung der USA – ihre Bedeutung für die Führung und Lenkung von Schulen*, Frankfurt a. M.

Mortimore, P. (1994), 'Schuleffektivität: Ihre Herausforderung für die Zukunft', in *Zeitschrift für Pädagogik*, 32. Beiheft: Bildung und Erziehung in Europa. Beiträge zum 14. Kongreß der Deutschen Gesellschaft für Erziehungswissenschaft vom 14.-16. März 1994 in der Universität Dortmund, 177-134.

Raschert, J. (1992), 'Entwicklung und Erfolge der Gesamtschule in Berlin', in Beller, K. (ed.) *Berlin und pädagogische Reformen. Brennpunkte der individuellen und historischen Entwicklung*, Berlin 129-142.

Roeder, P.M. (1986), 'Lehrerkooperation und Schulqualität. Beobachtungen aus Berliner Hauptschulen', in *Westermanns Pädagogische Beiträge* 7/8, 30-35.

Roeder, P.M. (1987), 'Qualitative Schulentwicklung am Beispiel einer Berliner Gesamtschule: Zielkonflikte und unbeabsichtigte Nebenwirkungen', in Steffens, U. and Bargel, T. (eds) vol. 2. *Fallstudien zur Qualität von Schule*, 87-123.

Roeder, P.M. and Schümer, G. (1986), *Kommunikation und Kooperation von Lehrern. Beobachtungen in Haupt- und Gesamtschulen*, Berlin.

Rolff, H.G. (1991), 'Schulentwicklung als Entwicklung von Einzelschulen? Theorien und Indikatoren von Entwicklungsprozessen', in *Zeitschrift für Pädagogik* 37, 6, 865-886.

Rutter, M., Maughan, B., Mortimer, P. and Ouston, J. (1980), *Fünfzehntausend Stunden – Schulen und ihre Wirkung auf Kinder*, Weinheim.

Seiring, W. (1993), 'Berliner Gesamtschule – status quo – wie geht es weiter?' Referat anläßlich des Berliner Gesamtschultages am 4. September 1993. Senatsverwaltung für Schule, Berufsbildung und Sport Berlin. Berlin.

Steffens, U. (1986), 'Erkundungen zur Wirksamkeit und Qualität von Schule', in *Die Deutsche Schule*, 3, 294-305.

Steffens, U. and Bargel, T. (eds) (1987ff), *Qualität von Schule*, vols 1-7, Hessisches Institut für Lehrerfortbildung. Wiesbaden.

Steffens, U. and Bargel, T. (eds) (1993), *Erkundungen zur Qualität von Schule*, Neuwied.

Tillmann, K.-J. (eds) (1989), *Was ist eine gute Schule?*, Hamburg.

Chapter 13

PATRONISING GOVERNMENTS AS BARRIERS TO SCHOOL IMPROVEMENT

What Can Be Done About Them?

Kees van der Wolf

Introduction

Many researchers have pointed out that the tendency of governments to over-regulate schools acts as an important obstacle to school improvement. At present, all over the world efforts are being made to reduce governmental interference in school policies. The aim is to enable schools to find their own solutions. Advocates of these new policies assume that new clients from minority and under-represented groups, in particular, can best be helped by autonomous schools, because quality can best be enhanced at the school level. Opponents of this 'neo-liberal ideology', on the other hand, argue that school autonomy will only create inequality between schools and that autonomy is used by governments as an instrument to divest themselves of their responsibilities. Schools are not equipped for autonomy and central, state reform ought to remain possible, they argue.

Many governments feel uncertain in this new situation. Some politicians seem to be afraid of an independently functioning school system, for which they could ultimately be held responsible. Political office-holders therefore manifest an understandable inclination to keep a grip on education from a distance, through systems of evaluation and accountability. However understandable all this may be, educational practitioners perceive it as bureaucrats continuing to patronise them despite a professed commitment to deregulation. There is a danger that this will in turn lead to a reduction in vitality, undermining the capacities of schools for self-renewal.

In this article an effort will first be made to find an explanation for the fact that schools are still being kept under control by the political world. The role of educational research in this process will be discussed.

Furthermore, it will be argued that bureaucratic control and lack of school autonomy impedes the school improvement process. Attempts to improve the quality of schools are better not exercised through top-down reform efforts. Such strategies tend to keep schools passively dependent on bureaucratic institutions. They strengthen the schools' inclination to pay more attention to signals from 'the great donor' (the government) than to those emanating from their 'customers'. This leads schools to take the needs and interests of the real 'educational' target groups (pupils and their parents) insufficiently into account and prevents them from developing policies guided by the wishes of those target groups.

The view will be presented that some market competition may be needed to encourage schools to re-orient themselves.

The Social Background to the Patronising Bureaucracy

The growth of post-war industry and of the public sector brought about an increase in the demand for well-educated employees. Educational improvement is no longer an ideal to be pursued only by a small progressive group. Good education for all is viewed as a necessary condition for procuring and retaining material prosperity. The need for well-educated employees becomes increasingly urgent.

One consequence of post-war political renewal has been that the existence of class differences is no longer taken for granted. Democratisation has made education common property. Owing to growing awareness, based on convincing sociological research, of the fact that children have unequal opportunities to profit from education, education is now assigned a central role in reducing social inequality and tracking down 'hidden talents'. After the disaster of the Second World War this led to a political climate which favoured huge investments in education. The extra finances necessary were readily available, because in many western countries economic and financial circumstances have been favourable during this period. In the Netherlands, between 1960 and 1975 public sector charges were doubled from about a quarter to roughly half of the national income. Expenditure on education rose to over 6.5 percent of the gross national product.

In educational circles (teachers, trade unions, inspectors and training staff) concern is felt over the failure of education to fulfil its social responsibilities. The school system was not equipped to handle the consequences of the post-war baby boom. It has suffered from a shortage of well-trained staff and classrooms, and worries have been expressed about class size in kindergartens and primary schools. Percentages of pupils not progressing up to the next grade and of referrals to special education proved to be rather high.

In the current discussion concerning the transition from the industrial era to the era of information technology the school is once again expected to play a crucial role. As in the post-war period, we are again going through a period of uncertainty and challenges. At such times the school is often given the responsibility for initiating youth into the secrets of the new age. 'Knowledge is power' still appears to be a valid adage. It is assumed that more education and better schooling will save us from an approaching catastrophe. The educational elite is only too ready to endorse this thesis, as it will tempt the government to set aside more money for education. The question should, however, be raised as to whether the school on its own should be assigned the role of solving potential social problems.

The points outlined above make it easy to understand why the political world is so reluctant to let schools themselves play a role in policy-making. The school has for a long time been used as an instrument for social renewal and restructuring. In referring to the U.S. situation, Reitman, however, puts it this way: 'I suspect that the best hope (...) for reducing American over-dependency upon the schooling system for resolving the nation's major social problems will not come from politicians, educational leaders, and teachers generally; rather from the American lay public itself' (Reitman 1987: 16).

This links up with a worldwide movement existing outside the profession of education, a movement away from centralised state monopolies in goods and services, a movement that can be detected in most developed countries.

The Contribution made by Educational Research to Bureaucratic Control

The 'black-box approach'

In order to check whether the large investment made in post-war education really has produced results, research was commissioned in the 1960s that can be characterised in terms of the 'input-output approach'. This approach views the school as a black box containing students. Resources are allocated to the students in the box, and there is a result in some form of output. Factors that may be influenced by policy, such as school size, facilities, teacher salaries and class size, were related to the average scores on standardised cognitive tests. The conclusion was often drawn that these variables, taken at school level, accounted for little if any of the differences in performance between pupils. Jencks, who showed a great preference for this type of input-output research, and whose main interest laid in long-term effects, notes at the end of his study: 'The long-term effects of schooling seem much less significant to us then they did when we began our work, and the internal life of the schools seems correspondingly more important' (Jencks et al. 1972: 13).

All this led to the incorrect conclusion that schools have no influence on the development of pupils, and that all the money invested in schools after Second World War had in fact been wasted.

The effective school-movement in fashion

Just when the U.S. government was about to radically reduce the education budget because of the disappointing results, the famous report 'A Nation at Risk' (1983) was published. This thirty-six-page report received an incredible amount of attention from the U.S. media. In particular, its recommendations contributed to the breaking down of the pessimistic views held by the political and educational world. The report made use of the so-called 'Edmonds' Five', derived from research on school effectiveness. These five factors, which were found to correlate highly with school quality, are as follows:

1. the principal's leadership and attention to the quality of teaching;
2. a pervasive and generally understood academic focus;
3. an orderly, safe climate conducive to teaching and learning;
4. teacher behaviour that conveys the expectation that all students are expected to obtain at least minimum mastery;
5. the use of measures of pupil achievement as the basis for school evaluation (Ellis and Fouts 1993).

These factors did not seem to be too expensive to introduce into schools and were so easy to understand, that even Ronald Reagan was able to publish a 'scientific' article on this subject under his own name during his 1984 presidential campaign. Furthermore, they concur well with intuitive knowledge about effective teaching.

The 'effective-school movement' was quickly adopted by the political circuit, especially in the U.S.A. By supporting the idea that school achievement can be influenced so that, given the right conditions, good results can be expected even from disadvantaged students, it supplied convincing arguments that could be used to obtain additional finances for schools with 'black' and poor students. Later on, procedures based on the effective-school reasoning were used by school boards to raise the quality of the education provided by their schools.

The concept has proven to be attractive to politicians and school boards, because, as has been mentioned, the solution is understandable to everyone, seems inexpensive and, in particular, because it has few consequences for the working methods of policy makers themselves! Bureaucracy, the primary cause of the problems according to many, gets off scot-free.

In the following we will report on a Dutch school project, based on the school-effectiveness principles, which was intended to serve an important goal (improving the quality of schools with a high proportion of migrant pupils), but which, in retrospect, did not produce the expected results.

An Amsterdam Initiative in Primary Education

The EGAA-project

The general standard of education in Amsterdam schools with a high proportion of migrant pupils has often been the subject of negative evaluation. In the Netherlands, the majority of ethnic minority groups are of Moroccan, Turkish, Surinamese, Yugoslavian, Spanish, Ghanese and Chinese origin. Pupil achievement in schools with a high percentage of minority students has been on average about one to two years below the Dutch norm. This presented a serious problem which needed to be addressed seriously in the view of Amsterdam politicians.

Prompted by this train of thought the city council of Amsterdam decided to set up an experiment aimed at improving the education in schools with a very high percentage of non-Dutch children. This school-improvement project, in which fourteen elementary schools with an pupil-age range of between four and twelve years participated, was launched on the first of May 1988. The project involved about 3,000 pupils, of which an average of 81 percent had a non-Dutch background, and more than 200 teachers. The project was called 'Experiment Gerichte Aanpak Amsterdamse Basisscholen' (Experiment with a targeted approach to Amsterdam primary schools), shortened to EGAA.

In this experiment, contracts were made between Amsterdam City Council as the supplier of subsidies, and the immigrant schools. The contracts contained the following points:

- the strong and weak points of the school were analysed;
- a plan of action was drawn up: this listed the activities to be undertaken in order to improve the education provided by the school;
- a survey was made of what was required in the way of staffing, financing, and equipment in order to implement these activities;
- a concrete list was made of things it was hoped to achieve by the end of the experimental period (expectations of results);
- a method was established for assessing the effects of the activities undertaken, both at pupil and teacher level.

A budget was provided to cover the activities undertaken: funds could be spent on extra staff, additional teaching aids and on in-service training for teachers.

On the basis of a literature study it was assumed that a combination of 'effective-school factors' (see the preceding section) would lead to good learning achievement on the part of the pupils, and that most of the children would move on to the more academic types of secondary education, with only a few changing track to special schools.

Some background reasons for the disappointing results

Based on effective school research many city council departments in the Netherlands have established programmes to encourage schools to develop more effective organisations. Schools are being instructed to raise their expectations, to establish priorities and to make decisions more cooperatively. The EGAA project employed intensive principal and teacher counselling and evaluation, and frequent standardised testing to keep track of student performance. The EGAA staff developed a fairly extensive research instrument in order to measure the results of the experiment. Teachers were given questionnaires, and pupils were given achievement tests on the subjects they had been studying, a questionnaire on non-cognitive factors, and a sociometric assessment.

The project was successful in the sense that the teachers from the participating schools found that 'politicians' were not blind to their problems and were prepared to pay attention to them. The net results at pupil level, however, were rather disappointing. No noticeable improvement of the standard of pupil achievements could be found. As often happens, the assumption that the innovation would be implemented at classroom level proved to be unfounded. The EGAA staff, by concentrating on effective school leadership, seem to have relied too much on the ability of the school leaders to promote the adoption of new strategies by teachers, which, by the way, is an example of 'top-down' thinking in itself. Teachers thought to be participating in the innovation, proved to be 'non-users'. Once again, this school-reform project has provided little evidence that the efforts have paid off. How can these results be explained?

Although some of the 'opinion leaders' put pressure on politicians to allocate large sums of money to school improvement in Amsterdam, teachers in 'immigrant' schools generally put up strong resistance at first to this 'school-improvement project initiated by the politicians'. They feared that new teaching methods might be imposed on schools, as had happened before in Amsterdam, or at least as they remembered had happened. Why, then, did the majority of teachers decide to join in this project? It was because the EGAA staff dispelled their negative feelings by emphasising that the EGAA project would 'merely' provide a structure inside which schools could realise the working goals agreed on.

The project would not actually focus on the methods teachers used in the classroom. Apart from this, the promise of a fair amount of money was extended. In order to realise the action items, the subsidy provider allocated the participating schools extra finances: a sum of US$ 14,000 was put at the disposal of each school for additional staff facilities. In real terms this meant nineteen hours per week. A sum of US$ 8,000 was provided as an extra budget for buying necessary educational tools and equipment, and a sum of US$ 5,000 to cover the schooling costs. The schools reacted with a certain eagerness to the EGAA offer, perhaps because they regarded it as an opportunity to solve some of their problems. In the pretest there was much concern about how much value the programme would have for the pupils. In general, teachers thought that the proposals, though often rather vaguely defined, could be implemented in their classrooms. In this respect, teachers felt confident. It is not clear whether this should be assessed as a positive or negative aspect. It might suggest ill-founded self-confidence. It could also mean that teachers did not actually intend to carry out the plans in their own classroom. Teachers seem to prefer the type of changes that do not interfere too much with the methods they use in the classroom. In this case, they could see that they were not expected to bring about radical changes in their role behaviour, teaching methods and views on teaching. This assessment would seem to have been correct, as the EGAA staff, as mentioned before, put great emphasis on school management, in the assumption that effective leadership and efficient organisation would lead to implementation of the selected 'working points' in the classroom, but they did not actually check the progress made in this in this respect. To put it in less charitable terms, the EGAA project provided the money to buy methods, without demanding radical changes in the classroom. Moreover, the project was of short duration, and ended after a period of only two years in each school. So, one did not have to worry too much about the investment of time. In addition, the fact that principals and teachers in 'immigrant' schools had put pressure on the politicians played a very important role. They had to participate once the politicians had met their own wishes.

On the whole, as has been stated, the results of the EGAA project were disappointing. The effects of a reform depend on how the programme affects those attributes of schools that are most strongly related to student achievement. These remain the educational content provided in the classroom, and the grip on the political context held by schools themselves.

Through focusing on the effective-school theories EGAA never came to ask or to answer the question: which interaction of internal and external factors causes schools to function badly? Research shows more and more clearly that the power of pressure from outside the school plays an important role. The more a school experiences pressure from politicians, trade unions, policy-makers and school counsellors, the smaller the chance of the internal organisation functioning well. Schools that have little say in the way their own budget is spent, in appointing or firing their staff, in choosing the projects in which to participate, usually function less well than schools that have control over these matters.

It is, consequently, becoming increasingly clear that it is not only factors that are internal to the school which are involved, but also, in particular, the ways in which schools handle external pressure of an administrative and political nature. Successful schools always deal well and creatively with their administrative surroundings!

Is Less Government Better Government?

The impasse

These experiences ought to make reformers sceptical of new efforts to improve education within existing school systems. Spending and regulation, using a project structure, have not been effective. When pressed by politicians to do something about failing city schools, school boards, superintendents and administrators tend to take the only action they can: they offer schools more money if it is available. If schools are given more money to spend in essentially the same way they spent it before, there is little reason to believe additional funding will bring about improvements.

Schools in the Netherlands, the U.S.A. and many other countries have organised effectively or ineffectively in response to various political, administrative, economic, and educational forces that demand organisational responses. How do these forces work? In this respect the fact that teachers have only a limited influence on the circumstances under which they do their work appears to be very important. They are caught in a web of hierarchical relationships. Bureaucratic control and lack of school autonomy impede the school improvement process. The mania for organisation that characterises Dutch authorities has only served to amplify this phenomenon. That is why the OECD welcomes the policy of deregulation currently being pursued by Dutch authorities. In other professions people have much more autonomy and much more 'room for free movement'. Lawyers and architects, for instance, are confronted with far fewer governmental whims and caprices and are able to establish their own rules to a greater degree. Teachers more often work in an atmosphere that requires a strong sense of duty and obedience. They are dependent on instructions and administration policies. All this has a negative influence on the way teachers feel about their competence and motivation. These bottlenecks are now increasingly attracting attention in the Netherlands.

Whether a school is effectively organised is not only connected with the calibre of the students in the school, but also, as has been stated before, with the pressures from outside the school.

It seems, then, that the Dutch educational system is at an impasse. In the following paragraph some thoughts will be presented on the direction in which possible solutions could be found.

Sketch of a possible way out

We tend to think that the system could be brought to move in the right direction if schools were to be given greater autonomy and a greater interest in investing in improving the quality of education in their own school. We agree with Chubb and Moe (1989) that the key to better schools is more effective school organisation.

The key to more effective school organisation is greater school autonomy and, finally, the key to greater school autonomy is school competition and parental choice. Schools would be given an interest in self-evaluation and self-improvement by strengthening the working of the market through better use of the constitutionally guaranteed freedom of school choice for parents. This would, of course, require a good system of information for parents on the educational (and other) qualities individual schools provide. If realised, such a system and the orientation on the 'mechanisms of the market' could stimulate schools to think through and formulate the concepts they want to present to parents as 'critical consumers'. Decisions about curricula, discipline, school counselling and guidance, teaching methods and priorities would be made by the schools themselves (teachers and principals) responding to their clients.

Autonomy seems to hold the key to school improvement. Parents and students must be given the right to choose the school that the student will attend. Proponents argue that competition would bring improved management and teaching and more efficient resource allocation. Opponents fear the influence of special interest groups and possible harm from subjecting teachers and curricula to the demands of the public. It is our opinion that if parents could choose their children's schools, additional learning opportunities would be stimulated. It is very important that in introducing these working methods the rights of minority groups and the poor are safeguarded.

Research indicates that school choice can offer a good opportunity for all children to get a quality education. Studies have indicated that higher levels of student achievement, teacher morale and parental involvement are associated with school choice, and students who have 'chosen' their school experience significantly fewer problems in school.

Government, in this view, should distance itself from school policies, apart from checking the qualifications of teaching staff, monitoring the attainment of minimum educational goals and, where necessary, taking measures to counteract discrimination against certain minority groups.

The role of school boards would, under those circumstances, be one of functioning as a source of inspiration and of supplying both the support and the pressure to realise necessary changes. No longer would they provide ready-made top-down solutions to problems or even to force them down reluctant school teams' throats. The solutions would in the first place be invented by the school leadership and staff, with a view to their own interest in maintaining or improving the quality of their organisation and in attaining the educational and other standards aspired to.

Educational research could play an important part, not by supplying politicians with easily understandable solutions, but by supplying schools with information which equips them to serve parents and pupils more effectively. At the same time research could check whether emphasising the role of parental choice (and, therefore, of the 'market') produces the expected and desired results and has no undesirable additional consequences.

Coleman (1992) argued that if the right intellectual agenda and research agenda are established, if appropriate questions are asked and the answers sought through diligent research, the social force capable of bringing about a new institutional order in education does exist.

Conclusion

In the recent past, the Netherlands has experienced increasing pressures toward centralisation and a steady increase in government control. There has been a significant growth in state-school bureaucracy over the last two decades. Educational research has played its own role in this process by first indicating that school 'does not matter' and then by supplying the framework for (over-) easy top-down solutions.

What is needed is school improvement through the full participation of parents in the development of educational policy.

The Netherlands could make a better use of choice. James (1982) noted that choice between Dutch schools 'exists with respect to the philosophy of education but only slightly with respect to funding or quality components which are dependent on funding'. The Netherlands could make a better use of choice, namely by using it to promote school quality.

References

Chubb, J.E. and Moe, T.M. (1989), *Give Choice a Chance. Answers to the Most Frequently Asked Questions about Mediocrity in American Education and What Can Be Done about It*, Washington D.C.

Coleman, J.S. (1992), 'Effective Schools and Educational Choice', in J. Bashi and Z. Sass (eds), *School Effectiveness & School Improvement*, Jerusalem.

Deal, T.E. (1985), 'The Symbolism of Effective Schools', in *The Elementary School Journal*, 5, 601-620.

Ellis, A.K. and Fouts, J.T. (1993), *Research on Educational Innovations*, Princeton Junction, N.J.

James, E. (1982), *The Private Provision of Public Services: A Comparison of Sweden and Holland*, New Haven.

Jencks, C., Smith, M., Acland, H., Bane M.J., Cohen D., Gintis, H., Heyns, B. and Michelson, S. (1972), *Inequality: a reassessment of the effect of family and schooling in America*, New York.

Reitman, S.W. (1985), 'American Educational Messianism: A View from a Nation Under Siege', Eric Report ED 250 822 (microfiche).

Chapter 14

THE MEANING OF 'SOCIAL CLASS' FOR TURKISH, MOROCCAN AND DUTCH 'SOCIAL CLIMBERS'

Guuske Ledoux, with *Piet Deckers* and *Pjotr Koopman*

Introduction

The question of whether the educational and social success of immigrant children is mainly determined by social class or by ethnic origin has been a point of discussion in The Netherlands for quite a while now. This discussion was prompted by the findings of several research projects, in which pupils from various ethnic groups were compared with each other. These projects showed that, *after controlling for social class*, the school achievement level of immigrant children did not appear to be significantly lower than that of native Dutch children (see for instance, Van 't Hof and Dronkers 1992; Van Langen and Jungbluth 1990).

In this kind of research 'social class' is generally based on the parents' educational and/or professional level, and 'ethnic origin' is based on the parents' country of birth. No matter how useful these kinds of measures are in quantitative research, they do not provide much insight into the mechanisms which give one group of children a better chance of success than another group. The discussion about 'social class' versus 'ethnic origin' would be more powerful if it focused on these mechanisms, and if the following questions were raised more often: What do these concepts of social class and ethnic origin actually stand for? If one argues that 'social class' offers the best explanation for differences in educational success, both for native Dutch children and for immigrant children, does this mean that social class means the same thing to both groups and is reflected in the same processes? Can we assume that social differences between 'higher' and 'lower' classes are the same for each ethnic group? Are we talking about the same gap between school and home environment? Are the obstacles experienced by children from various disadvantaged groups in education, both in social and cognitive domains, the same? And if it is assumed that 'ethnic origin' does have an independent influence on children's educational opportunities, which 'ethnically determined' processes and characteristics are responsible for this? Are these processes really completely different in nature from those stemming from 'social class'?

In this chapter we will focus on some of these topics, in particular on the meaning and implications of social class. We will try to find an answer to the question of whether the mechanisms that are supposed to explain why social class is so important for educational success operate in the same way for immigrant children and for native Dutch children. In other words, we are looking for differences and similarities between these two groups in the components of social class. The main purpose here is to contribute to the discussion mentioned above.

We will first turn our attention towards the hypotheses that lie behind the umbrella term 'social class'. Subsequently, we will check to what extent and in what way these hypotheses apply to a specific group: Turkish, Moroccan and Dutch young adults who have climbed (very) high on the social ladder compared to their parents and, by doing so, have – as it were – changed their social class. Finally, we will summarize and discuss the differences and similarities found between the immigrants and the native Dutch group.

Hypotheses on Social Class

Research on social class and inequality in education has been conducted for more than three decades. Since 1960 several theories about the origins of this type of inequality have been developed and, in part, subjected to empirical testing. We do not have the scope to review all these theories within the context of this chapter. We will therefore use our own classification of hypotheses from the literature. We make no claim to be exhaustive, but we think that the overview presented here will be reasonably workable for the purpose of this part of this discussion; that is: to elaborate on the nature of inequality arising from social class and to identify themes which can be used to compare immigrant and native Dutch participants in education.

Hypothesis 1: direct educational support

This hypothesis implies that the more parents are able and prepared to give practical support to their children in their school education, for instance, by helping them with their homework, keeping in touch with the teachers and participating in parent activities in school, the greater the children's chances of educational success in school. We are talking here, among other things, about the level of understanding parents have of their child's school life and school requirements, and about the degree to which they can actually help their children in this respect. Highly educated parents would be more capable of doing this.

Hypothesis 2: indirect educational support

This hypothesis implies that the more parents are able to stimulate the cognitive (intellectual) development of their child, the greater the child's chance of educational success. We are talking here about parental influence on the development of thinking, language, and the acquisition of general knowledge, through their daily interaction with their children. The amount of reading and reading aloud is important, as is the way in which parents communicate with their children, the amount and kind of attention parents give to their children individually, the degree of participation in artistic and cultural activities, and the opportunities children get from their parents to extend their experience and knowledge. An important role is reserved for the language the child learns to use at home.

Hypothesis 3: aspirations for the future

This hypothesis implies that the higher parents' expectations are for the future educational achievements of their children, the 'higher' those achievements will be. According to this hypothesis, the lower classes tend to hold the view that higher education is not accessible 'to our kind'. Less importance is attached to education, either out of fatalism or due to a positive appreciation of (manual) occupations that do not require much school education. The hypothesis also implies that in the higher classes further education is self-evident. Parental aspirations are transmitted to the children, thus influencing children's motivation for education.

Hypothesis 4: the influence of the social environment

The idea here is that the routine and frequent events occurring in the social environment of the child which are seen as 'normal' within this environment, have their own influence on the child's future opportunities. Growing up in a family where no one is highly educated, in a neighbourhood where this is also the case, attending a school where almost all the children have the same family and neighbourhood characteristics, makes it inconceivable that one would reach higher education. We are talking here essentially about the presence or absence of certain role models.

Hypothesis 5: child-rearing patterns

This hypothesis implies that certain kinds of child-rearing behaviour and attitudes are more or less suited to (implicit) educational requirements concerning the behaviour and attitude of children. The best-known examples are more disciplinary versus more transaction-oriented child-rearing styles, and more role-oriented versus more person-oriented styles.

Hypothesis 6: class-specific selection processes in education

This hypothesis concerns the way in which schools respond to class differences. The central idea here is that, in education, preferential treatment is given to children coming from higher classes because their knowledge, language usage, social world and behaviour are implicitly used as educational standards. Another element in this field is teachers' expectations: by expecting more from children from higher social classes than from those from lower classes teachers influence children's motivation to learn, and through this their achievement levels.

Up until now we have been attempting to order the mechanisms that lie behind the concept of 'social class'. Our next step is to investigate to what extent and in what way the processes described in the hypotheses occur in the lives of immigrant people on the one hand and native Dutch people on the other hand. For that purpose we have used a research project on individuation processes in young immigrant adults.

'Individuation Processes' Research: Setup and Characteristics

Little research has been done into the processes going on 'behind' social class and ethnic origin. The study we are using here was not primarily directed at answering these issues. It was a study of the individuation processes of young immigrant adults (aged between 20 and 35) of Turkish and Moroccan origin, who have 'succeeded' socially. Social success was defined in this study as follows: completion of a course in higher vocational education or at university rounded off with a diploma, followed by employment appropriate to their qualifications. There were two main questions in this study. The first question was which factors could be held responsible for the educational success and the social success of these immigrants. The second question was whether there have been any changes in their value patterns during their lives up to the point in time when the research was carried out. This last question is based on the assumption that in Turkish and Moroccan families there are some culture-determined value patterns which contradict the dominant value patterns in Dutch education. This would mean that Turkish and Moroccan children must cross extra barriers, or put in an extra amount of effort to learn the cultural codes that are a condition for successful participation in Dutch education. It is conceivable, however, that native Dutch children from disadvantaged groups also experience changes in values and attitudes when they take up studies in higher education. Therefore, a control group of socially successful Dutch young adults was selected in this study to verify whether the (assumed) differences in cultural codes are based mainly on ethnic-cultural differences or mainly on cultural differences related to social class. To obtain two comparable groups, only those young adults who have obviously attained a better social position than their parents were selected.

In depth interviews were held with the selected subjects (27 young adults: 10 Turkish, 9 Moroccan, 8 Dutch, both men and women), in which their educational career was reconstructed, and various elements in their upbringing were charted retrospectively. We used a biographical method of interviewing, resulting in detailed information on the life of each individual, especially their home and school life. Owing to the nature of this data it is possible to carry out secondary analyses on research questions other than the original ones, which is what we have done for this chapter. We looked into the data to find out whether, and how, the mechanisms mentioned in the hypotheses present themselves in the life stories of our 'successful' subjects, focusing in particular on the question of whether these mechanisms are similar or different for the various ethnic backgrounds.[1]

1. Of course, there are severe limitations in our research material with regard to the central question of this chapter. The sample was small and very specific, comprising only young people who had climbed up the social ladder relative to their parents. Their experiences in life are not typical and cannot be considered representative of lower-class children and adults in general. Furthermore it must be stressed that while our interviewing method did

We have chosen to present the results as follows. For each hypothesis we will indicate whether we found examples of the phenomena mentioned in that particular hypothesis and if so, whether there were any differences between immigrant and native Dutch youngsters. We will then go on to discuss the nature of these differences. We will use the term *gradual* when the differences found are essentially the same for immigrant and Dutch youngsters and only vary in scale. We will use the term *fundamental* when the differences found point to really different experiences or characteristics for immigrants on the one hand and native people on the other. In addition, if we are talking about fundamental differences, we will discuss whether they could be characterized as 'ethnic' components. Based on our findings on each hypothesis we will then return to the question of whether, and to what extent, it is useful to differentiate between social-class explanations and ethnic-origin explanations.

Social Class Hypotheses and the Individuation Research

1. Direct educational support

On this subject our research results show a clear difference between Turkish and Moroccan families, on the one hand, and Dutch families, on the other. To start with the Dutch families: there is no active, substantial help with school work in these families, especially in secondary education. The low educational level of the parents does not enable them to give their children substantial help with their school work, for instance by explaining the subject matter. Still we can see that these parents, especially the mothers, maintain regular contact with the primary school, and sometimes even participate in parental activities like helping with reading. At secondary school contacts become less frequent, but in this phase we can still see that parents discuss school activities at home, and occasionally try to supervise their children's homework.

In Turkish and Moroccan families parents are obviously less involved with their children's education. In primary education there is almost no parental participation (only one father had participated in a representative advisory body). Most parents do their best to attend parents' evenings, but they are often confronted with language problems. They do

indeed reveal a lot of information relevant to the question in this chapter, this was only as a 'byproduct', not as the central topic in the conversation. It would be better to carry out a research project with the specific aim of analysing the processes described in our hypotheses. Nevertheless, we think that we can provide some initial insight into the question about the meaning of social class for different ethnic groups. We do not claim to have come up with definite answers or to be representative.

not help with school work. Often this is truly impossible as one or both parents are illiterate, even in their own language. In these families parents obviously have a more limited insight into their children's school life. As the respondents in our study were good learners and often very independent at an early stage, many Turkish and Moroccan parents saw no reason for intensive contact, as there were no problems. They took it for granted that their children and the school were doing their work properly. They often had to depend on the advice of other people when choosing a primary school for their children.

In these families there are even fewer contacts between parents and school in secondary education than in primary education. It is usual for the children in these families to take the choice of the secondary school upon themselves, sometimes guided by their primary school: visiting various schools, choosing a school, planning the enrolment. Also, during secondary education children take care of all the formalities required themselves. They take on the responsibility for organizing their homework and solving problems at school (which occur quite often in the secondary education phase). When they are offered help by their family, this comes from brothers or sisters. Real communication with their parents about educational matters is usually impossible.

In summary, and not taking into account all the differences existing within the ethnic groups, we can say that on the subject of 'direct educational support' Turkish and Moroccan parents are distinguished specifically by:

- fewer opportunities to give actual help to their children,
- less contact with the school,
- a much more limited knowledge of education (content and system),
- a much more limited knowledge of everyday school life,
- strong confidence in their child and in the school ('as long as things are running smoothly, we don't need to interfere').

Are these differences between native Dutch and immigrant parents gradual or fundamental? Both, in our opinion. On the first two points we can talk about a gradual difference, stemming from the fact that the educational level of the immigrant parents is even lower than that of the Dutch parents. But the last three points are typical of the immigrants. It would not be true to say that Dutch parents have virtually no knowledge of education at all, and, either out of necessity or because of a different attitude towards the school ('the school knows what is best'), leave the organization of all school activities entirely to the school and the child. Nor would it be true to say that Dutch parents hardly, if ever, discuss school experiences with their child. For the time being these factors are typical of the immigrant families (in our study Turkish and Moroccan families), but it is expected that these differences will disappear in future generations. By then, the parents will have at least some experience of Dutch education.

2. Indirect educational support

The Individuation study provides only limited information on this subject. The nature of the study (retrospective questioning with just one 'party' in the educational process) does not allow any statements about, for instance, interaction processes and language use in the family. In a general sense we can say that none of our respondents was raised in a family showing the typical characteristics of the highly educated, such as an extensive reading culture and an active participation in art, culture and other forms of leisure activities that may have an 'educative' effect. Only in a few cases parents did have a lot of books at home, but in general parents were not enthusiastic readers. Marked differences between native Dutch and immigrant parents were not present in this area, even though many of the immigrant parents were illiterate.

A striking fact is that many parents (in all ethnic groups) had unfulfilled desires regarding their own education. They had wanted to learn much more when they were younger, but owing to various circumstances they did not get round to it. This may suggest that there is more learning potential among the parents in our study than their low educational levels show. From this we can deduce that the parents of the individuals examined in this study may have had more 'knowledge of the world' than other parents from lower social backgrounds. An indication of this is that several respondents described their parents, or one of their parents, as a person with broad interests and a rather open attitude towards learning new things. This is, however, neither a general pattern nor a characteristic difference between native Dutch and immigrant families.

Another relevant fact here is the way in which our respondents, in their own judgement, have changed in comparison to their parents. When they were asked this question, they often mentioned a change in their *way of thinking*: more balanced, less straightforward, departing less from established facts, more flexible than their parents'. This indicates that, in these cases, a shift is actually occurring, which corresponds with assumptions about the differences between social backgrounds on this point. But this is not a general pattern either. There were also respondents, Turkish, Moroccan or Dutch who did not describe their parents as people with limited horizons. There are examples of parents who were active in political and religious issues and liked to initiate discussions in the family about all kind of social issues.

We found no specific 'ethnic' components on this subject, and we cannot make any univocal statements about gradual differences in 'background', since the life stories are too diverse for this purpose.

3. *Aspirations for the future*

The hypothesis referring to relatively 'low' aspirations in lower social class families has not been confirmed anywhere in our research, either for native Dutch or for immigrant families. Nearly all parents wanted their children to continue their studies. Often, parents passed the message on to their children that they 'should achieve more than we did'. This varied from a non-specified wish that the children 'study as much as possible', to a particular high-status profession such as lawyer or doctor. This was especially the case among immigrant families. For many parents the desire to climb the social ladder was very explicit and it was often a compensation for their own unfulfilled desires for more education ('my mother would have loved to continue studying, but she never had the chance, so her children are expected to do it').

The idea that higher education would be beyond their reach, or that education was thought to be unimportant is definitely not characteristic of our target group. One might assume that we have found here an explanation for their success. However, we must make some comment on this. It is true that the parents of immigrant respondents in our research have a high aspiration level, but this is not comparable to the high aspiration levels in higher social classes. For the latter the aspiration level stems from their familiarity with higher education and high status professions, and from the natural assumption that these are accessible to their own children. In immigrant families the higher aspiration level is related to their wish to reach a higher status, parents being only oriented towards some generally known professions with a high status. There is very little knowledge of the means of getting there, and therefore people know too little about the actual 'level' of the education or profession desired.

Bearing this in mind, we return to the question of whether the differences found in our study on this hypothesis are gradual or fundamental. It seems unlikely that they would be gradual. According to the hypothesis, high social background corresponds with higher aspirations. One would therefore expect that the Dutch parents, who have received comparatively more education, would have higher aspiration levels. However, the reverse was found. It is probable that we are dealing with a specific characteristic of immigrants. The purpose of migration, also among our respondents, is usually an improvement of status. If adults who took the migration step have not yet managed to achieve this improvement, and this was the case in most of the families examined in this study, it is only natural that they pass this wish on to their children. The latter have to fulfil the purpose of migration and prove to themselves and their environment that it is possible to 'succeed'. It is also possible that this typical characteristic among immigrants is only temporal and will disappear in future generations. This, however, is still very uncertain.

4. *The influence of the social environment*

According to the hypothesis referring to the influence of social environment (more specifically the presence of role models) one might expect our target group, a 'successful' group coming from low social backgrounds, to have been stimulated by acquaintances who have proved that it is possible to reach higher education and achieve a high social status. However, we found very few indications of this. Positive role models in the family circle outside the direct family were not found. In secondary education, in particular, our respondents were often exceptions at school, in the sense that they had only a few schoolmates from similar backgrounds. Sometimes there were examples of an older brother or sister at a higher type of secondary school or studying at university, and sometimes there were younger brothers and sisters who followed the same education as the respondents. Turkish and Moroccan respondents in particular were often the first or only members of the family who had really succeeded in completing a higher vocational or a university course. The respondents themselves did not ascribe this success to the impetus given by positive examples in their environment, but much more often to their own characteristics and parental support, and to their own need to live up to the expectations of their parents. Therefore, our findings specifically suggest an absence of the influences described in this hypothesis. For this reason, questions about differences of a gradual or fundamental nature cannot be answered.

5. *Child-rearing patterns*

For this hypothesis our research material has the same limitations as for the hypothesis on indirect educational support. However, we can make some statements here on a fairly superficial level.

Characteristic of many of the parents in our research is that they had given their children free rein to choose their own career. We also found that nearly all parents were very positive about their children's decision to continue studying. Furthermore, immigrant parents were forced to leave many decisions about further education to their children. Therefore, our respondents were given a great deal of responsibility and freedom in this field. This did not always apply to other domains in their lives. Immigrant families often struggled with questions concerning how much freedom they should give to their children in their leisure time and to participate in other areas of school life apart from 'studying'. Not only the parents, but also the respondents themselves, sometimes had problems with these questions. There are examples of things that were forbidden by the parents, but also examples of situations in which the children learned to anticipate their parents' ideas, therefore limiting themselves. A difficult issue in several families was when it was considered 'decent' for children to start to live independently, away from the family. This was especially true for girls, but for boys too it was not an easy decision.

The conflicting desires of parents and children on this type of issue cannot easily be put into a simple framework. For instance, it is almost impossible to classify such controversies in terms of child-rearing styles that leave more or less room for negotiation. It appears that it is frequently very hard for children to negotiate with their parents, because they do not want to manoeuvre their parents into awkward positions in relation to their environment, or deprive themselves of the large amount of practical support that they receive when they live with their family.

It is also very difficult to affirm that the model of a more or less role-reinforcing type of child-rearing is applicable here. At first sight this does indeed appear to be the case. Immigrant families have more rigid ideas about what can be considered 'decent' for boys and girls than Dutch families. On the other hand it is true that the parents of our Turkish and Moroccan respondents were remarkably more liberal on this point than other Turkish and Moroccan families in their environment. Furthermore, a very considerable proportion of the respondents had drifted away from their parents' lifestyles at a certain point in time. This also applied to our Dutch respondents, who did not meet their parents' expectations concerning role and status. To complicate matters further, there are also examples of immigrant families who did offer a great deal of freedom to their children, not only in the field of education, but in all areas.

To summarise, there are some differences, but they do not simply run parallel to the distinction immigrant-native Dutch, and cannot easily be typified as 'gradual' or 'fundamental'.

6. *Class-specific processes in education*

As we have indicated, the central concept in this hypothesis is that education favours children from higher social backgrounds by implicitly using the knowledge, language use, social world and behaviour of these children as a standard, and by having higher expectations of them. The Individuation study setup is not suitable for supplying information about the way in which teachers actually perform. So, we have confined ourselves to the domain of expectations, on which we do have some material from our interviews.

First there are several examples of teachers in primary education who gave lower recommendations for secondary education to our respondents than the respondents themselves thought appropriate, based on their achievements and test scores (especially compared to their classmates). On almost every occasion this occurred with Turkish and Moroccan respondents. We found that many immigrant respondents felt they were being treated unequally.

Secondly, again mainly among Turkish and Moroccan respondents there were several examples of implicit low expectations from teachers in secondary education. Some of our respondents had the very strong feeling that they had to prove, much more so than other students, that they could keep up with the level and pace of education. Generally there was little stimulation and understanding of the circumstances in which immigrant students had to complete their studies. The attitude of many teachers, especially in higher school types, ranged from 'expectant' to 'sceptical'. The fact that many respondents were almost alone in a secondary school might have played a role here. There were only a few immigrant students in these schools during this period.

It is remarkable that the information we have on teachers' expectations refers almost exclusively to pupils from immigrant families. Dutch respondents obviously did not feel that they were being judged or treated on the basis of their social backgrounds. These differences can also be observed later, in the work situation for instance. This raises the question of whether we are talking here about more than a gradual difference resulting from possible prejudices about immigrants and their social background. For the time being this seems very likely.

Conclusions

In this chapter we have tried to find out whether the same mechanisms are being used as a cover for 'social class' among immigrant and non-immigrant people, by using information on the careers of a specific group, namely social climbers. Not surprisingly, the answer to this question appears to be 'yes' and 'no'. In some hypotheses (the ones about child-rearing patterns and indirect educational support) we have not found marked differences between our immigrant and native Dutch respondents. The differences that were found in this respect did not run along ethnic dividing lines and could not be captured in the dimension 'more-less'. For other hypotheses there was simply little or no support in our material (for instance, the assumption of positive role patterns), neither for native Dutch nor for immigrant respondents. In the remaining hypotheses we found more indications for *fundamental* differences than for *gradual* differences. A gradual difference is for instance that Turkish and Moroccan parents are even less able than poorly educated Dutch parents to help their children with their school work and maintain adequate contacts with the school, because they have received even less education. The differences that we have called 'fundamental', that is real differences between immigrant families on the one hand and Dutch families on the other, are the following:

- Turkish and Moroccan parents are not able to help their children with their school work and with choosing schools, not just because of lack of familiarity with higher forms of education, but due to the fact that they have very little knowledge of education in general, and of Dutch education in particular (hypothesis 1, direct educational support).
- Turkish and Moroccan parents have less contact with schools because of a different attitude towards education. They take it for granted that teachers know what they are doing, and do not consider it their task to interfere with education, unless 'problems' are reported by the school (hypothesis 1, direct educational support).
- Turkish and Moroccan parents and their children have high aspiration levels stemming from the fact that they are immigrants (improving one's position is the purpose of emigration). Their aspiration levels do not correspond with their class (hypothesis 3, future aspirations).
- There are indications that in education there are specific 'ethnic' prejudices against immigrants, resulting in lower expectations and/or inadequate support (hypothesis 6, class-specific processes in education).

These points indicate that social background does not mean the same thing for immigrants and for native Dutch people. Owing to the limitations of our research, we cannot claim that the elements which are specific to immigrants are more numerous, or even more important, than the general mechanisms that may account for inequality in education in both groups. However, we do think we can reject the statement that 'social class' functions in the same way for immigrants and non-immigrants.

The question is whether what we have referred to as 'specific to immigrants' should also be called an ethnic factor. Perhaps it is better to reserve this term for processes to be described in other hypotheses, namely hypotheses about ethnic origin.[2] The factors to be mentioned in those hypotheses are in principle not of a temporal nature and refer to systematic differences between immigrant and native Dutch people. The above-mentioned 'fundamental' differences within social class hypotheses are in fact differences that may disappear in a generation of parents from ethnic groups that have been educated in Holland from the start. Therefore, these factors should rather be seen as *migration factors*.

In this chapter we have not dealt with hypotheses on ethnic origin. We expect that the impact of this factor could confirm the conclusion that, for the time being, it is useful to distinguish between 'social-class explanations' and 'ethnic-origin explanations'. We think this is important for the present discussion, because there is a great deal of uncertainty about what is actually meant by 'social class' and 'ethnic origin'. Whether the distinction will remain theoretically relevant in the long run, however, is another question. On a somewhat higher level of abstraction it can probably be argued that ultimately the same processes are involved.

2. Analogous to the hypotheses on social class it is possible to formulate hypotheses on ethnic origin based on literature. These hypotheses would refer to ethnic-cultural and migration-related processes and would be specific to immigrants.

References

Braat, H. and J.Veenman (1990), 'Sociale ongelijkheid en sociale mobiliteit' in J. Veenman (ed.), *Ver van huis. Achterstand en achterstelling bij allochtonen*, Groningen.

Dagevos, J. and J. Veenman (1992), *Succesvolle allochtonen. Over de maatschappelijke carrière van Turken, Marokkanen, Surinamers en Molukkers in hoge functies*, Meppel/Amsterdam.

Deckers, P. (1993), *Literatuurstudie individuatieprocessen: belemmerende en faciliterende factoren voor maatschappelijk succes. Concept*, Amsterdam.

Fase, W. (1994), *Ethnic Divisions in Western European Education*, Münster/ New York.

Hoek, J. van der and M. Kret (1992), *Marokkaanse tienermeisjes: Gezinsinvloeden op keuzen en kansen*, Utrecht.

Hof, L. van´t and J. Donkers (1992), 'Onderwijsachterstanden van llochtonen: klasse, gezin of cultuur?' Paper for the Educational Research Days 1992, Amsterdam.

Langen, A. van and P. Jungbluth (1990), *Onderwijskansen van migranten. De rol van sociaal-economische factoren en culturele factoren*, Forum 6. Amsterdam/Lisse.

Ledoux, G., P. Deckers, E. de Bruijn and E. Voncken (1992), *Met het oog op de toekomst. Ideeën over onderwijs en arbeid van ouders en kinderen uit de doel-groepen van het onderwijsvoorrangsbeleid*, Amsterdam.

Leij, A. van der, R. Rögels, H. Koomen and J. Bekkers (1991), *Turkse kinderen in onderwijs en opvoeding. Meningen en ervaringen van Turkse basisschoolkinderen, hun ouders en leerkrachten*, Amsterdam.

Meijers, F.J.M., H.J. van Houten and F.D. von Meijenfeldt (1993), *Ingepast of aangepast? Loopbaanstrategieën in etnische perspectief. Een vergelijkende studie naar jongeren en hun ouders*, Amsterdam.

Niekerk, M. van (1990), *Kansarmoede. Reacties van allochtonen op achterstand*, Documenten en Onderzoek PSCW, no. 4. Amsterdam.

Pels, T. (1991), *Marokkaanse kleuters en hun culturele kapitaal. Opvoeden en leren in het gezin en op school*, Amsterdam/Lisse.

Pels, T. (1993), 'Het belang van een cultuurbeleid in het onderwijs' in *Comenius*, 49, 42-55.

Risvanoglu-Bilgin, S., L. Brouwer and M. Priester (1986), *Verschillend als de vingers van een hand. Een onderzoek naar het integratieproces van Turkse gezinnen in Nederland*, Leiden.

Chapter 15

NEW FRAMEWORKS FOR INTERCULTURAL EDUCATION IN A CHANGING CITY

*Gerd R. Hoff**

Intercultural Education (IE) is understood by our institute as a process which has to prevail in all curriculum development [1] and remains a major part of all educational efforts inside and outside schools.

Recently I was in London where I watched a television programme called 'Postcard from Berlin' in which the city was described as the only one in the world that is 'constantly changing'. An ideal place to promote any pedagogical principle that understands itself as being dynamic. There are a whole new set of frameworks in establishing IE in the multicultural city of Berlin.

In this chapter I aim to demonstrate how the practice of IE needs to change in the new city. I will discuss the following:

1. The development of IE in the former West Berlin. Which structures were in place when the wall came down?
2. The conditions which have changed – and may keep changing – in Berlin.

* Parts of this paper draw on some materials from Gerd R. Hoff, 'Multicultural Education in Germany: Historical Development and Current Status', in James A. Banks and Cherry A. McGee Banks (eds), *Handbook of Research on Multicultural Education*, New York, 821-838.

1. I understand curriculum development as being dynamic, reflecting the changing needs of a society.

3. What new strategies are needed to meet these conditions? Do we have to rephrase our goals?

The Development of IE in the Former West Berlin. Which Structures Were in Place when the Wall Came Down?

While the overall percentage of so-called *Ausländer* (foreigners) slowly developed from about 11 percent to 13.2 percent in 1989, when the wall came down, the percentage of immigrant pupils in state schools has always been significantly higher, about 22 percent in 1991[2] but mounting up to 46.8 percent in Kreuzberg and exceeding 30 percent in three more boroughs. More than 43 percent of the immigrant population was Turkish. However, by 1992 the Turkish population was reduced to only 36 percent of the non-German population of the re-unified Berlin (while the absolute figures steadily increased from 128,112 to 138,738).[3]

Subsequently most of the compensatory measures, the special initiatives, and the accompanying academic research focussed on the Turkish community, our own institute not to be excluded. By 1989 there were some 300 Turkish teacher assistants, working in West Berlin schools, and permanent in-service training opportunities were included. There were and still remain projects of Turkish/German pre-school groups; some twenty primary schools are participating in bilingual reading programmes; a few secondary schools offer special arrangements for Turkish pupils, and there are after-school and leisure-time opportunities for Turkish youths, including some for women and girls separately.

These schemes may sound adequate. However, aiming at the Turkish community only, it left the other 60 percent of immigrants unfairly neglected. Even here, the special initiatives were never able to cover as much as a quarter of the actual needs. Very few attempts were made to provide special assistance for Yugoslav,[4] Greek, or Polish pupils, although there had been some initiatives in this direction. All merits and failures were the result of more than fifteen years of struggle by passionately engaged teachers, parents, social workers, researchers, and even some local politicians. It should be kept in mind that I am referring to the year 1989, which was the peak of the modest successes in IE in West Berlin schools, this being due in part to a slightly more supportive than previously Red-Green coalition in the city government. Even so, the solutions

2. The year 1991 is the last year that statistics show figures for German migration from East to West Germany separately for East and West Berlin.

3. Data from Statistisches Landesamt Berlin, Einwohnerregister.

4. Yugoslavia was, at the time of research, still a united state.

provided – the special courses on offer – hardly ever outgrew experimental status, and many initiatives were firmly objected to by parts of the educational and or political establishment.

At a more basic level, we had to struggle with the general matter of political insecurity for migrant workers, refugees, and other 'unofficial' immigrants. Although we can register a slight improvement during the last couple of years after re-unification[5] it was and still is a fact, that Germany has one of the lowest levels of naturalisation of any Western country: only about 0.5 percent of resident foreigners a year become German citizens, compared with 2.0 percent in Britain, 1.2 percent in France and 5.2 percent in Sweden (Ardagh 1991:288).

Here lie the roots of the very problem German schools were facing in trying to provide education programmes for the children of immigrants and guest workers. Given the large numbers of people who are unsure of how long they will remain in Germany, it is extremely difficult to define the core subjects and major goals of education. Politicians, teachers, parents, and children are undecided as to whether pupils in school should be prepared to succeed in the German society or in their country of origin (Hoff 1992).

While the Berlin senate, as with most of the more liberal and social-democratic governments of German Länder, favoured a laissez-faire attitude according to their understanding that a fundamental schooling according to the much more advanced German education system would be useful everywhere in the world (DECS/EGT 1986), the educational profession was divided between two major policies:

Assimilation policy: compensatory approaches, providing single or group tuition to help children with language 'disabilities' (e.g., not speaking and understanding German) to acquire quickly the necessary skills to follow the teaching provided for German children in schools. This was and still is summed up under the conception of *Ausländerpädagogik* (education for foreigners).

Cooperative Policy: emancipatory approaches, trying to establish cultural identity, guarantee mother-tongue alphabetisation, modify general curriculum towards a multicultural representation of values, offer an introduction into all major and locally represented religions, very often focussing on bi-cultural comparison. The term used in Germany and most (non-English-speaking) Western European states is *Interkulturelle Erziehung* (intercultural education). The 'interculturalists' in Germany defined their position in relation to those who favoured 'anti-racist education' in

5. The East Germans use the term *Wende* (turning point) while the West Germans more frequently use the term *Wiedervereinigung* (re-unification), both terms being equally inaccurate.

Britain or in the Netherlands, but struggled for many years to retain the term 'Intercultural Education'. This was because 'racism' and 'anti-racist' initiatives, in the German language of West Germany, were exclusively reserved for the behaviour and discrimination against Jews, especially during the era of Nazism and therefore highly tabooed.

Only in the last five years, in particular since re-unification, has it become possible to suggest that racist thinking and racist behaviour exist in modern Germany. To challenge this development, some scholars prefer to describe themselves today as being 'anti-racist' educators; others remaining in the field of multicultural or inter-cultural education reflect anti-racist goals in their work without explicitly changing their terminology.

The Conditions Which Have Changed – and May Keep Changing – in Berlin

Race relations have become headline news since the wall came down. German society as a whole is undergoing a fundamental change of its self understanding as a consequence of the collapse of the Communist countries and the reunification of 1989. It is a sort of mass identity crisis, resulting from the fact that no positive understanding of nation and nationality exists in Germany.

Contrary to the experiences of the population in the West both at work and at home, with *Gastarbeitern* the people in the East had little experience of dealing with 'foreigners'. While the West Berliners had opportunities to meet other people while travelling abroad, the East Berliners could only get permission to travel to the other countries of the Eastern bloc, very often explicitly as a reward for politically correct behaviour. Only as the economy of East Germany became more prosperous did the authorities begin to finance 'international solidarity' programmes, which brought over students and workers from distant countries such as Cuba, Vietnam and Angola. However, these migrants were kept isolated in secluded living quarters; they came as single men and women and were forbidden to marry. In the German Democratic Republic people were officially given the slogan 'workers of the world unite' and they had to pay individual financial contributions to international solidarity programmes, but in everyday life people were discouraged from mixing with 'foreigners'.

The files of Stasi, the former state security service, indicate that neo-fascist activities had been observed since the end of the 1970s according to reports in the daily newspapers in October 1992. This means there is a history of a neo-Nazi underground within both parts of Germany.

For East Germany the old Nazi traditions lingered on under another name: obedience, politeness, and order were the dominant virtues inside the family (Sturzbecher 1990). This was complemented by flag appeals and torchlight processions, compulsory membership of the state youth organisation, and the army seen as a main pillar of values in society. This has all been swept away by re-unification and replaced by a weak central government, the national problems of a divided economy and unemployment or frozen wages combined with soaring rents.

While the world recession cut jobs in the West, reduced social security, and taxes were raised to finance the 'Aufschwung Ost' (Eastern stimulus), Germany had to absorb 3 million asylum seekers from 1989 onwards, twice as many as the U.S.A. in the 1920s (Guardian 1992). As a result, in August 1992, 67 percent of Brandenburg's youth in a representative survey, agreed that there were too many foreigners in Germany (the actual rate in Brandenburg being two percent), while 15 percent supported the opinion that 'Every foreigner is one too many!' (Tomic 1993).

'Foreigners' were one of the main concerns of young people in the former East German state of Brandenburg, which surrounds Berlin. Fifty-four percent were worried about a possible 'flooding of foreigners', following a representative survey in this state, conducted by the regional Ministry of Education in autumn 1991.

These results are not surprising; there are few concepts existing for an understanding of the new German nation. Legal decisions have already been handed over to Brussels (seat of the E.U. bureaucracy), but 'United Europe' is still a utopia and will remain so for many years to come. People are reluctant to face the fact that there are millions of immigrants living in the country who will have offspring, and that there will be more immigration into their territory, no matter how preventive the legislation might be. 'There is the choice between 'apartheid' and an open society and in a multicultural society we must retain the optional character of cultural autonomy for the individual.'(Brumlik and Leggewie 1992:435)

In this chapter I am not able to do more than highlight a few aspects of life in the re-united city. I will therefore briefly summarise the most important political, economic and cultural facts which – from my point of view – characterise the ever-changing multicultural city of Berlin in 1995:

- The city has a very humane and just constitution – nevertheless, this is deeply rooted in racist thinking, because it discriminates between rights granted to everybody and those reserved for Germans only.
- Unification has lead to a merging of heterogeneous experiences, values, lifestyles, habits, fashion and even use of local dialect.

- Berlin is now the capital of Germany -this though, is an illusion; it provides an insecure 'role-model', and a fear of loosing identity in the local neighbourhood (Kiez).
- There is a general teleological crisis; felt particularly among ex-East Germans but not completely unfamiliar to Western 68ers – the left-wing reformers of university life during the 1970s – who are aware that the new society lacks any central goal or plan and is not prepared to help solve any of the world's problems (Dieckmann 1995).
- The city has over-strengthened impoverished public resources, accompanied by sharp cuts in funding of social services, education, culture, etc.
- There are rising taxes; accompanied by the fall of special allowances in West Berlin and therefore these are felt more strongly than in other parts of Germany.
- The city has a 'two-thirds society'; with rising unemployment figures[6] especially among young people (astonishingly even higher in the West than in the former East Berlin), sky-rocketing rents, most severely felt in the Eastern satellite towns and the Western neighbourhoods, which are known as being 'where the scene is', resulting in a growing number of homeless people.
- There is evidence of neo-fascism and radical right-wing activism of fringe groups, particularly among young people.

However, but in spite of all this Berlin remains:

- an outstanding attraction for immigrants,
- a city with a tradition of religious tolerance,
- and a city which offers an extraordinarily varied range of cultural activities.

What New Strategies are Needed to Meet These Conditions? Do We Have to Re-phrase our Goals?

I will attempt to outline some of the principle strategies which are needed to meet the new conditions in a changing Berlin. There is no doubt, that given the facts of Berlin society in 1995, immediate political action is needed. Educational programmes can only support developments in soci-

6. In a recent comparison of five West European capitals Berlin came first in unemployment figures (13.2 percent compared with the last which was Vienna with 6.8 percent) and last in the percentage of ethnic minorities (12.1 percent compared to the first which was Brussels with 29.1 percent). *Der Spiegel*, no. 8 1995:49.

ety when there is definite public agreement about the direction in which the nation wants to go.

Some changes do at last seem possible. 'Guest worker' organisations, the Frankfurt City Directorate of Multicultural Affairs, and the Berlin Ombudsperson for Foreigners, have been pressing for the acceptance of immigrants as German citizens, to make dual citizenship possible.

Berlin's 'ombudsperson for foreigners' published a review in February 1993, which gives evidence that the majority in East and West Berlin object to xenophobia and support legal equality for non-Germans.

It was only after the second horrific arson attack against a house inhabited by a Turkish family, this time in Solingen, in which five Turkish women and girls lost their lives (30 May 1993), that for the first time, politicians from all political parties stood up to demand a change of the constitution giving 'guestworkers' the right to German citizenship. It is significant that after Solingen, the most influential political magazine, *Der Spiegel*, changed its terminology from 'foreigners' to 'immigrants' and from 'Turks in Germany' to 'Turkish Germans' (*Der Spiegel* 1993).

We should probably consider the deconstructionalists' critique of the theories and practices of IE. It argues, that in effect IE serves to distance and disempower minorities and immigrants by naming and emphasising cultural differences between the indigenous majority of Germans and ethnic minorities of immigrants. We have to be aware of the social construction of minorities as the marginalised 'Cultural Other', and it would help to deconstruct this artificial paradigm, which has been created by some sociologists as an instrument of power provided for them. Bukow and Llaryora (1993: 168-178) and Steiner-Khamsi (1992:199-208) ask why those groups of the population, which are formed by migration processes, are especially marked and stigmatised. The processes of ethnicisation and labelling as such are generally seen to be interdependent. They refer to the making of 'ethnicity' for political purposes to the 'unifying' effect of alienating minorities from the 'native' groups of a population, and to promote the rights of those who have been in a particular country first. To overcome this sort of social mechanism they argue that ethnic differences have no constitutive meaning in modern societies. They do not deny their existence but want ethnicity to be placed into the private lives of people, to 'enjoy their given diversity'. In the fields of politics and education the concern should be for the particular economic and social problems which exist in any society.

The deconstructionalists see the need to extend existing inter-cultural programmes (e.g., those concerning social learning, role play, teaching styles) to offer a more inclusive view of society. It is necessary to have significant and positive representation in all school books and audiovisual media from black and ethnic minority groups. It is not enough for our children to be told that they are living in a multicultural society – they must experience it. This should include black television presenters (e.g., Cherno Jobatey) and actors in all German television productions (not just the dubbed Anglo-American imports, which would once again transport exotic flair), especially those addressing young people.

Likewise Brumlik and Leggewie (1992:441-442) plead that 'positive discrimination' of ethnic minorities apparently does not work. What is needed is active protection against discrimination, based on equal treatment and an equal legal position given to all inhabitants. The 'ombudspersons', responsible for immigrants, need more executive power. The traditional methods of state intervention (force, money, law) will have to be used to guarantee effective changes, as persuasion has not succeeded.

To accomplish this kind of intervention means:

- We must lobby in favour of changing the *Grundgesetz* (constitution). We should adjust to European standards and get rid of the *ius sanguinis* and adopt the *ius terrae*.[7]
- We should agree to an annual immigration quota as well as welcoming the fact that Germany has become an immigration country, because the German economy will need a continuing immigration process of about 300,000 people a year to keep the usual rates of economic growths and secure old-age pensions for its citizens after the year of 2020.
- We should develop special anti-discrimination laws to protect everybody against insecurity, fear, and physical harm. To do so would, in addition, help those people to refocus their ideals, who complain about having lost their basic goals in the event of the disintegration of world socialism.
- We should use our tax revenue to invest in education and cultural projects, which can help us to develop our identity, explore and make use of society's diversity, learn to respect differences, and to object firmly to the denial of equal rights and opportunities to anybody who has chosen to live in our community.

As Berlin pupils have one of the longest compulsory schooling periods in the Western world, one might question whether the existing schools are able to handle the problem of racism and discrimination at all. A system of hiring teachers, where promotion is often the only means of getting rid of

7. These terms are taken from Roman law, meaning the right of citizenship is founded in blood relationships or generated according to birth place, respectively.

incompetent personnel and a streaming system in secondary schools where general educational tasks are neglected in favour of subject teaching, show that the education system itself is in desperate need of a major reform.

There are promising proposals and well researched alternatives,[8] but the crucial question is whether there will be a strong public demand for school reform to open the gates for IE in mainstream classrooms, especially in mainly German neighbourhoods. Schools need to open themselves to the needs of the community and attempt to implement today's problems into school life, and, of course, major changes need to be implemented in all schools in the general curriculum and in the materials and textbooks used.

However, there still remains a major task for teachers and researchers in the field of multicultural education, 'to institutionalise learning for all children, to enable them to develop their own culture – not just one adapted from a group, to communicate with other cultures, and to become self-determined in a growingly differentiated world' (Krüger-Potratz 1993).

To help the teachers to do so we need two things:

1. A political field which offers perspectives for qualified school leavers and supports teachers, acting according to the above demands. It is extremely short sighted to cut grants for apprenticeships, for youths clubs, for youth and social workers.
2. Intensified and extensive in-service training for all types of teachers in inter-cultural and anti-racist work.

8. There are new initiatives: the authorities in the city of Nuremberg developed '100 ideas for projects' in anti-racist education, focussing on social studies in pedagogical practice (Erziehung und Wissenschaft 1993) and there are new examples of learning second languages, e.g., those represented in the classroom as mother-tongues, in elementary schools (Landesinstitut für Schule und Weiterbildung 1992).

References

Ardagh, J. (1991), *Germany and the Germans* (3rd edn), London.

Banks, J.A. and C.A. McGee Banks (eds) (1995), *Handbook of Research on Multicultural Education*, New York.

Brumlik, M. and Leggewie, C. (1992), 'Konturen der Einwanderungsgesellschaft', in K.J. Bade (ed.), *Deutsche im Ausland – Fremde in Deutschland,*Munich.

Bukow, W.D. and Llaryora, R. (1993), *Mitbürger aus der Fremde. Soziogenese ethnischer Minoritäten*, (2nd edn) Opladen.

DECS/EGT (1986), 'The Education and Cultural Development of Migrants', *Project No. 7. Final report*, Strasbourg.

Der Spiegel (1993), 'Die Deutschen Türken – Weder Heimat noch freunde', 7 June, 16-31.

Der Tagesspiegel (1992), 'Informationsdienst des Bundestages. Pressemitteilung', 14 September,14.

Der Tagesspiegel (1992), 'Vorurteile und Meinungslosigkeit in der Wende', 31 October,13.

Dieckmann, C. (1995), 'Dresden klagt nicht an', *Die Zeit*,7 March.

Erziehung und Wissenschaft (1993), '100 Projektideen für die Pädagogische Praxis' vol.3, 23-26.

Guardian Weekend (1992), 'Hitler's Youths', 5 December, 6-10.

Hoff, G.R. (1992), 'Culture in transition: A view from West Berlin', in K.A. Moodley (ed.) *Beyond multicultural education: International perspectives*, Calgary, 66-77.

Krüger-Potratz, M. (1993), 'Die (ehemalige) DDR auf dem Weg in eine multikulturelle Gesellschaft?' in S. Kroon, D. Pagel and T. Vallen, *Multiethnische Gesellschaft und Schule in Berlin*, Münster/New York, 69-91.

Landesinstitut für Schule und Weiterbildung (1992), *Begegnung mit Sprachen in der Grundschule*, Soest, NRW.

Steiner-Khamsi, G. (1992), *Multikulturelle Bildungspolitik in der Postmoderne*, Opladen.

Sturzbecher, D. (1990), 'Comparative Survey on Dominant Goals in Family Education', Unpublished manuscript, University of Potsdam, Institut für Familien- und Kindheitsforschung.

Tomic, B. (1993), 'Weiternin rechtsradikal', *Der Tagesspiegel*, 24 March,19.

Chapter 16

INTEGRATION OF PEOPLE WITH A MENTAL HANDICAP INTO THE COMMUNITY

Adrian van Gennep

Introduction

The end of the Second World War was a victory for democracy. In democratic societies the notion emerged that a society can only be democratic if all of its members are given the opportunity to participate equally in societal life. This notion led in the 1960s to integration movements for minority groups. People with a mental handicap constituted one such minority group.

The premise of this chapter is that the integration of people with a mental handicap must be pursued. The concept of integration is defined and discussed in section 1, followed by a description of the developmental process towards integration in the Netherlands in the following three sections. Unlike Scandinavia, Britain and the United States, large-scale segregated care in institutions has continued in the Netherlands. Section 2 analyses this problem. However, parallel to this segregated care, small-scale care in the community developed in the 1970s; the normalisation principle being the motor of this development. However, integration was only limited in this phase, which is described in section 3. In recent years we have entered upon a new phase in the development towards integration. Supported living is an example of this and is described in section 4. In section 5 I shall argue that normalisation and integration are essentially different. It is not right to equate these two concepts. In the final section some conclusions are drawn.

1. The Concept of Integration

The efforts being made to integrate mentally handicapped people into the community should be regarded as a reaction to their segregation in institutions. In the 1970s these institutions increasingly came to be regarded as a segregating form of care. Integration was consequently defined as deinstitutionalisation. According to Scheerenberger (1976:125-129) deinstitutionalisation implies a certain attitude, a principle and a complex process. We are talking about an attitude that puts great emphasis on freedom, independence, individuality, mobility, personalised life experiences and a high degree of interaction in a free society. The principle pertains to the right of an individual to receive treatment and programmes of care in the least restrictive environment. The key component is independence, i.e., the right to self-determination, the right to seek self-realisation, to be an individual, and to move about at will. Finally, deinstitutionalisation encompasses three interrelated processes: (1) prevention of admission by finding and developing alternative community methods of care and training; (2) return to the community of all residents who have been prepared to function adequately in appropriate local settings through programmes of rehabilitation and training; (3) establishment and maintenance of a responsive residential environment that protects human and civil rights and contributes to the expeditious return of the individual to normal community living whenever possible.

It has gradually been realised that integration involves more than just placing mentally handicapped people back in the community. Wallner (1982) distinguished three levels of integration: physical, functional and social integration.

1. *Physical integration* means that mentally disabled persons live among people without disabilities.
2. *Functional integration* means that mentally disabled persons make use of public transport, go shopping, visit restaurants, cinemas, theatres, libraries, and are members of sports clubs, hobby clubs etc.
3. *Social integration* means that persons with a mental handicap are equal partners and respected persons in the community.

The following observations need to be made here:

a. If we define disability as a disadvantaged position of an individual, as a consequence of impairment or disability, which limits his/her normal role-playing in the environment, then *optimal* social integration of a person with a mental disability is, by definition, impossible.
b. Many persons without disabilities are also not well integrated.
c. The mentally disabled individual must want to integrate.

In the development of care for mentally disabled persons we distinguish three periods: segregation, normalisation and integration. I propose first to explain and discuss these three periods. Then I shall compare normalisation and integration. Finally, some conclusions will be drawn. The situation as it has developed in the Netherlands will be emphasised.

2. Segregation

Until about 1970, it was the protection of people with a mental handicap which was emphasised in the Netherlands: protection by creating special situations, such as special schools, sheltered workshops and institutions. Currently, about 30,000 people with mental disabilities are living in institutions. This number will fall in the future for the following reasons:

1. A higher percentage of institutional residents will die because of old age.
2. Parents/families of younger residents and of residents who have only been living in the institution, for a few years now prefer small residential facilities in the community.
3. More than 80 percent of parents whose children have been placed on a waiting list for an institution prefer small residential facilities in the community.

Which people are not eligible for integration? In other words, which people will remain in the institution where they already live, and which people living in the community will be admitted to an institution?

Based on three studies of waiting-lists (Van Gennep and Calis 1990, 1991, 1993) the following conclusions can be drawn. People urgently waiting for admission to an institution have the following characteristics. They mostly have a severe or profound disability. About 25 percent are non-ambulant, about 33 percent are incontinent, and about 50 percent have severe behavioural problems. Only 10 percent appear not to have those characteristics. Admission to an institution may be preferred in cases of severe behavioural problems or severe mental disabilities. These findings agree with Haney (1988) who states that behaviour is the best predictor of unsuccessful integration. The level of the mental disability (personal appearance, vocational skills, social skills, personality) has some relation to unsuccessful integration.

Based on this research we expect that the number of admissions to institutions will fall, and that only a small proportion of current residents will be deinstitutionalised. Nevertheless, the reduction in institutional places will proceed more slowly than in other countries, for the following reasons.

In the first place there is a shortage of places in residential facilities in the community. As long as there is such a shortage, the existing places in institutions will continue to be used, although a place in the community is always preferred.

In the second place, many parents/families of mentally disabled adults who have lived in an institution for many years, prefer to continue this situation. They are satisfied with these institutions. And, indeed, Dutch institutions are generally better than comparable institutions in the United States, for instance. Table 16.1 compares data from a U.S. study (Raynes et al. 1979) with data from a Dutch study (Van Gennep 1989). The data was gathered by means of three measurement instruments: RRMP, ICI and IPE. The RRMP (Revised Resident Management Practices Scale) assesses the resident-orientation of management, in daily and other activities; flexibility, individuality, privacy, for instance. The ICI (Index of Community Involvement) assesses contact with the community; the percentage of residents who used various community amenities (buses, cinemas, churches), and had been on vacations, for instance. The IPE (Index of Physical Environment) assesses the 'normal' aspect of the environment, such as the ratio of bedrooms, bathrooms and armchairs to the number of residents, etc.

Table 16.1 Quality of Care in Dutch and American Institutions

	Netherlands		**United States**	
	low level	high level	low level	high level
RRMP	9	3	29	17
ICI	37	24	43	32
IPE	28	19	68	43

Notes:

RRMP	0 = most resident-oriented	56 = least resident-oriented
ICI	0 = most integrated	52 = least integrated
IPE	0 = most 'normal'	88 = least 'normal'

For the two reasons already given, the reduction in institution places may be limited in the Netherlands. However, the policies of the government, and of the Dutch Association of Care for Disabled Persons and the Federation of Parents Associations, are directed towards integration in the community. Admissions to institutions are to be restricted as much as possible, and admissions to residential facilities in the community will be promoted. An important impetus to this policy came in the form of the normalisation principle.

3. Normalisation

The normalisation principle originated in the 1970s in the Scandinavian countries. The normalisation principle means making patterns and conditions of everyday life available to mentally disabled persons, which are as close as possible to the patterns and conditions of mainstream society. 'As close as possible' means that one must not force the issue. The normalisation principle means equal rights for all individuals, with or without a disability.

The introduction of the normalisation principle in the Netherlands has had the effect that, since 1970, more and more mentally disabled persons have stayed in the community, and that only a limited number of mentally handicapped people have been institutionalised. We now have a continuum of residential facilities in the community.

1. *Socio-homes*. About 2,000 deinstitutionalised residents presently live in a home in the community. These people still receive their day care on the institution grounds. We call these residences *socio-homes*.
2a. *Group homes*. Normally, these homes accommodate several groups containing four to eight residents. In total, there are about twenty-five residents in a group home. In the last ten years, group homes have evolved into administrative entities. This means that residents increasingly live in ordinary houses, with some distance between these houses.
2b. *Annexes of group homes*. Annexes are houses in the neighbourhood of a group home, accommodating four to six former residents of the group home, who are more independent than the average population of the group home.

Currently about 15,000 mentally disabled persons live in group homes (annexes included).The main difference between socio-home residents and group-home residents is that socio-home residents function on a slightly lower level. There is also some difference in the quality of care between socio-homes and group homes. Living conditions and lifestyles in group homes are more normalised than in socio-homes. Table 16.2 gives an overview of the quality of care in residential facilities for comparable residents, namely adults with a high level of functioning (Van Gennep 1989:58-62).

Table 16.2 Quality of Care in Three Types of Residential Facilities

	Institution	Socio-home	Group home
RRMP	3	0	1
ICI	24	28	26
IPE	19	14	11

Note: Scoring as per table 16.1

The main difference between the three types of residential facilities is the physical environment. Adult residents with a higher level of functioning, and without severe behaviour problems profit from deinstitutionalisation.

The three types form a continuum, from less to more normalised living. Residents can be placed on a parallel continuum, from lower to higher levels of functioning. It seems as if residents 'are allowed' to live more normalised lives as they function on a higher level. This is a flow-model.

However, integration remains limited in the more normalised residential facilities too. The 'institution culture' appears to be still present in small residential facilities in the community. This is called 'micro-institutionalisation'.

4. Integration

The period of normalisation was a major step forward, compared with the period of segregation. Nevertheless, its limitations have also gradually become manifest. First, the continuum of residential facilities is understood as a flow-model: a mentally disabled person is 'allowed' to live in a certain type of residential facility if he/she is ready for it. Others make this decision, not the person in question. Furthermore, integration is realised only in a limited way. Physical and functional integration have been especially successful. Social integration has not been a success. That is why self-determination and social integration of people with a mental handicap are now being emphasised more strongly.

The social world of a person with a mental disability consists of a social network and a social safety net. The social network consists of parents, family, friends, neighbours and volunteers. The social safety net consists of the care system: counselling, facilities and finances, amongst other things. According to the new model, the social safety net does not become operative until the social network can give sufficient support to the mentally disabled person. The resources of the care system are directly linked to the social network, so that the people in the network maintain the responsibility. The system of supported living is an example. In this system the mentally disabled person is offered (possibly through the mediation of a foundation) a place to live by him/herself (or with another person if both want that). Support is given when necessary, by a foundation in cooperation with parents, family, friends, neighbours, volunteers. So, social integration is built into this system.

The first experiences with the system of supported living in the Netherlands (in the Rotterdam district) proved to be positive. Most participants in this project are functioning on a level slightly higher than the average level of functioning shown by residents in a group home. However, the idea here is that, in principle, all residents of group homes or socio-homes are eligible for supported living. I shall now discuss two cases.

The first example relates to a man, Didi, aged thirty-five and a woman, Maria, aged thirty. Both people function slightly above the level of the average population of a group home. Maria had a relationship with a man, but this was not successful. Afterwards, for a short time, she lived in a group home. At that time, Didi still lived at home with his parents. They became acquainted with each other and, after a year, they decided to live together. They have been living in a flat for about two years. Support is given by their parents and by two caregivers from a group home. Initially, the emphasis of the support was on time structuring, finances and housekeeping. When this support proved to be successful, the emphasis shifted towards supporting the relationship, which was characterised by conflict due to communication problems. Maria is hard of hearing and Didi often does not have the patience to listen to her. So, their relationship requires a great deal of support, and the support offered has been successful.

The second example concerns a young man, Manta, aged twenty-one and living alone. He functions below the level of the average population of a group home. Until recently, he lived independently and received some guidance. This situation was not a success. Housekeeping was too difficult for him, he got tired and overslept quite often. He now lives in an apartment consisting of four bed-sitting rooms, two showers (including toilet) and a common kitchen. The apartment is situated in a newly built district, with public transport in the neighbourhood. Manta has good contact with another resident in the apartment. He gets support in getting up on time, housekeeping, money management, building and maintaining relationships. Manta reacts strongly to stimuli. He used to use the telephone quite a lot, and spent too much money. Consequently, he was faced with financial problems and quarrelled with his mother, who was in charge of his money. Since then, his caregiver has taken charge of his money. Housekeeping is still problematic. He currently gets extra support in housekeeping, four evenings per week. There were also problems in the work environment. Consultations in the workshop were successful. As a consequence of the temporary absence of the resident with whom Manta had a good relationship, he began to wander about in the neighbourhood. Children teased him in the street. His caregiver talked with the children and the problem was solved. Comprehensive support is now bearing fruit, but the situation is not yet satisfactory. For a long time it was doubted whether supported living was really appropriate for this young man. He himself thinks it is, but one must proceed with caution in this kind of situation.

In a longitudinal research project carried out over seven years, Lazano (1993) evaluated the functioning of about 1,500 people participating in supported living projects. He found that those who received a great deal of support were more likely to remain in their own homes. Those who had been previously trained to develop living skills and maintained or improved these skills, were also more likely to remain in their own homes. The skills of people who had not had any previous training also improved as a result of the experience of living on their own. So, the real experience of living in one's own home is most important. The essence of these results is that we must not give a mentally disabled person the opportunity to live in his/her own home *after* he/she has proven to have the necessary living skills. What we must do is give those people who wish to live in their own home the opportunity to do so, and then offer them all the support they need. The learning of specific skills must take place within the context of supported living.

5. Normalisation versus Integration

During the period of normalisation in the Netherlands, a consensus was gradually reached on the best way of living for mentally disabled persons, namely, in small groups of residents with the same needs. These groups had to be housed in ordinary homes administered by a foundation, with a guarantee of care and government subsidy, supported by caregivers working on a duty rota and offering professional care aimed at advancing the independence of the residents. There is a continuum of care facilities and this continuum is understood as a flow model. This idea of a continuum has some disadvantages:

- it emphasises facilities and buildings instead of caregiving;
- it justifies the most restrictive type of living facility;
- it confuses intensity of care with restriction in the living situation;
- it assumes that persons must be 'ready' to live in the community;
- it suggests that people have to move to a new type of living facility as they develop further new skills;
- it merely pays lip-service to the specific needs of the individual, because *individualised* means in fact that the choice of the individual is restricted to what is available;
- it obscures a fundamental question of human rights: why is it necessary to restrict the rights of mentally disabled persons, namely, the right to be free and to participate in community life?

In essence, the continuum of residential facilities transfers bureaucratic management from the institution to the community. Living in the community is defined as group living. We can ask to what extent residents of group homes and socio-homes can shape and give content to their own lives independently. We can also ask questions related to the fact that living in small residential facilities in the community might sometimes entail as little integration as living in institutions.

Supported living assumes that mentally disabled persons must be given the opportunity to live agreeably and safely in a home of their own choice, and must have the opportunity to participate in community life, with guidance and support. Flexibility is essential, the need for support is continually changing. Essential support must be given by relations in the community: the social network.

We need to warn against two dangers:

1. the danger that overenthusiastic caregivers 'dump' persons with a mental handicap in a bad or dangerous environment in the name of giving these persons their own place;
2. the danger that caregiving-fashion freaks are wrongly beginning to call small residential facilities 'supported living'.

To escape both dangers we must be clear about what it means to have one's own home. O'Brien distinguishes three dimensions of the *own home*:

1. *Feeling at home*. People who feel at home decorate their house in a nice and personal way. They decide how to spend their time and energy on housekeeping (cooking and cleaning, for instance), and on activities in and around the house (cutting grass, growing vegetables, painting the house, for instance). They enjoy personal protection through rent protection, recognition as legal residents, and participation in the district, or through a supportive family or other social networks. Feeling at home gives one a physical and emotional base, from which to go out and come back.
2. *Control*. Controlling the home gives one the power to invite people to come in, or to shut them out. Those who control their own home can choose where and with whom they live, and who will be their caregiver. Some mentally disabled residents choose to do most things by themselves, with support from their family, friends and neighbours. Others delegate part of their power to caregivers from foundations, for instance. For residents with a more severe mental disability, an advocate (preferably a parent or family member) will take action.
3. *Possessing one's own home*. Owning a home or having the status of tenant gives one a sense of self-esteem and respect in the community. It is also an incentive to take care of the residence.

Supported living originally emphasised the person involved. Subsequently emphasis was placed on the person involved and the caregiver. Gradually, the emphasis started shifting towards the whole social network: person in question, caregiver, parents, family, friends, neighbours, employers, colleagues in the work situation. The most important objective is to advance integration. Therefore, we must use ordinary support whenever possible.

Conclusions

Living in the community, i.e., living among other people in big cities, seems feasible for most people with a mental disability.

Individual living offers the best opportunities for optimal integration. At this moment it is not clear whether individual living is feasible for most mentally disabled persons. For the time being it seems sensible to start supported living with persons that have a moderate mental disability and live in a group home or socio-home.

Group living seems feasible for most people with a severe or profound mental disability, who are still living at home. They continue to live in the community, in small group homes, with intensive support. In this case, there is a stronger emphasis on normalisation than on integration.

Up to now we have concentrated on the living situation. But a comparable development has taken place in the area of day-time activities. In the segregation phase, day activities in the day-activity centre were emphasised. In the normalisation phase, the emphasis shifted towards special day-care centres, special schools and sheltered workshops. Now, in the period of integration the emphasis is shifting again, from special towards regular day-care centres, from special schools towards regular schools, and from sheltered workshops towards supported work.

Figure 16.1 Development in Living and Day Activities.

Period	Living	Day activities
Segregation	Institution	Day-activitiy centre
Normalization	Socio-home	Special school
	Group home	Special day care centre
	Annex	Sheltered workshop
Integration	Supported living	Regular school
		Regular day care centre
		Supported work

Normalisation was a necessary, but not a sufficient condition for optimal integration. Support by a social network is a guarantee of integration.

References

Gennep, A.T.G. van (1989), 'Quality of Care in Dutch Residential Facilities', *The British Journal of Mental Subnormality*, vol.XXXV, Part 1, no 68, p.58-62.

Gennep, A.T.G. van, and W. Calis, (1990), *De achterkant van de wachtlijst*, Nunspeet.

Gennep, A.T.G. van, and W. Calis, (1991), *Waar wachten we op?*, Rotterdam.

Gennep, A.T.G. van, and W. Calis, (1993), *Zorg in Zicht*, Aalsmeer.

Gennep, A.T.G. van (1994), 'Quality of Care in Dutch Residential Facilities: Towards an Orthopedagogical Approach.', *The British Journal of Developmental Disabilities*, vol.XL, Part 2, 79, 104-110.

Haney, J.I. (1988), 'Toward successful community residential placement for individuals with mental retardation', in L.W. Heal, J.I. Haney, and A.R. Novak Amado (eds) *Integration of developmentally disabled individuals in the community*, 2nd edition, Baltimore.

Lazano, B. (1993), 'Independent Living: Relations Among Training, Skills and Success'. In *American Journal on Mental Retardation*, 98, 2.

O'Brien J. (z.j.) *Naar beneden over treden die nooit eigen zijn*. Paper.

Raynes, N.V., M.W. Pratt and S. Roses (1979), *Organizational structure and the care of the mentally retarded*, London.

Scheerenberger, R.C. (1976), *Deinstitutionalization and Institutional Reform*, Springfield.

Wallner, T. (1982), 'Die Wohnversorgung geistig Behinderter in Schweden', in *Humanes Wohnen, seine Bedeutung für das Leben geistig behinderter Erwachsener*, Marburg/Lahn.

Chapter 17

THE DEVELOPMENT OF DAYCARE PEDAGOGICS IN THE NETHERLANDS

Elly Singer

Introduction

There is a growing consensus among daycare experts that defining quality child daycare involves more than the development of an expert view on what is good for the child (Moss and Pence 1994, Singer and Miltenburg 1994). The quality of a service refers to the extent to which a service meets its goals or objectives. In the case of daycare services there are several parties involved, each of them defining their own goals and objectives: the children, the parents, the providers, and financers like employers and governments. The children may be primarily interested in meeting other children, and their parents in joining the labour force or forming a support network. The goals of providers are probably related to their career perspectives and professional standards, employers are interested in continuity of work from employees, and governments are concerned with attaining their social policy goals. Finally, there are also the experts, most of them devoted to their own theoretical frame of reference and concerned with their career perspectives in that context.

Quality is a dynamic, multi-defined, context-bound and value-laden concept. The question of quality in daycare, is not only related to assessing the extent to which the goals are met. We also have to ask how the goals were set, and whose views of quality were included or not taken into account. According to Moss and Pence (1994:5): 'The question of who is the Ruler should precede the question of which ruler should be used for measurement'.

In this chapter I have taken this context-bound, multi-defined and value-laden concept of quality as my starting point for analysing the process of the development of daycare pedagogics in the Netherlands. I want to demonstrate the drawbacks of the strong expert-dominated tradition in pedagogical thinking in my country, and of the still dominant ideology of traditional motherhood. I also want to point to urgent questions which Dutch experts have to address to support the development of daycare pedagogics that will fit in with the needs, wishes and opportunities of parents, children and professional caregivers.

I will start with a brief sketch of the current daycare policy, and of the attitude towards daycare of the Dutch government, the media and of experts. Then I will confront the government's policy and the experts' view with the experiences and wishes of parents. Finally I will point to the most urgent theoretical issues to be tackled in the process of developing pedagogical methods for daycare centres.

The Social-political Context

Daycare for children has been a controversial subject in the Netherlands for a long time. Up to the mid-1980s, along with Ireland, the Netherlands had the lowest percentage of mothers with children under the age of ten working outside the home, 18 percent and 24 percent respectively (European Commission Network on Childcare 1992). This percentage has risen rapidly during recent years to roughly 46 percent in 1991. However, this remains low in comparison with countries such as Denmark (86 percent) and Belgium (69 percent), and in addition, most Dutch mothers work part-time. A new type of middle-class family life is developing: a full-time working father and a part-time working mother, with one or two children in part-time daycare (Singer 1991; Van Dijke, Terpstra and Hermanns 1994).

Until 1990 there were very few daycare centres in the Netherlands and most of them were subsidised by the government. The greatest problem was the enormous shortage of daycare centres. All daycare centres had long waiting lists. This situation changed in 1990 under the influence of the Government's 'Stimulative Measure on Childcare'.

The most important aim of this Stimulative Measure was a growth in the number of child-care facilities for working parents (*Stimuleringsbeleid*

Kinderopvang 1990-92). Local governments and employers are subsidised to buy child-care places in daycare centres and organisations for family daycare. The formerly subsidised daycare organisations are now being forced to work on a commercial basis (*Kinderopvang* 1993).

The stimulation programme has been very successful in several ways (*Nieuwsbrief Kinderopvang* 5 1994). Within three years the capacity of Dutch daycare organisations doubled (47,849 new child places). However, it has been the well-educated parents with better jobs who have profited most from this programme. Employers invest less in daycare for the children of their unskilled and easily replaceable employees. Daycare on a commercial basis is too expensive for parents with low incomes (Ibid.).

The national stimulation programme is due to end in 1996 and the problems that this will bring are now becoming clearer. In the near future only 30 percent of the costs of daycare will be subsidised. So 70 percent has to be paid by employers or parents; or 70 percent of the child places have to be sold on the daycare market.

The need to work on a commercial basis has brought about a culture shock and many organisational and financial problems in previously subsidised daycare organisations. It is not known how many daycare organisations will survive, and at what cost. This leads me to the next problem, the problem of guaranteeing quality daycare.

With regard to ensuring and encouraging the quality of formal daycare facilities, the government has chosen to keep a low profile. In future, only minimal basic standards will be laid down at a national level, and these only for a period of five years. The control of these basic standards is handed over to local inspectorates (*Commissie Kwaliteit Kinderopvang* 1994; *Nieuwsbrief Kinderopvang* 5, 1994). Up until 1994 only half of the local authorities had actually organised any form of inspection. According to the Dutch government, the daycare organisations themselves are primarily responsible for quality control. Within five years they have to develop a 'self-regulatory system'. So far though, nobody really knows what a self-regulatory system means, especially in the case of commercialised daycare services. Competitive prices for child places could be created at the expense of quality, particularly if the external control and quality demands are minimal or even totally absent.

To sum up according to the national government daycare is primarily an instrument in their labour-market policy. Quality is first and foremost the responsibility of the daycare organisations. It is up to local governments to subsidise daycare for children at risk or from disadvantaged families.

The Media on Child Daycare

The general attitude towards daycare seems to have become a great deal more positive as a result of the Stimulative Measure. An evaluative paper on the Stimulative Measure produced by the Ministry of Welfare, National Health and Culture (WVC) in 1992, informs us that 'Daycare for children is on the way to becoming an accepted social phenomenon in the Netherlands'. However, discussions on daycare in the media are more heated than ever.

Nothing has changed in the Netherlands as is apparent from a study carried out at the University of Amsterdam into how national newspapers, magazines, women's magazines and academic literature write about the effects of daycare on children (Singer and Paardekooper 1992). Since the beginning of the 1970s, working mothers have been shocked to attention at least once or twice a year by experts, politicians or worried parents publicly making emotional statements against daycare. They speak of babies as 'little wet bundles being delivered to the crèche' (ex-minister Bot 1979); only 'extremely strong children will be able to cope with this' (Professor of Child Psychiatry Sanders-Woudstra 1986); daycare for children is 'trading in child-meat' (feminist and lawyer Pessers 1992).

In spite of this, during the past twenty years there have been fewer negative articles about the effects of daycare than the above would lead us to believe. Out of the 71 articles we found concerning the effects of daycare, only 14 were completely negative. However, it is true to say that most of the articles in favour of daycare were defensive. They have titles such as: 'Will my child survive a crèche?' and 'Are the children of working mothers insecure?'Apart from this, 47 of the 71 articles point out the great advantages for social development. It is interesting to note that only those in favour of daycare actually refer to scientific research.

Experts on Daycare

The daycare requirements of working parents have inspired very few Dutch researchers to carry out research on this subject (Singer 1992a). During the last twenty years Dutch research on the care and education of children under the age of four years has been, and still is, primarily interested in the upbringing of children in the family. The main topic has been the mother-child relationship and only recently have fathers been 'discovered'. The dominant theoretical frame of reference was and is attachment theory, especially the modernised versions based on the work of Van

IJzendoorn et al.(1982) and Belsky (1984) that are broader in scope than the original theory by Bowlby (1969).

Besides the mother-child relationship, studies on home-based prevention-programmes, programmes for early detection of developmental disorders and educational programmes in child-care centres for ethnic minorities are popular (Van Loggem and Bekkers 1994, Rispens and Van der Meulen 1992, Vedder et al. 1996).

There is a strong tradition of problem- and prevention-oriented research. This tradition is based on the assumption that all parents are in need of expert guidance, and at-risk groups urgently need expert guidance to cope adequately with their children (Singer 1992b, 1993). Very seldom are the experiences, needs, educational values and coping strategies of the parents taken as the starting point for theoretical thinking. In fact there is hardly any research available about daily life and upbringing in the minority groups or at-risk groups, at whom the intervention programmes are aimed.

Children are mostly studied in a dyadic relationship with an adult. The advice of experts is mainly concerned with how to handle an individual child. The most popular advice recommends being sensitive and responsive to the signals of the individual child, and is based on attachment theory. There is very little theorising and research on relationships between young children and interactions between two adults and a group of children, which is what happens in daycare centres. In this respect, our research at the University of Amsterdam on the parents' perspectives, and on groups of young children, represents a new theoretical trend in the Netherlands. Research into daycare for children of working parents has been, and to a great extent still is being, neglected.

Parents' Experiences

The parents' voice is seldom heard in discussions about daycare. What are their experiences and needs? We have carried two studies into this: a study of 144 parents who make use of daycare centres (Singer 1991), and a study of 754 parents who make use of various forms of daycare including baby-sitters, family daycare and centre-based daycare (Van Dijke, Terpstra and Hermanns 1994). In both research projects it was clear that parents with a higher level of education make the most use of formal daycare facilities.

The experiences and wishes of middle-class parents appeared to be profoundly different from the experts' thinking on quality daycare. Take for instance the issue of guilt about using daycare. In both studies we found that working parents rarely suffer from the feelings of guilt that some experts feel they should. Working parents do not suffer feelings of guilt more often than parents who have chosen to bring up their children at home. Apparently guilt feelings are, to a certain extent, just all part of parenting (Van Dijk, Terpstra and Hermanns 1994). If working parents feel guilt, it is usually caused by some concrete situation, in which they feel they have reacted inadequately. For instance if their child is ill and has to remain at home, and all the parents' attention is taken up with trying to find a suitable solution for the care problem which has arisen (Singer 1991). A relatively small group of parents have doubts about whether daycare is good for their children (Van Dijke, Terpstra and Hermanns 1994). It should be remembered though, that most Dutch mothers work part-time and the parents we interviewed only made use of daycare for two or three days a week.

A large number of parents did find it difficult to get used to leaving their child with someone else, particularly if the child was still a baby (Singer 1991). Among experts daycare for babies is much more controversial than daycare for children older than twelve months. But in fact, according to the experiences of parents, babies younger than seven months familiarise more easily with the new situation than older children. Parents often felt separation problems when the child was younger than seven months; but the children experienced separation problems more often if they started when they were older than seven months. However, most parents and children quickly get used to the new situation and the doubts experienced by some parents soon disappear. A positive attitude by the caregivers and individual attention for the parents and the child was most helpful during the period of settling-in. The important factor is the feeling of parents that they can trust their child's caregiver.

Parents have two simple criteria when judging the quality of child daycare facilities. 'Can I leave my child here when I am at work?' and 'Is the daycare good for my child?' (Van Dijke, Terpstra and Hermanns 1994). With regard to the first quality criteria, parents have a number of complaints. The opening hours of daycare very often do not correspond with parents' working hours; also, children who become ill are not cared for – they have to be sent home. Childminders and baby-sitters at home can, of course, react more flexibly to the hours needed by parents, in the evenings, during the weekend and changeable hours, but childminders and baby-sitters can resign or be taken ill themselves, leaving the parents with no child care. From research carried out in other countries it can be seen that the lack of correspondence between daycare opening hours and parents working hours, and/or care unexpectedly failing (being withdrawn), causes an extensive amount of stress for working parents, which, in turn has a negative effect on family life (Hughes and Galinsky 1988).

With regard to the question of whether daycare is good for their children, Dutch parents have very modest wishes. In the first place they want good interaction between all of the people involved: is the atmosphere and the way staff treat the children pleasant, homely, relaxed, warm and loving? (Van Dijke, Terpstra and Hermanns 1994). They also look at the way staff treat parents, and whether, at the end of the day they can say something personal about their child (Singer 1991). It is important to parents that their children learn how to behave with other children in a daycare centre and learn good manners, obedience and social rules. Many parents admitted that disciplining at home is difficult, and is partly unwanted, because they do not want to disturb the spontaneity of their child. They therefore welcomed this supplement to discipline provided by daycare education. Besides this, many parents wanted caregivers to encourage the creativity and fantasy life of their children. When care is given by childminders or baby-sitters, the smaller environment and homeliness are valued.

Middle-class parents have little affinity with the extra pedagogic goals formulated for daycare facilities by local governments and some experts. A development toward a more 'schoolish' form of daycare is considered by most parents to be unnecessary and unwanted. They also feel no need for guidance and expert advice from staff in their methods of upbringing. What they would like is more discussion and exchange of views, about their children, with staff on an equal footing (Singer 1991).

According to parents, one disadvantage of care in a daycare centre is the fact that they are badly informed about the pedagogic policy of the centre (Mutant 1993, Singer 1991). Parents also say that they have more influence on the childminder or babysitter than on the staff at a daycare centre (Van Dijke, Terpstra and Hermanns 1994). The formerly subsidised daycare centres have no strong tradition of client-centredness, or of giving parents power in decision-making processes. I will return to this point later.

Parents of Ethnic Minorities

Special attention has to be given to the needs and wishes of parents of ethnic minorities. As far as ethnic minorities are concerned we have to mention the national and local government preventive policy. Within this framework, child-care centres, especially playgroups, are seen as a means of giving parents from ethnic minorities information on upbringing and as a means of stimulating the development of children from disadvantaged backgrounds (*Opvoedingssteun op maat* 1991, *Ouders ondersteunen* 1994). This preventive policy is, therefore, particularly aimed at the groups who are threatened with being excluded altogether from daycare by the commercialisation of child daycare facilities. As I said before, it is the well-educated parents with better jobs who have profited most from the national stimulation programme. Employers invest less in daycare for the children of their unskilled and easily replaceable employees, which is what immigrant parents often are. The fact that a lack of good daycare facilities can actually cause a number of problems in upbringing is ignored, even by the majority of experts in the field of early education for minority groups (Geense 1994, Van der Zwaart 1995).

There is very little information about how different ethnic minorities organise daycare for their children. Formerly, when daycare centres were subsidised institutions, they were quite popular in families with a Surinam or Antillean background. Now, however, whether they can keep their subsidised places depends upon local government policy. Other minority groups such as Turks or Moroccans, seldom entered formal daycare in the Netherlands. Some daycare centres have developed a special policy to make their centres attractive to Turkish parents and children. However, since commercialisation, we have had daycare centres with qualified Turkish caregivers, but almost no Turkish children.

It is likely that many young children of working immigrant parents are cared for in the informal circle of family and friends. There is no public knowledge about their situation, only anecdotal evidence about the way parents try to cope with their daycare problems. For instance, leaving the child alone in a room above the restaurant where the parents work; keeping older girls at home to take care of the younger ones; sending the child back to Turkey until it has reached school age; or parceling the child between many relatives who take care of him/her (Geense 1994, Van der Zwaart 1995).

Our daycare policy has, until now, strongly favoured formal daycare in centres with qualified caregivers. In addition, many experts have stressed the need for caregivers to have training and qualifications. Most baby-sitters, childminders and grandmothers do not have certificates and diplomas in childrearing. However, many parents, including the immigrant parents we interviewed, favour informal daycare in a family context and are very satisfied with it. Minority groups appear to have a strong preference for informal daycare. Policy makers and experts need to change their negative image of informal care, and support the preferences of the parents.

We really need more information about the wishes and experiences of immigrant parents. We need to break through our concepts of daycare to find ways to support forms of daycare that are compatible with the practical needs, values and customs of upbringing of different (sub)cultural and ethnic groups of parents.

Daycare Centres: What is Quality?

It is clear that parents differ in their needs and wishes regarding daycare. Parents' demands are, by definition, always unique, based on the balance of the various interests involved such as working hours, financial means and pedagogic wishes (Hughes and Galinsky 1988, Van Dijke, Terpstra and Hermanns 1994). Institutions cannot possibly accommodate all of the wishes of every parent. Besides, accommodating the needs of parents could be at the expense of the children and/or quality as defined by professional caregivers. For instance it is impossible to foster strong attachments between children, a goal of professional caregivers, if the composition of the group is totally different every day, because the children's mothers – as most Dutch mothers do – work only two days a week.

Therefore, from my point of view the challenge for daycare institutions is: how can daycare be organised in such a way that it accommodates the requirements and wishes of specific groups of parents and children, and also meets the standards of the professionals involved?

To try to answer this we conducted a study into pedagogical organisation in six daycare centres (Singer and Miltenburg 1994). In each daycare centre we investigated the basis of their pedagogic policy and policy toward parents. What did they do to meet the special needs of parents and children? We hypothesised that the content of the pedagogic and parental policy, and the structure of the organisation would both be strongly related to the aims of daycare centres. Because of this we selected daycare centres that were very different in terms of their basic principles, aims and/or target groups. They were:

A. A daycare centre aimed at inter-cultural care for Turkish and Dutch children.
B. A daycare centre aimed at group upbringing and the development of methods for working with young children in groups.
C. A daycare centre aimed at mainstreaming handicapped children.
D. A daycare centre for children at risk aimed at help and prevention.
E. A daycare centre for employees of a large hospital.
F. A parent-run crèche, where parents take turns in working with the children.

The main results of this study are outlined below:

- A strong relationship was found between the special goals of daycare centres and their quality standards. All daycare centres have special quality demands in order to meet the needs of specific groups of parents and children or to achieve special goals. For example: in the intercultural daycare centre the main aim is the emancipation of minority ethnic groups, taking their particular needs into account. For this reason they have an extremely consistent policy of bilingualism towards children and parents and cultural diversity is emphasised. The daycare centre for children at risk (including many immigrant children) makes individual work plans for each child and demands the cooperation of parents both in the centre and at home. In contrast with this, the hospital daycare centre makes no extra pedagogic demands, but measures are taken to assist parents, for instance by giving their children breakfast when they arrive very early in the morning.

  Without these special quality demands, special groups (handicapped children, children at risk, children from disadvantaged families) would probably be excluded from daycare centres. So diversity is crucial to meet the special needs of parents and children.
- The higher the pedagogical goals of the daycare centre, the less attention was paid to the needs of employed parents. Parents were in the weakest position at the daycare centre for children with problems, where the parents are seen mainly as people in need of help. In the daycare centre for group upbringing it is also the institution's own pedagogic perspective that dominates. For instance, 'second children from one family' are not given priority; when admitting new children the required age of the child is decisive with regard to the range of ages in the group. This has led to stormy debates with parents, as it has forced parents with two or more young children to search for different solutions for the care of their children.
- The professional knowledge of teachers is to a great extent 'tacit knowledge'. A clear pedagogy for working with young children in a group is lacking. As a consequence of this, teachers made a number of pedagogic rules at group level, without being aware of basic pedagogical principles. This led to misunderstandings and conflicts. Systematic evaluation and improvement of pedagogical quality was lacking and was not possible because there were no basic common principles or rules to evaluate.
- Teachers think of their daycare centre as 'one big family' or as a 'second home'. Informal chats with parents about their children are highly valued by the teachers. However, parents have little

> influence at policy-forming level. They do not participate in the informal communication circuit of the professionals, where the decisions are made. On the one hand, the informal 'family behaviour' of the teachers is highly valued by both teachers and parents. But on the other hand parents are placed in the position of 'outsiders' in this 'homely' organisational culture.
>
> Priority was given to the interests of the 'second (daycare) home' in the pedagogic policy of most centres. One consequence of this professional dominance is insensitivity to the needs of the child that is growing up in at least two social contexts.

This study makes clear that daycare centres define quality in professional terms. It also makes clear, and other Dutch studies confirm this conclusion (Mutant 1994), that the position of parents is weak. Immigrant parents have the least information about what is going on in the centre with their children (Bouwer and Vedder 1995). Dutch daycare centres are often 'inward-looking', preventing parents from having any influence on, or even information about, the daycare centre's pedagogic policy. Daycare centres still have a long way to go with regard to the development of a client-centred attitude. This is not only necessary to meet the demands of a commercialised daycare system. There is also a need to develop a daycare system that is really supportive to parents and children, and which complements the upbringing at home in a positive way (McKim 1993, Larner and Phillips 1994).

Developing Daycare Pedagogics in the Dutch Context

I began this chapter with the statement that in the case of daycare many parties are involved. I have showed that in the Dutch situation different parties have different or even opposing definitions of quality. They are often unaware of this because of their inability or unwillingness to take into account the perspective of the other parties, the legacy of traditional thinking about young children is probably still present in the background. Experts and professional caregivers still find it difficult to support the needs of working mothers/parents and their children.

To sum up my main conclusion about developing daycare pedagogics in the Netherlands:

1. In order to make child care correspond to the needs of parents, it is necessary that governments and experts start to put their own (pedagogic) ideals and goals into perspective. They have to take

the reality of parents, children and caregivers as a starting point of their policy making and theoretical thinking. Special attention has to be given to the position of poor families in a commercialised daycare system.

2. Experts have to break through problem-oriented tradition and their assumption that all parents need expert guidance. This assumption is deeply embedded in developmental psychology, and not only in the Netherlands, as I have demonstrated elsewhere (Singer 1992b, 1993). There has been little interest in the theories, values and needs of parents. The main aim of developmental psychologists has been to discover universal laws of child development and context-free theories of development. Having had their training within this scientific tradition, we should not be surprised when teachers 'forget' the perspectives of parents and the family context of the child.
3. Dutch daycare centres need a stronger theoretical framework for working with groups of young children, and for cooperation with parents. The complex network of relationships in daycare centres is a far cry from the mother-child dyad which (Dutch) researchers have concentrated on in the main (Singer 1992b, 1993). For example, many Dutch experts strongly advise teachers to be sensitive and responsive to individual children, advice that is founded on attachment theory. But teachers have to work with at least fourteen toddlers: how do they deal with all these children signalling for attention? A dyadic theory does provide some clues about how to handle the interrelationships between young children and their teachers. Daycare centres need theoretical concepts and operational methods in order to translate general pedagogical principles into daily practice, and to evaluate their effectiveness.

References

Belsky, J. (1984), 'The determinants of parenting: a process model', in *Child Development*, 55, 83-96.

Bowlby, J. (1969), *Attachment and Loss*, Vol.1, *Attachment*, New York.

Bouwer, E. and Vedder, P. (1995), *Kleine verschillen. Intercultureel werken in de kinderopvang.* Utrecht.

Commissie Kwaliteit Kinderopvang (1994), *De kunst van de kinderopvang. Vier beleidsadviezen.* Utrecht.

European Commission Network on Childcare (1992), *Employment, Equality and Caring for Children*, Brussels.

Geense, P. (1994), 'Opvoeding in Chinese gezinnen', in T. Pels (ed.) *Opvoeding in Chinese, Marokkaanse en Surinaams-Creoolse gezinnen*, Rotterdam.

Hughes, D. and Galinsky, E. (1988), 'Balancing work and family lives: research and corporate applications', in A.E. Gottfried and A.W. Gottfried (eds), *Maternal employment and children's development, Longitudinal Research*, New York and London:233-268.

Kinderopvang. Regeringsstandpunt over het beleid na 1993 (1993), Minister van W.V.C. H. d'Ancona, 's Gravenhage.

Larner, M. and Phillips, D. (1994), 'Defining and valuing quality as a parent', in P. Moss and A. Pence (eds), *Valuing Quality in Early Childhood Services. New approaches to defining quality,* London.

Moss, P and Pence, A. (1994) (eds), *Valuing Quality in Early Childhood Services. New approaches to defining quality,* London.

McKim, M.K.(1993), 'Quality child care: what does it mean for individual infants, parents and children?', in *Early Child Development and Care*, 88, 23-30.

Mutant (1993), *Uitspraken over inspraak, onderzoek, analyse en aanbevelingen over de positie van ouders in de kinderopvang*, Nijmegen (in opdracht van de Commissie Kwaliteit Kinderopvang).

Nieuwsbrief Kinderopvang 5, informatie van het Ministerie van WVC (1994), Rijswijk.

Opvoedingssteun op maat. Hoofdlijnen pedagogische preventie in het kader van het jeugdbeleid (1991), Rijswijk.

Ouders ondersteunen. Een notitie over opvoedingsondersteuning (1994), Rijswijk.

Rispens, J. and Meulen, B.F. van der (1992) (eds), *Gezinsgerichte stimulering van kinderen in achterstandssituaties,* Amsterdam.

Singer, E. (1991), *Kijk op kinderopvang, ervaringen van ouders*, Utrecht.

Singer, E. (1992a), 'Family policy and preschool programs in the Netherlands', in G.A. Woodhill, J. Bernhard and L. Prochner (eds), *International Handbook of Early Childhood Education*,, New York/London.

Singer, E. (1992b), *Child Care and the Development of Psychology,* London/ New York.

Singer, E and Paardekooper, B. (1992c), *Effecten van kinderopvang. Een literatuurstudie*. Amsterdam.

Singer, E. (1993), 'Shared care for children', in *Theory and Psychology*, 3, 429-449.

Singer, E. and Miltenburg, R. (1994), 'Quality in child daycare centres: how to promote it?', in *Early Child Development and Care*, 102, 1-16.

Stimuleringsbeleid Kinderopvang 1990-1993. Resultaten over 1990-1991 (1992), Ministerie van W.V.C., Rijswijk.

Stimuleringsbeleid Kinderopvang 1990-1992 (1992), Rijswijk.

Van Dijke, A., Terpstra, L. and Hermanns, J. (1994), *Ouders over kinderopvang. Een onderzoek naar meningen, ervaringen, wensen en keuzen van mannen en vrouwen*, Amsterdam.

Van IJzendoorn, M.H., Tavecchio, L.W.C., Goossens, F.A. and Vergeer, M.M. (1982), *Opvoeden in geborgenheid: een kritische analyse van Bowlby's attachmenttheorie*, Van Loghum Slaterus.

Van Loggem, D. and Bekkers, B. (1994) (eds), *Het jonge kind tussen onderwijs en welzijn*, Amsterdam.

Van der Zwaart, J. (1995), *Hoe vrouwen moderen. Buurtgesprekken over opvoeding*, Utrecht.

Vedder, P., Bouwer, E., and Pels, T. (1996), *Multiclutural Child Care*, Clevedon.

Chapter 18

EARLY CHILDHOOD EDUCATION AND CARE IN GERMANY

History, Current Issues and Policy Perspectives

Wolfgang Tietze

Early Education in the Context of the Bourgeois Family Model

Early childhood education and care, as a more or less clearly articulated educational concept, has been developing in Germany and other central European countries over the past two centuries. Its origins must be seen against the background of the formation of the bourgeois notion of the family, which came into being during the second half of the eighteenth century. This notion, which has generally been distinguished by an increase in warmth in the climate of family bonds, assigns a central role to the mother-child relationship (Shorter 1975). Accordingly, a woman 'discovers' within the family her 'natural' vocation as wife and mother. Hence, the previously prevalent attitude of a certain degree of indifference towards children was replaced by one characterised by constant concern for, and attention paid to, children's upbringing. As a result of this cultural-historical development, childhood began to be perceived as a separate state of being (Ariès 1962), a state needing to be observed, interpreted, and subjected to deliberate molding. Educational theorists, particularly those of the circle of Philanthropism (Basedow, Wolke, Salzmann, Campe, among others), drew attention to the great importance of the earliest phase of human life and expounded on what was pedagogically appropriate for the child (Heiland 1987).

However, members of a large number of social strata lacked the material means necessary to attain such a bourgeois family ideal. This discrepancy was further aggravated by growth of the proletarian population due to industrialisation. Owing to the poverty of the lower classes, all capable family members, mothers as well as older children, were obliged to work to obtain the means of subsistence. The mother's employment was ranked as more important than the care and upbringing of her small children, who represented a burden on the household and, indirectly, a further source of additional poverty. While their mothers were at work, many children, who often lacked supervision from a very early age, were left to their own resources. They were confined to their accommodation and were in some cases even given sedatives or alcohol to keep them quiet. Accidents among children were common, and a considerable number were in danger of complete dereliction (Barow-Bernstorff et al. 1986:123ff., G. Erning 1987, Reyer 1985:65ff.). As a consequence of such a cluster of developments, various local establishments for the care and education of young children came into being. In most cases, their founding was initiated by members of the bourgeois class and the aristocracy, and the cost was borne by private societies. Reyer (1987:252), one of our historians of early childhood education, speaks of the dual motivation of publicly organised child care and education inasmuch as the objectives were to enable the mother's employment (and with this to stabilise socially and economically lower-class households) and to educate their small children according to bourgeois principles. In practical terms, the aims were to preclude the physical and psychological dereliction of children, to instill in them morals appropriate to the circumstances of their class, to relieve the burden on public relief funds, and to free the emerging school system from looking after young children, a task it had begun to adopt (G.Erning 1987a). Government authorities swiftly recognised the stabilising effects such institutions had on the status quo of society and advocated their dissemination, although without providing funds for their support.

An important role in the propagation of early childhood education was played by the writings of the Englishman Samuel Wilderspin, which were translated into German in 1826. Wilderspin propounded the importance of education for young impoverished children between the ages of one-and-a-half and seven. Around the middle of the century, parochial preschools, which had goals similar to Wilderspin's and which were run according to methods described by the Protestant minister Theodor Fliedner (1800-1864), gained wide acceptance. Similar efforts were made in many regions by the established churches, and they formed a starting point from which, during the second half of the nineteenth century, the

Protestant and Roman Catholic churches gained decisive influence on early childhood education and care in Germany.

A major influence on further developments is due to the philosophy and projects of Friedrich Fröbel (1782-1852). His 'kindergarten' was not primarily intended to be a new institution. He conceived it as a pedagogical principle, with the aim of providing a new basis for the education of children within the family itself (Heiland 1987). Fröbel's intention was to aid and instruct mothers to provide a better early education for their children by means of didactic toys and games.

Nevertheless, it was not the kindergarten in the form of a pedagogical model for mothers, but rather the kindergarten as a pedagogical institution utilising play and games in an educational manner that made its reputation and created its enduring influence both in Germany and far beyond its borders. It is a mark of this influence that the term kindergarten, as the label for preschool education, has been adopted either in this form or in translated form in so many languages (Tietze 1989). Fröbel's concept of the kindergarten also included intensive personnel training.

Fröbels's conception of early childhood education and care played an important role in the aspirations and efforts to create a national plan for education during the bourgeois revolution of 1848. This inclusion of the kindergarten in the proposed democratic national system of education was one of the reasons for the prohibition of the kindergarten in Prussia for ten years, from 1851 to 1861, after the failure of the bourgeois revolution (Barow-Bernstorff et al. 1986:197).

Towards a Uniform Concept of Center-based Early Childhood Education

A continual increase in the number of preschool institutions characterises developments in the second half of the nineteenth century. Existing side by side were a number of differing types of institutions: there was the Fröbel kindergarten, for instance, which emphasised educational goals. Kindergartens were generally open for only a few hours a day and attended largely by middle-class children. There were also the preschools and asylums for the poor, in which social welfare functions were emphasised and where children often spent the whole day. When an attempt was made to incorporate the pedagogical methods of the Fröbel kindergarten into the conceptual framework of the institutions with a largely welfare character, this resulted in the establishment of the conceptual framework of the 'Volkskindergarten' (people's kindergarten). Thus began a process of drawing together the various conceptions of the differing institutions.

Since the end of the last century child-oriented motives have been advanced as a justification for centre-based preschool education. At least part of the three to six-year-old age group was offered a socialisation that was independent of and supplementary to family upbringing. The process of becoming recognised as a system independent of specific family conditions was attended by a growing state regulation of kindergarten teacher training. These enactments represented the beginning of an increasing commitment on the part of the state towards kindergarten education.

After the end of First World War and the transition from empire to republic, a fundamental revision of the educational system was undertaken. However, those who wished to include kindergarten in the educational system and to make it the bedrock of a uniform educational system for all children failed to achieve their objective. Even today, the regulations laid down in the 1922 Youth Welfare Act are still valid in principle. The law acknowledged the right of every child to an education, which the public authorities were obliged to provide indirectly or directly – if the family itself was unable to do so. The law gave priority in the founding and running of kindergartens to organising bodies of independent social welfare organisations. This meant that kindergartens sponsored by public authorities were only established if the need for such institutions was not met by the churches or other philanthropic organisations (the principle of subsidiarity). As a result of the economic crises in Germany in the 1920s and also of the growing power of politically reactionary forces, the planned system could not be fully realised. Compared with the level achieved prior to the First World War (see Table 18.1), there were in fact slightly fewer kindergarten places. Early childhood education was nevertheless seen from that period onwards as a peremptory public duty to be furthered and regulated by the state.

In the so-called Third Reich, kindergarten was, like all other educational institutions, placed in the service of National Socialist ideology and its desire for power (Berger 1986). The extension of National Socialist influence into the kindergarten system, which up to that time had been pluralistic in its structure, was achieved by various means. In some cases the organising bodies were brought into line with National Socialist ideology; in others, the church kindergartens were taken over by the National Socialist welfare organisation Nationalsozialistische Volkswohlfahrt (NSV), although in many instances the NSV founded its own institutions. Kindergarten teachers' professional organisations were treated in the same manner. For instance, the Fröbel association, with its long tradition, was forced to disband (Reyer 1987a).

Table 18.1 Historical Perspective of the Growth of Kindergartens

Territory	Year	Number of Provisions	Number of Places	Supply Ratio %
Kingdom of Prussia	ca. 1850	400	26,000	1.0
City of Berlin	ca. 1850	33	3,800	7.5
German Empire	ca. 1910 1930 ca. 1940	7,300 7,300 20,000	559,000 422,000 1,123,000	13.0 13.0 31.0

Note: Derived from Tietze 1993: 103

As a result of the exigencies of the war economy in particular – women and mothers having to replace men in factory work – the number of kindergarten places was greatly increased (see Table 18.1).

After the end of the Second World War and the collapse of the structures of National Socialism, the prevailing function of the kindergarten was that which characterised it at the time of the origin of the institution in the nineteenth century: kindergartens again became institutions whose task was to save children from the threat of dereliction. A considerable number of children were orphans, many fathers had fallen at the front or were prisoners of war, so women and mothers formed the primary source of labour potential for securing their families' bare existence. The fact that many buildings – whether factories, offices, or dwellings – had been destroyed in the bombing and the fact that several million refugees and displaced persons from former German territories in the eastern part of the country had arrived in the Western Zones exacerbated the problems.

Different Paths of Early Education in East and West Germany

Different paths were taken in the re-establishment of the kindergarten system in East Germany (the future German Democratic Republic) and in West Germany (subsequently the Federal Republic of Germany). In East Germany the inclusion of a kindergarten level in the education system was planned as early as 1946 and was later confirmed in law. Thus kindergarten came to be defined as an educational institution; correspondingly, it was free of charge and the system was rapidly expanded so that, in the 1980s at least – every child had the chance to become enrolled in a kindergarten (Boeckmann 1973). Similarly, the provisions for the under-three-year-olds (Krippen) were extended considerably from the early 1950s onwards so that the GDR became the country with the highest coverage rate in the world for this age group (Weigel and Weber 1991). The extraordinary growth and investment of the GDR in centre-based care and education for all preschool-aged children came about for three major reasons. From the very beginning of the GDR, all female labour potential, including that of mothers with young children, was considered necessary for the intended economic development. Therefore public provisions for children at no cost to parents were necessary to incorporate mothers into the labour force. In addition, mothers being bound to the home because of child-care duties was regarded as not in line with the equal rights of women which were strongly emphasised in the emerging socialistic society. Finally, centre-based education – instead of uncontrollable family education of young children – was seen as a measure that would provide a socialistic education at an early stage and would allow the state to control education from its very outset (Boeckmann 1993).

Table 18.2 Expansion of the Kindergarten System in West Germany (FRG) and East Germany (GDR) since 1950

	FRG			GDR		
year	provisions	places	supply ratio %	provisions	places	supply ratio %
1950	8,648	604,698	29.1	-	-	-
1955	11,122	749,195	29.4	8,527	350,332	37.0
1960	12, 290	817,200	28.1	11,508	158,678	49.4
1965	14,113	952,900	28.0	12,921	555,472	56.6
1970	17,493	1,160,700	32.9	13,105	654,658	69.1
1975	23,130	1,478,900	56.1	12,218	701,809	90.6
1980	23,938	1,392,500	67.5	12,233	664,478	98.8
1985	24,476	1,438,400	67.7	13,148	788,232	96.3
1989	-	1,440,000	67.7	13,453	747,140	97.4

Note: Derived from Tietze 1993: 109

In contrast, a different path was chosen in West Germany. As in the case of the school system, the kindergarten system turned to the example of the Weimar Republic. Kindergarten remained the administrative responsibility of the youth welfare service, and its function was limited to that of supplementing family upbringing where needed. In essence the regulations of the 1922 act were adopted (Barow-Bernstorff et al. 1986: 415ff, Neumann 1987).

The state's contribution to the setting up and further development of the kindergarten system in the Federal Republic of Germany was trifling

Table 18.3 Expansion of the Care and Education System for Under 3 Year Old Children in West Germany (FRG) and East Germany (GDR) since 1950

	FRG			GDR		
year	provisions	places	supply ratio %	provisions	places	supply ratio %
1950	170	7,491	0.4	194	4,674	6.3
1955	360	16,043	0.7	1,586	50,171	5.9
1960	374	18,351	0.7	2,517	81,495	9.9
1965	438	18,108	0.6	3,317	116,950	1.8
1970	520	17,457	0.7	4,323	166,700	2.6
1975	829	24,251	1.3	5,576	234,941	4.2
1980	995	26,104	1.5	6,415	284,712	4.5
1985	1,028	28,353	1.6	7,315	338,676	4.8
1989	-	-	-	7,707	348,058	55.2

Note: Derived from Tietze 1993: 114

up to the second half of the 1960s. Social policy and the concomitant public debate largely reflected a return to the traditional image of the family (Neumann 1987). A widespread summary critique, although it was somewhat exaggerated, contained more than a grain of truth when it suggested that women and mothers should perceive their tasks within the triple K of 'Kinder, Küche, Kirche' (children, kitchen, church). This family image implied a lack of a general need for an additional system of preschool education beyond that of the family. Such a system of care and education outside the confines of the family served its purpose only in cases in which family adversities made it unavoidable. There was, in addition, a widespread belief that preschool education in kindergarten might even pose a threat to the family, inasmuch as the institution enabled mothers to take on jobs outside of the family circle. This attitude is expressed in remarks of the Minister for Social Affairs in 1957 which were made in response to the suggestion that the number of kindergartens be expanded: 'We must consider very carefully to what extent the family, although protected on the outside by the creation of such social institutions, exhausts itself internally as a result' (cited in Haensch 1969).

This kindergarten-pedagogy was, at the time, embedded in conceptions of developmental psychology, according to which the child's development is effected as an internally controlled process of maturation (Schmalohr 1970), kindergarten pedagogy considered its most significant task to be providing the child with a protective environment – an environment that would secure an undisturbed development of children's talents and abilities and that would shield children both from overwhelming stimuli and from their own precocity.

This situation changed dramatically in the mid-1960s, when a remarkable phase of expansion and reform in West Germany's education system took place. Kindergarten, although not an element in the education system, was rapidly caught up in the reform process. Indeed, early childhood education was even accorded a key role. The immediate post-war restoration of the education system, which had been oriented towards older models, no longer seemed adequate to meet the demands of a developed industrialised nation. The conviction that the German education system was heading towards a catastrophe (Picht 1964) was widespread. As a result, the debate on education became the dominant theme in social policy during the second half of the 1960s. As an expression of a general consensus regarding the need for improving the education system, the Deutscher Bildungsrat (German Council on Education), a committee consisting of scientists, members of the government, and representatives of important social groupings, was established in 1965. Its task was to make recommendations for a fundamental reform of the entire education system.

Particular attention was paid to early childhood education in the hope that it would be capable of making a special contribution to the main goal of educational reform. It was assumed that the deficits of underprivileged children could be adjusted by compensatory early childhood education prior to school entry, thus providing equal opportunity for all children in the general school system. It was furthermore assumed that by a systematic utilisation of the potential of early childhood learning, the general standard of education among all children would be raised (Deutscher Bildungsrat 1970). As a consequence, these goals caused great uncertainty in the traditional kindergarten system and led to a dramatic reorientation of its pedagogy. Kindergarten education had previously set as its task the furthering of play and games and of the child's innate developmental potential. These earlier postulates were now regarded, at least polemically, as 'passive spectator pedagogy', and the kindergartens were decried as institutions in which children were artificially kept stupid (Lückert 1967).

The great importance ascribed to early childhood education, regardless of the various controversies, was expressed in a new assessment of the kindergarten as an educational instrument, as well as in a massive expansion of the number of kindergartens. To a much greater degree than before, kindergarten was given an educational task independent of the state of affairs in the family; it was perceived as a distinct and fundamental stage in the total system of education. The German Council on Education (Deutscher Bildungsrat 1970) coined the term 'Elementarbereich' (elementary level) for this new stage, which was to precede the primary (ages six to nine) level of education. Although kindergarten attendance would not be compulsory, it was assumed that all children would be reached by provision of an ample supply of kindergarten places that were to be filled voluntarily.

Within this period, an enormous improvement in the provision of kindergarten places was achieved in West Germany (see Table 18.2) . The strong growth in the supply ratio (percent of children served) was also partly due to a substantial reduction in the birthrate during the same period.

However, in the 1970s, as a result of a generalised exhaustion of educational reform efforts, kindergarten lost its position in political priorities and in public attention. Except for insignificant fluctuations, the supply ratio of kindergarten places has remained until today what it was in the late 1970s.

Since the middle of the 1980s, the kindergarten has again been brought to public notice. Changes in the structure of the family, the increase in single-parent families, the improvement in the standard of education of young mothers and their desire for employment outside the family, as well as the remaking of women's image that has resulted from the feminist movement, all appear to be causes for the appeal for institutions that are more capable of responding to the changing needs and lifestyles of families and children (Tietze 1987). The demands are directed at the inadequate supply of kindergarten places that exists in many residential areas. Other demands concern a greater flexibility of attendance hours – wanting them to be coordinated with family needs, for example, or wanting an increased supply of full-time kindergarten places.

One central demand relates to the improvement of care for children under three years of age, who have not generally been counted among kindergarten clients. Krippen, which are institutions specialising in the care of children younger than three years, came into being later than the kindergartens did and have not received the same educational approval up to now (Reyer 1985). They are to be found largely in major urban centers. With some 60,000 places, they cannot serve even two percent of the birth-to-three-years age group. In the last few years a series of mixed-age kindergartens have been established in which children from birth up to the age of six are cared for.

Conclusion

For the future, four major issues have to be observed when considering the development of the early childhood education and care system in Germany.

1. In connection with a new federal law on abortion each child in the age range from three years to school entry will be entitled to a kindergarten place *(Rechtsanspruch)* at the start of 1996. This calls for an enormous expansion of the system in West Germany and for great investments in this educational and social sector. There are serious doubts that the goal set by the law can be reached in time. Another realistic concern relates to the fact that the necessary quantitative expansion of the system will be achieved at the cost of lowering quality standards such as group size, educator/child ratio, training of educators or reduced space standards. The financial investments needed to reach the goal set by the law will amount to some DM 20 billion (Deutscher Bundestag 1992). For East Germany the quantitative capacity of the system is sufficient. Moreover, because of the tremendous reduction in birth rates occurring in East Germany after reunification, an over capacity can be observed and many provisions are going to be closed down due to a lack of children. Both the insufficient capacity in West Germany and the lack of children in East Germany provide for an unbalanced system in Germany with its specific problems in both parts of the country.
2. The reunification of the two Germanies brought together two completely different early childhood education and care systems. Both systems differ considerably not only in regard to coverage rates, especially for the under-three-year-olds, but also in other characteristics such as educator training and pedagogical orientation and functions of the provisions in the society. The tension between the two systems has not automatically disappeared after reunification and will presumably determine the situation in Germany for the next few years. In East Germany, after the break down of a socialistic society with its corresponding educational system, disorientation and a need for a renewed educational approach can be observed.
3. Centre-based care and education of young children can no longer be seen in isolation. There is an increasing need in Germany to develop a more comprehensive perspective which includes the various measures such as centre-based care, family day-care and support for care in the family of the child such as parental leave regulations, job guarantee for caring parents or tax reductions. There is still a long way to go until Germany reaches a coherent system of the various support measures which provides parents with the opportunity to select the form of support that best fits their family needs.

4. The growing integration of the European Union based on the Treaty of Maastricht has produced increased insight on the part of all those active in the field of early childhood education and care, i.e., decision makers, administrators, educators, researchers, so that further developments and improvements in this field should not be carried out in isolation but with respect to endeavours and developments in the other European countries.

References

Ariès, P. (1962), *Centuries of Childhood: A Social History of Family Life*, New York.

Barow-Bernstorff, E., Günther, K.-H., Krecker, M. and Schuffenhauer, H. (1986) (eds), *Beiträge zur Geschichte der Vorschulerziehung*, (7th edn), Berlin.

Berger, M. (1986), *Vorschulerziehung im Nationalsozialismus. Recherchen zur Situation des Kindergartenwesens 1933-1945*, Weinheim, Basel.

Boeckmann, B. (1993), 'Das Früherziehungssystem in der ehemaligen DDR', in W. Tietze and H.-G. Roßbach (eds), *Erfahrungsfelder in der frühen Kindheit. Bestandsaufnahme, Perspektiven*, Freiburg.

Deutscher Bundestag. Sonderausschuß Schutz des ungeborenen Lebens. 12. Wahlperiode. Ausschußdrucksache 0088. 18.5.1992.

Deutscher Bildungsrat (1970), *Strukturplan für das Bildungswesen*, Stuttgart.

Erning, G. (1987), 'Geschichte der öffentlichen Kleinkinderziehung von den Anfängen bis zum Kaiserreich', in G. Erning, K. Neumann, and J. Reyer (eds), *Geschichte des Kindergartens*, vol.1, Freiburg.

Erning, D. (1987), 'Quantitative Entwicklung der Angebote öffentlicher Kleinkinderziehung', in G. Erning, K. Neumann, and J. Reyer (eds), *Geschichte des Kindergartens*, vol. 2, Freiburg.

Haensch, D. (1989), *Repressive Familienpolitik*, Reinbek.

Heiland, H. (1987), 'Erziehungskonzepte der Klassiker der Frühpädagogik', in G. Erning, K. Neumann, and J. Reyer (eds), *Geschichte des Kindergartens*, vol. 2, Freiburg.

Lückert, H.-R. (1967), 'Begabungsforschung und basale Bildungsförderung', *Schule und Psychologie*, 14 (1), 9-22.

Neumann, K. (1987), 'Geschichte der öffentlichen Kleinkinderziehung von 1945 bis in die Gegenwart', in G. Erning, K. Neumann, and J. Reyer (eds), *Geschichte des Kindergartens*, vol.1, Freiburg.

Picht, G. (1964), *Die deutsche Bildungskatastrophe. Analyse und Dokumentation*, Olten/Freiburg.

Reyer J. (1985), *Wenn die Mütter arbeiten gingen – Eine sozialhistorische Studie zur Entstehung der öffentlichen Kleinkinderziehung im 19. Jahrhundert in Deutschland*, (2nd edn), Köln.

Reyer J. (1987a), 'Geschichte der öffentlichen Kleinkinderziehung im deutschen Kaiserreich, in der Weimarer Republik und in der Zeit des Nationalsozialismus', in G. Erning, K. Neumann, and J. Reyer (eds), *Geschichte des Kindergartens*, vol. 1, Freiburg.

Reyer J. (1987b), 'Entwicklung der Trägerstruktur in der öffentlichen Kleinkinderziehung', in G. Erning, K. Neumann, and J. Reyer (eds), *Geschichte des Kindergartens*, vol. 2, Freiburg.

Schmalohr, E. (1970), 'Möglichkeiten und Grenzen einer kognitiven Frühförderung', *Zeitschrift für Pädagogik*, 16 (1), 1-26.

Shorter, E. (1975), *The Making of the Modern Family*, New York.

Tietze, W. (1987), 'Flexibility in preschool education: Current issues in West Germany's kindergartens', in M.M. Clark (ed.), *Roles, responsibilities, and relationships in the education of the young child*,Birmingham.

Tietze, W. (1989). 'Vorschulerziehung', in D. Lenzen (ed.), *Pädagogische Grundbegriffe*, vol. 2, Reinbek.

Tietze, W. (1993), 'Zur Entwicklung vorschulischer Erziehung in Deutschland', in W. Tietze & H.-G. Roßbach (eds), *Erfahrungsfelder in der frühen Kindheit, Bestandsaufnahme, Perspektiven*, Freiburg.

Weigel, I. and Weber, C. (1991), 'Research in nurseries in the German Democratic Republic', in E. C. Melhuish and P. Moss (eds), *Day Care for Young Children. International Perspectives*, London.

Chapter 19

PARENTS' ATTRIBUTIONS REGARDING THEIR CHILDREN'S DEVELOPMENT

Heleen A. van der Stege

Abstract

Dutch parents with young children in the cities of Rotterdam and Maastricht (N=94) were asked to indicate the degree of importance they ascribed to factors like genetics, parenting, environment and past events for the development of their children. An instrument (known as VIVOO) was developed to measure these parental beliefs or attributions. The first question this study set out to answer concerned the variability of parental beliefs. The study has shown that parental ideas vary significantly across the developmental domain of their children (learning, social skills and personality). The second research question concerned the relation between parental attributions and the number of children in a family (parents with one child and parents with several children participated in this research). The covariation hypothesis based on scores on a parenting scale was tested, and an alternative covariation hypothesis was developed based on the perceived influence of 'genetics'. Empirical support has been found for this alternative covariation hypothesis. This means that parents with two or more children ascribed more influence to 'genetics' than parents with one child.

Introduction

Research on the beliefs or cognitive processes of parents concerning their children's development has received increasing attention during the last twenty years (Sigel 1985, Goodnow and Collins 1990, McGillicuddy-DeLisi 1985). This recent rise of interest in cognition started with Bell's concept of 'the thinking parent' (1979) and Parke's critique of research which only focused on the overt behaviour of parents and children (1978). Operant conditioning or simple stimulus-response reactions are not sufficient to explain the behaviour of parents. Parents are thinking, organising beings and 'their beliefs play an important role in their lives as well as in the lives of their children' (Sigel 1992:454). Knowledge about parental beliefs (content and related variables) is necessary for future research. Beliefs are a significant ingredient in a complex model of causal interrelationships between parental beliefs, emotions, behaviour, and child outcomes.

In addition to its scientific importance, the study of parental beliefs serves a pragmatic purpose. Professionals in health centres, schools, day-care centres and social institutions for parental support or youth assistance, communicate with parents as a client or customer. To counsel, support, or advise 'customers' it is important to know what they think and how their beliefs vary. Research into parental beliefs should enable better communication.

This study focuses on parents' beliefs. Parents are rather like psychologists. They ask themselves: why are children the way they are and why do they behave the way they do? Parents have certain ideas about what determines the way their children turn out and they have views on which factors, such as genetics, parenting or environment, are important in the development of their child. In this study we have examined two variables related to parents' beliefs, namely, the developmental domain of the child, and the number of children the parent has. With regard to the first variable we have been concerned with the variability of parental beliefs. With regard to the second variable we have been concerned with an important topic of attribution theory.

Attribution theory provides a conceptual framework or useful perspective for studying 'why-questions' asked by parents or common-sense explanations of causality (Dix and Grusec 1985, Gretarsson and Gelfand 1988). Within this framework the focus is on what people actually believe, and not on what is true or reasonable. In this study, a principle from attribution theory has been used to shed light on these parental beliefs. This principle is called *covariation*. The research has examined whether parental beliefs bear any relationship to 'the number of children'. The covariation principle (Heider 1958, Kelley 1967, Himelstein,

Graham and Weiner 1991) explains how people attribute cause and effect: a certain condition is considered responsible for the effect, if condition and effect co-vary. This means that, when the condition is absent, the effect is absent too, and when the condition is present, the effect is also present. Himelstein, Graham and Weiner (1991) have applied this principle to the beliefs of parents. They stated that parents with one child have different attributions from those with several children, because the latter are confronted daily with the fact that children are different. Therefore, parents with more than one child do not easily experience a systematic relationship between their own child-rearing behaviour (the condition) and the way their children finally develop (the effect). What they experience is a discrepancy between their child-rearing behaviour and the fact that their children differ from each other. As these authors stated: 'Parents with multiple children therefore should tend to discount the importance of their own actions in influencing the characteristics and achievements of their offspring. Rather they should ascribe their children's behaviour and characteristics more to peers, schooling, and genetic variation'. This is different for parents with one child. Because they are not confronted with behavioural and personality differences, they tend to believe that there is a strong relationship between their behaviour and the development of the child.

According to the covariation principle the 'child-rearing practices' factor (or 'parenting' factor) is more important for parents with one child than for those with several children. Himelstein, Graham and Weiner (1991) measured the perceived influence of genetics, child-rearing practices, and environment and found empirical support for the covariation hypothesis in a sample survey of 194 parents with children aged between five and seventeen. They found differences between parents with one child and parents with multiple children on the factor 'child-rearing practices', however, they found no differences on the two other factors: genetics and environment. This is strange, especially for the influence of genetics. When parents are confronted daily with the fact that children are different, they tend to have different ideas about the genetics, more specifically, they will attribute more influence to genetics, because of the differences they notice between their children. In fact, this is an alternative covariation principle. Parents with more children are able to ask themselves 'why are children in the same family so different?' Parents of multiple children who experience differences will relate those differences to uncontrollable and variable influences, such as genetics or the environment outside the family. The latter perceived influence is probably less important when considering parents with young children. According to parents of very young children the child's environment is merely an extension of the parental influence. As one parent of two young children in a pilot study put it: 'I choose the environment for my children'. In this way the perceived influence of the environment is strongly connected with the perceived influence of parenting.

To sum up: in daily life parents with two or more children will notice that children within the same family differ enormously. In view of the fact that parents with multiple children tend to think that their child-rearing practices are relatively constant between their own children, they will tend to attribute differences between the children to influences outside their control, such as genetics. For parents with one child it is quite different. Those parents are not confronted with behavioural and personality differences between children of their own, so they tend to attribute a strong influence to their own parenting.

In this study we will investigate whether the covariation principle based on 'parenting' also holds for a population of Dutch parents with young children (two to six years old) and whether parents with one child differ from those with several children in the influence they attribute to 'genetics'.

The question of the variability of parents' ideas is an important one. Parents can attribute differently in areas such as learning, social skills and personality. In this study the variable of 'the developmental domain of the child' is taken into account. Do parents' ideas vary across the developmental domain of the child? Himelstein, Graham and Weiner (1991) found no significant effects or interactions involving domain for either the parenting or the environment ratings. Domain was only a significant factor in ratings on genetics. This means that parents reported different perceived influences of genetics across the three developmental domains. The fact that there was no variability found for ratings on parenting or environment across the developmental domain, may have been caused by the extent of the instrument used. The Parent Questionnaire developed by Himelstein, Graham and Weiner contains nine questions with three on the domain of 'personality', three on 'social skills' and three on 'school performance'. In this study we have examined the variability of parental ideas in a population of Dutch parents with young children using a new questionnaire which contains more topics, so that the parent can give more differentiating answers. In this questionnaire (named VIVOO) parents were asked to indicate the degree of importance they attribute to factors such as genetics, parenting, environment and past accidental occurrences, in considering the development of their child.

The research questions in our study read as follows:

1. Do the attributions of parents vary across the developmental domain of the child?

2a. Does the covariation hypothesis (based on 'parenting' scores) hold true in a sample of Dutch parents with young children? In other words, will parents with one child find the influence of parenting more important than parents with more than one child.
2b. Will parents with multiple children find the influence of genetics more important than parents with one child.

Method

Sample and procedure

The sample consisted of 94 parents in Rotterdam (N=55) and Maastricht (N=39). In Rotterdam, 85 percent of parents take their child to a health centre to have his/her growth and health monitored. In this study, 150 parents were approached via ten health centres in Rotterdam. The ten centres were chosen out of thirty-three health centres existing in Rotterdam. Two centres were chosen from each part of the city, and parents from all kinds of neighbourhoods participated. Professionals in the health centres asked parents to participate in this research project and gave each of them an envelope containing a questionnaire. The parents filled out the questionnaire at home and were given a small reward when they returned the questionnaire in a postage-paid envelope. In Maastricht the questionnaires were sent to parents with children at a elementary school.

Of the parents approached in the health centres in Rotterdam, 37 percent responded and in Maastricht the response of the parents with school children was 72 percent. Parents were asked to fill in the questionnaire for one of their children age between two and six years old. In our research we have used all the questionnaires that were filled in for children between one and seven years old.

Subjects

The parents that participated in the study were aged from 25 to 48 years (M=36.2) and had between one and four children. The children ranged in age from one year to seven years. The subjects comprised 12 men and 82 women. The target children were 45 girls and 49 boys. The professional and educational level of the respondents was higher than the national average; 47 percent of the parents that participated in our research had received higher education (higher vocational education, university), 46 percent secondary education and 5 percent had received only lower education (elementary school). By way of comparison, according to CBS data for 1990 in the Netherlands, 20 percent of women and

25 percent of men between 25 and 44 years old had received higher vocational and university education.

Questionnaire

A new questionnaire was developed for this research, entitled the VIVOO questionnaire. This abbreviated Dutch title stands for 'Questionnaire on parents' ideas about the development of their child as a person'. The questionnaire measures parents' ideas about genetics, child-rearing practices, environment and a fourth factor 'past accidental occurrences'. Although this factor is not taken into account in our attributional analysis, we include it in the questionnaire because 'past occurrences' were frequently mentioned by parents in open interviews (Van der Stege 1992). Parents' ideas about genetics, child-rearing practices, environment and past accidental occurrences are measured in two different ways. Actually, we are talking about two different instruments. The scores obtained on these instruments provide insight into the so-called 'convergent validation'. The two instruments will be briefly examined below.

The first instrument (VIVOO part 1) measures parents' ideas on seventeen issues related to the development of the child's personality. For each issue the first question is how often the child presents some specific behaviour. Then, parents have to indicate on an eight-point scale how much influence the following factors have on the development of their child: genetics, child-rearing practices, environment and past accidental occurrences. Each page of the questionnaire contains a framed explanation for these factors. This explanation reads as follows:

- genetics: the nature of the child/innate features;
- child-rearing practices: the way in which the parent handles his/her child;
- environment: the way in which the child is handled by other children and adults outside the family;
- past accidental occurrences: important events in the life of the child that occurred by accident.

The seventeen issues used in the first part of the VIVOO questionnaire are concrete issues closely related to daily child-rearing practices. By being requested to describe their ideas on these seventeen issues, parents are given the opportunity to differentiate. Consequently, this is expected to provide a more reliable picture than the one obtained by asking parents to describe their ideas on only three issues, as the instrument developed by Himelstein, Graham and Weiner did (1991). At a later stage in the process, the seventeen VIVOO issues can be summed up in larger categories, or development domains. The three development domains are social skills (or social contacts), personality, and learning skills (cognition and attitude towards learning). So, the field of social skills incorporates the following VIVOO subjects: playing with other children, making new friends easily, making contact with strangers easily, acting the boss with other children, being obedient. The following subjects come under the field of learning (cognition and attitude towards learning): intelligence, oral proficiency, ability to concentrate, inquisitiveness. Finally, the following subjects belong to the personality field: liveliness, self-confidence, aggressiveness, obstinacy, hot temper, anxiety, timidity and boisterousness.

The second instrument (VIVOO part 2) also checks the degree of influence ascribed by the parents to genetics, child-rearing practices, environment and past accidental occurrences. However, this is done differently. Part two consists of thirty-three Likert items. Parents can indicate whether they agree or not to certain statements. The genetics scale consists of eight items. An example of an item used on the 'genetics' scale is 'There are some characteristics which I have noticed from birth in my child, which I think are just "innate features"'. An example of an item on the 'child-rearing' scale is 'By giving my child a good education and lots of love I can prevent him/her from becoming a criminal later in life'. An example of an 'environment' item is 'Other adults (like the school teacher or the nurse in the day-care centre) have a great deal of influence on the development of my child'. Finally, an example of items belonging to the 'past accidental occurrences' scale is 'Some events (pleasant or unpleasant) have made a deep impression on my child, influencing the development of his/her personality'. The second part of the VIVOO questionnaire contains eight genetics questions, eight child-rearing questions, eight environment questions and eight questions relating to past accidental occurrences in the life of the child.

The advantage of measuring parents' ideas by means of two instruments is that this type of measurement gives insight into 'convergent validation'. The intention is that the genetics scales on both instruments should correlate strongly with each other, and weakly with the other scales. This also goes for the child-rearing scale, the environment scale and the scale for past accidental occurrences.

Results

General results relating to the VIVOO questionnaire

The reliability or internal consistency of the eight scales in the VIVOO questionnaire was examined. On three of the four scales used in the first part of the VIVOO questionnaire, alpha was higher than 0.90. On one of the four scales alpha was higher than 0.80. (According to Nunnally's rule of the thumb alpha should be at least 0.70, if one wants to speak of internal consistency). Regarding the second part of the VIVOO questionnaire, on the 'genetics' scale alpha was higher than 0.80, and on the 'parenting' scale, alpha was higher than 0.70. Both on the 'environment' scale and on the 'past accidental occurrences' scale, alpha was moderate, namely, 0.57 and 0.58 respectively. In this study the two 'genetics' scales and 'parenting' scales are of greatest importance.

A correlation matrix (Multi-trait Multi-Method Matrix) of the eight scales of the two instruments is useful to study the convergent and discriminant validation of the instruments (Campbell and Fiske 1959). In this study we only focus on the convergent validity. There are four traits (genetics, parenting, environment, occurrences) measured by two instruments (part 1 and part 2 of the VIVOO). Correlations between two corresponding traits measured by two different instruments, have to be sufficiently large: the minimum requirement is positive significantly different from zero. In our study, the two genetics scales related positive significant ($r = 0.58$, $p < 0.001$ one-tailed), as also did the two parenting scales ($r = 0.47$, $p < 0.001$ one-tailed) and the two environment scales ($r = 0.29$, $p < 0.01$ one-tailed). The correlation of the two occurrences scales was not significant ($r = 0.24$, $p > 0.01$).

To sum up: the reliability and validity of the genetics and parenting scales is sufficient. This is not the case for the environment and occurrences scales of part 2, the reliability is moderate, and the validity correlates are less convincing.

The variability of beliefs

The means and standard deviations of the VIVOO scores in part 1 are presented in Table 19.1 specified according to the developmental domain of the child. The mean overall score on genetics and parenting were equivalent (genetics M=5.99, SD=1.10, parenting M=5.90, SD=0.83). Table 1 shows that the level of the mean scores varies for each domain of development. Parents' ideas with respect to genetics or parenting, for instance, appear to fluctuate.

An analysis of variance (number of children x domain, MANOVA with repeated measurements on the last factor) was carried out for each of the four attribution areas (genetics, parenting, environment, occurrences). The 'domain' appeared to be a significant factor in all the analyses ($p < 0.001$). We are able to state that the answers varied significantly with each development domain of the child.

Table 19.1 Mean Attribution Scores of 94 Parents on Eight-Point Scales, Specified for Domain.

	learning		social skills		personality	
	M	SD	M	SD	M	SD
Genetics	6.46	(1.18)	5.80	(1.20)	5.85	(1.24)
Parenting	6.32	(1.02)	5.92	(0.95)	5.68	(1.02)
Environment	5.60	(1.39)	5.81	(1.17)	5.45	(1.14)
Occurrences	3.41	(1.91)	3.72	(1.75)	3.78	(1.73)

Apart from fluctuations by development domain, the attributions also differ from each other. So, the mean scores for parenting are higher than the mean environmental scores or the occurrences scores. To verify whether attributions do, indeed, differ significantly from each other, we have calculated a mean total score for each attribution. By means of an analysis of variance we checked whether these mean total scores differed from each other (number of children x attribution, MANOVA with repeated measurements on the last factor). The 'attribution' factor proved to be a significant main factor ($F[3,255]=71.35$, $p < 0.001$). The answers show that attributions differ significantly from each other.

Concerning interaction effects, we are able to state that the degree to which genetics, parenting and environment are found to be important, depends on the development domain of the child. Parents attach more importance to 'genetics' than to 'environment', when they refer to their child's learning capacity. However, this does not hold true for the child's 'social skills': here, the score on 'parenting' is the highest. When we verify this interaction effect by means of an analysis of variance (MANOVA with repeated measurements on the twelve attribution clusters) a significant interaction appears to exist between attribution and development domain, ($F[6,515] = 19.19$, $p < 0.001$).

We are able to state that the answers on the attribution scale and the answers referring to the development domain are not independent of each other.

The covariation hypothesis and genetic ratings

Table 19.2 presents the means of the four attributions (across all domains), divided over the number of children. Several ANOVAs (with education level as a covariant) were conducted to determine whether the attributions on the factor 'number of children' differed from each other. Attributions concerning parenting did not vary significantly on the factor 'number of children'. The means in Table 19.2 show that attributions concerning 'parenting' in VIVOO part 2 are greater for parents with only one

Table 19.2 ANOVA Results and Mean Attribution Scores of 94 Dutch Parents on Eight-Point Scales, Specified for the Number of Children.

Attributions		M	SD	F	*p*
Genetics (part 1):					
One child	(N=20)	5.92	1.00	0 .11	NS
Multiple children	(N=68)	6.01	1.14		
Parenting (part 1):					
One child	(N=20)	5.97	0.93	0.51	NS
Multiple children	(N=69)	5.88	0.81		
Environment (part 1):					
One child	(N=20)	5.69	1.18	0.49	NS
Multiple children	(N=69)	5.55	1.05		
Occurrences (part 1):					
One child	(N=20)	3.87	1.84	1.12	NS
Multiple children	(N=67)	3.52	1.56		
Genetics (part 2):					
One child	(N=21)	4.04	0.70	5.22	< .05
Multiple children	(N=73)	4.43	0.79		
Parenting (part 2):					
One child	(N=21)	4.50	0.65	2.47	NS
Multiple children	(N=73)	4.22	0.75		
Environment (part 2):					
One child	(N=21)	4.05	0.47	0.19	NS
Multiple children	(N=72)	3.97	0.62		
Occurrences (part 2):					
One child	(N=21)	3.95	0.69	0.26	NS
Multiple children	(N=72)	3.85	0.63		

child than for parents with more children. However, the difference is not significant. This means that there is no empirical support for the covariation hypothesis of Himelstein, Graham and Weiner (1991). There is a significant difference, however, between parents with one child and parents with multiple children on the 'genetics' scale part 2. Inspection of the means in Table 19.2 reveals that attributions were greater for parents with multiple children. This supports the alternative covariation hypothesis.

Discussion

The results do not agree with the results of the attributional study of Himelstein, Graham and Weiner (1991). First, regarding the parenting and environment ratings, they found no main effects or interactions involving the domain. This means that parental beliefs did not vary across topics such as school performance, social skills or personality. In our study, however, the variability of beliefs is quite clear. The attributions of parents vary significantly across the different developmental domains of the child.

Second, our findings concerning the covariation hypothesis are different. In the study of Himelstein, Graham and Weiner (1991) parents with only one child did ascribe more influence to parenting than parents with more children. Parents with one child experienced a systematic relationship between their child-rearing behaviour (the condition) and how children finally turn out (the effect). We could not find empirical support for the covariation hypothesis based on the differences on the parenting scale. Although there seemed to be a trend, the differences between the means were not significant. Scores on the genetics scale in part two, however, differed significantly. The number of children proved to have an influence on parents' ideas, not regarding the importance of parenting, but regarding the perceived influence of genetics. This effect can easily be explained from attribution theory as well. This finding is related to the same covariation hypothesis. Parents with one child have different attributions from those with several children, because the latter are confronted daily with the fact that children are different. Parents with multiple children who experience differences between their children will relate those differences to an uncontrollable and variable influence, such as genetics.

Himelstein, Graham and Weiner (1991) noted in their discussion: 'Having more than one child increases the likelihood that parents might subscribe to a naive belief in the importance of genetics'. In their study, however, the effect of family size was not found to be significant, though they did find relatively higher attributions to genetics in multiple-children families. The evidence for the covariation hypothesis was based on scores on the parenting scale. In our study we found support for their statement.

In this study we focused on parents' attributions. A very interesting area of research is the focus on the relationship between beliefs and actualisation of beliefs into action (Sigel 1992). In this light a good question would be: some parents find genetics more important than others. What are the consequences for parental behaviour? Scarr and Dunn (1987) suggested that parents, who believe that children develop more or less by themselves, can relax and observe their children's development. More time and effort is demanded of parents when they think that intensive interaction and instruction is necessary for optimal development.

References

Bell, R.Q. (1979), 'Parent, child, and reciprocal influences', *American Psychologist*, 34, 10: 821-26.

CBS (1990), *Statistisch jaarboek 1990*. 's-Gravenhage.

Campbell, D.T., and Fiske, D.W. (1959), 'Convergent and discriminant validation by multitrait-multimethod matrix', *Psychological Bulletin*, 59, 2:81-105.

Dix, T.H. and Grusec, J.E. (1985), 'Parent attribution processes in the socialisation of children', in I.E. Sigel (ed.), *Parental Belief Systems: The Psychological Consequences for Children*, Hillsdale, NJ.

Gretarsson, S.J. and Gelfand, D.M. (1988), 'Mothers' attributions regarding their children's social behaviour and personality characteristics', *Developmental Psychology*, 24, 2: 264-69.

Goodnow, J.J., and Collins, W.A. (1990), *Development According to Parents. The Nature, Sources and Consequences of Parents' Ideas*, Hillsdale, NJ.

Heider, F. (1958), *The Psychology of Interpersonal Relations*, New York.

Himelstein, S., Graham, S. and Weiner, B. (1991), 'An attributional analysis of maternal beliefs about the importance of child-rearing practices', *Child Development*, 62, 2:301-10.

Kelley, H.H. (1967), 'Attribution in social psychology', in D. Levine (ed.), *Nebraska Symposium on Motivation*, Lincoln, Nebraska.

McGillicuddy-DeLisi, A.V. (1985), 'The relationship between parental beliefs and children's cognitive level', in I.E. Sigel (ed.), *Parental Belief Systems, the Psychological Consequences for Children*, Hillsdale, NJ.

Parke, R.D. (1978), 'Parent-infant interaction: Progress, paradigms, and problems', in G.P. Sackett (ed.), *Observing behaviour: Vol.1 Theory and Applications in Mental Retardation*, Baltimore.

Scarr, S. and Dunn, J. (1987), *Mother Care/Other Care. The Child-Care Dilemma for Women and Children*, London.

Sigel, I.E. (1985) (ed.), *Parental Belief Systems, the Psychological Consequences for Children*, Hillsdale, NJ.

Sigel, I.E. (1992), 'The belief-behaviour connection: a resolvable dilemma?', in I.E. Sigel, A.V. McGillicuddy-DeLisi, and J.J. Goodnow (eds), *Parental Belief Systems, the Psychological Consequences for Children*, Hillsdale, NJ.

Van der Stege, H.A. (1992), 'Waarom kinderen zijn, zoals ze zijn: ideeën van ouders', *Kind & Adolescent*, 13, 4:185-188.

Chapter 20

UNIVERSITY ENROLMENT IN THE NETHERLANDS 1815 TO 1935

Bibi van Wolput

Introduction

In this chapter I will describe the change in enrolment in higher education in the Netherlands during the period 1815 to 1935. This will be related to the transformation of the higher education system.

First I shall discuss the theory and the hypotheses of the research project of which this paper forms a part,[1] followed by a discussion of the data gathering process. Next I will describe the institutional transformation of the higher education system. Finally, the changes in enrolment will be presented and related to the development of the system of higher education. This will be done for:

1. Enrolment as a whole.
2. The differences in enrolment between the existing institutions of the time.
3. Female students.
4. The nobility.

1. This paper forms part of a research project investigating the social transformation of the higher education system in the Netherlands from 1815 until 1935.

Theory and Hypotheses

In other countries there is already quite a tradition in research on the transformation of higher education. The most important impulse came from F. Ringer's pioneering study, *Education and Society in Modern Europe* (1979), in which he investigates the different ways enrolment developed in higher education in Britain, France and Germany.

In 1983 another major work on this topic appeared, *The Transformation of Higher Learning 1860 - 1930*, edited by Konrad Jarausch. In this book the expansion, diversification, social accessibility and professionalisation of higher education in Britain, the United States, Germany and Russia is investigated. In his research Ringer introduces the important differentiation between inclusiveness, progressiveness and segmentation of education systems. Jarausch uses a slightly different terminology: expansion instead of inclusiveness and social accessibility instead of progressiveness. His diversification is not totally interchangeable with Ringer's segmentation.

My own research focuses on the influence of the institutional transformation[2] of the higher education system on the increase in the number of students (expansion) and the broadening of social recruitment (the social accessibility). The institutional diversification of the higher education system – as Jarausch termed the emergence of new types of higher learning which differ in prestige from the old traditional forms – is an important direct factor in accounting for expansion and increased social accessibility. According to Bourdieu's theory (1969, 1979, Rupp and de Lange 1989) on cultural capital, these new fields of learning and new institutions had less status than the traditional sciences and therefore recruited many more students from the middle and lower classes. So according to this theory the institutional development of higher learning had an effect not only on the number of students (absolute and relative), but also on the social background of students.

In addition to this there were, of course, many indirect factors affecting expansion and social accessibility, such as increasing demand for an educated workforce, a rising supply of pupils from secondary education as a result of population growth, economic growth and the growing level of prosperity, the situation on the labour market (unemployment), etc. All these factors are associated with modernisation in a general sense (Jarausch 1983). Other authors (Boli 1985, Meyer 1992) have stressed the importance of state formation processes, but they have looked mainly at primary and secondary education.

2. The sociologists Martin Trow (1962) and Clark Kerr (1973, 1991), stressed the importance of researching the institutional transformation of higher education, as they have done for the American situation.

Diversification as a concept is too general and needs to be specified. Two kinds of diversification are discernible, leading to the following hypotheses:

First of all there was the modernisation of the higher education system. As a result of the modernisation of society, new fields of learning arose and were added to the old ones. This could be within existing institutions or in new institutions. These new fields of science and these new institutions had lower status than the traditional ones and recruited many more students from the middle and lower classes, especially when the new subjects were taught in the new institutions. This led to further expansion and increasing social accessibility.

The second kind of diversification was denominational segregation. Institutions were founded on denominational grounds. It is thought that these universities would have recruited relatively more students from lower social backgrounds, as for them this was a way to emancipate themselves (van Kemenade 1968), especially while the elite of these denominated groups continued to go to the old universities. It is expected that the religious split increased expansion by attracting new groups to higher education and, in this way, also brought about an increase in social accessibility.

Before the start of the institutional transformation, we assume the system was highly elite and relatively closed to groups other than the upper classes. The expansion and opening up of the system as a whole would have remained stable. There would however, have been differences in social accessibility between the institutions and subjects.[3] The hypotheses under investigation can be summarised in the research model (Figure 20.1).

Figure 20.1 The Research Model

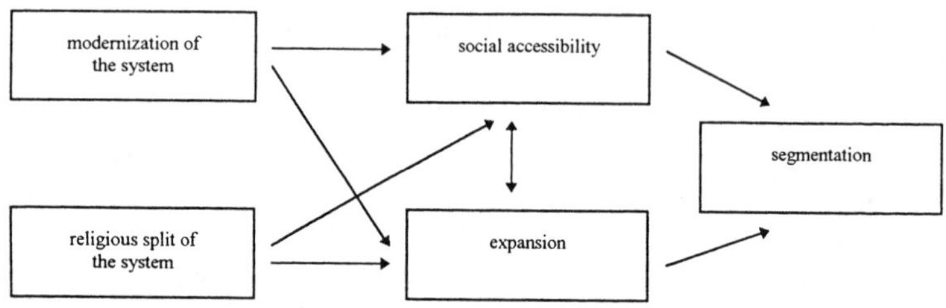

3. For example we expect to find a difference in the social composition of the student population between theology on one hand, and law and medicine on the other hand. The university of Leiden would have been even more elite than the other two universities of Utrecht and Groningen. The law faculty of Leiden would have been the most exclusive. In the Netherlands the law faculty at Leiden was the route to high political functions for the Dutch nobility (Frijhoff 1981). The faculty of theology was the route followed by middle and lower-class students (Wingelaar 1989).

In this chapter only one of the aspects investigated comes up for discussion. This is the expansion of the higher education system (in the Netherlands). Expansion (increase in enrolment) is measured by the proportion of the relevant age group (eighteen to twenty-five years of age) taking part in higher education.

The other two concepts (social accessibility and segmentation)[4] are not at issue here, although the hypotheses make predictions about social accessibility as well as expansion.[5]

Data

To investigate the social transformation of the higher education system, a large data set was created. Stratified samples of 750 students at a time were taken out of the registration lists of the institutions of higher education existing at the time, every ten years from 1815 until 1935. This created a database consisting of more than 10,000 students.

The following data were gathered: name of student, date of birth, place of birth, gender, university, faculty, first year of enrolment, final grade, year of graduation, father's occupation and religion. The social origins are indicated by father's occupation.

Most of the data mentioned were collected from the university archives, apart from father's occupation and religion, and for part of the data set, date of birth.

From 1910 onwards there are books in which genealogical trees of the most important Dutch families are published, there also is a series on the Dutch nobility. Those books were used initially to find the student's fathers. For the remaining students, the data needed was mainly collected from birth registers and registry offices.

4. Increased social accessibility (the broadening of social recruitment) is measured by the proportion of lower and middle-class students in higher education relative to the number of upper-class students. A relative increase (or decrease) in the number of students from lower and lower middle classes means that access to higher education has become more open (or closed).

Segmentation means the existence of separate tracks within the higher education system leading to particular occupations and social positions, based upon the social backgrounds of the students.

5. This is because expansion and social accessibility are interrelated. However, at this time the data is not yet ready to allow this part of the hypothesis to be investigated. Before investigating the social accessibility of higher education, it is worthwhile to look at the expansion of enrolment, without differentiating on the basis of social origins of the students. In theory, it is possible to find a broadening in social recruitment, without an increase in attendance at higher education. In reality however, this is not very likely to have happened.

The Institutional Transformation

During the period under research, Dutch higher education developed from a system consisting of three universities (called academies) and five faculties (or only three if you take the importance of the faculties into account), into the great mass of higher education of today, consisting of thirteen universities and over forty faculties, not taking into account all of the academies/vocational colleges. Two periods can be distinguished within the period under research.

The First Period, 1815 – 1876

This first period begins in 1815, the year in which the Kingdom of the Netherlands was proclaimed after the end of the French occupation. With this event a turbulent period of Dutch history came to an end (Schama 1977).

One of the first things the government did was design a plan for higher education which resulted in the 'Organic Law' *(het Organiek Besluit)* of 1815. This placed the existing universities under the central control of the government. However, this did not mean that a totally new situation emerged, in fact the existing situation was legalised (Groen 1987).

There were some changes however. Leiden regained its status of most important university, which meant more money and more professors (Otterspeer 1992).

The number of universities was reduced to three: Leiden, Utrecht and Groningen. The former universities of Franeker and Harderwijk lost their right to confer degrees and became athenea.[6] The athenea were not a big success, one after the other closed its doors.[7] The atheneum of Amsterdam was the only one which was successful and became a university in 1877.

Another major change concerned the faculties. Two faculties were added to the old ones of theology, medicine and law: language and philosophy and natural sciences and mathematics. Before being admitted to the faculty of medicine students had to pass an examination in the faculty of natural sciences. Theology and law students had to pass this examination in the faculty of language and philosophy. An examination in one of the two new faculties was a certificate to teach at the Latin schools.

During this period there were numerous discussions about the changes desirable in the higher education system. The discussions centred around the following questions (Gedenkboek Universiteit Groningen 1864):

6. These were institutions of higher education without the right to confer degrees. To graduate, their students had to go to one of the three universities.

7. First Harderwijk in 1818, then Franeker in 1843 and finally Deventer in 1876.

1. Are there too many universities? Should higher education be concentrated in fewer institutions?
2. Are there too many students? Should there be an entrance examination?
3. What is the place of scientific research at the universities?
4. What is the place of technical, business and agricultural education in the higher education system?
5. What is the position of religious minorities?

The Second Period: 1876-1935

The discussions mentioned above resulted in the First Law on Higher Education of 1876, which replaced the Organic Decree of 1815. This law, for its part, was not replaced until 1960, but by then it had been changed repeatedly.

With this law Leiden lost its position as the premier university, all universities were given equal status. The atheneum of Amsterdam was transformed into a university, along with Leiden, Utrecht and Groningen. From this point onwards the national system of higher education started to expand. Its aims were extended, and the number of institutions, faculties and grades increased. The higher education system was becoming modernised. The requirement of having passed an examination in the faculty of language and philosophy or natural sciences before being admitted to one of the other three faculties disappeared. These two faculties, which were mainly meant as training for teachers at the Latin schools, grew into fully fledged sciences after 1876. With this law, Latin was legally abolished as the academic language.

A new task for universities was scientific research. From 1876 onwards the Dutch government invested large amounts of money in founding laboratories for the natural sciences (Otterspeer 1992, Wachelder 1992, Oosterhoff 1987). The first change in the law occurred in 1905. The polytechnic school of Delft was upgraded to a technical academy and was raised to tertiary level.[8] It became an academy with the right to confer degrees. This also meant a decision was made about the place of technical education. It was placed in separate institutions. In 1913 a separate academy for economics was created, and in 1921 the University of Amsterdam was allowed to open an economics faculty. Later, in 1937, the other universities were given the same right. The same happened with agricultural education. In 1917 the agricultural school in Wageningen

8. Strangely enough, before 1905 it had belonged to secondary education.

was changed into an agricultural academy. The old difference between the universities (Hoogescholen) and the athenea was replaced by a new one: universities and academies (Frijhoff 1992).

The freedom to found schools on religious grounds was based on the constitution of 1848. In 1880 the first denominational university was founded, the Protestant University (VU). Until the change in the law of 1905, it had, like the athenea during the first period, no right to confer degrees. This was followed by the founding of the Roman Catholic University of Nijmegen in 1923 and the Roman Catholic Economic Academy of Tilburg in 1927.

In 1917 there was another change in the law. Pupils from the former Dutch High School (HBS) were formally allowed to study medicine and natural sciences. Previously, this had only been possible following grammar school education (gymnasium). The former Dutch High School was founded in 1863 as a final secondary school for the upper-middle classes (Goudswaard 1981,1986, Idenburg 1964, Boekholt and de Booy 1987). With dispensation from the minister, it had been possible to study medicine since the founding of this type of school, and since 1878 passing a matriculation had legally opened the way to university for those pupils. Almost from the beginning more than half of the pupils from the former Dutch High School went to university (Groen 1987, Idenburg 1964). Finally, in 1920 a new degree was introduced: the *doctorandus* which is so typical of Dutch higher education. This became the standard grade. Before 1876 the doctorate had been the standard, now there were the doctoranduses, the lawyers and the engineers.

Student Enrolments

Table 20.1 and figures 20.2 and 20.3 show the enrolments in higher education for the period 1815 to 1935, both absolute and relative.
As predicted by hypothesis 3 relative enrolment shows a stable pattern during the first period, at a level of about 0.35 percent of the relevant age group.[9] There are some fluctuations,[10] but smaller and temporary institutional changes account for these. The sharp increase in the period 1815 to 1835 was probably caused by the fact that theology students were exempted from paying lecture fees from 1820 until 1836.

9. The percentage of 18 to 25 year olds taking part in higher education.

10. This was probably the cause for the academic authorities' complaint about the number of students. In times of growth they complained there were too many students, in times of falling numbers they also complained.

Table 20.1 University Expansion 1815 to 1935.

Year	Total number of students	Number 18-24 years of age	Expansion in % of 18-25 year-olds	Total population of the Netherlands in millions
1815	767	244,400	0.31	2.2 (1815)
1825	1,511	309,184	0.49	2.86 (1830)
1835	1,712	364,769	0.47	2.86 (1840)
1845	1,288	385,459	0.33	3.06 (1849)
1855	1,406	429,885	0.33	3.31 (1859)
1865	1,325	414,054	0.32	3.58 (1869)
1875	1,681	450,187	0.37	4.01 (1879)
1885	1,974	534,189	0.37	4.51 (1889)
1895	2,847	633,909	0.45	5.10 (1899)
1905	4,392	673,993	0.65	5.54 (1905)
1915	5,069	857,589	0.59	6.43 (1915)
1925	9,438	943,091	1.00	7.42 (1925)
1935	12,628	1,041,185	1.21	8.48 (1935)

Figure 20.2 Expansion in Higher Education

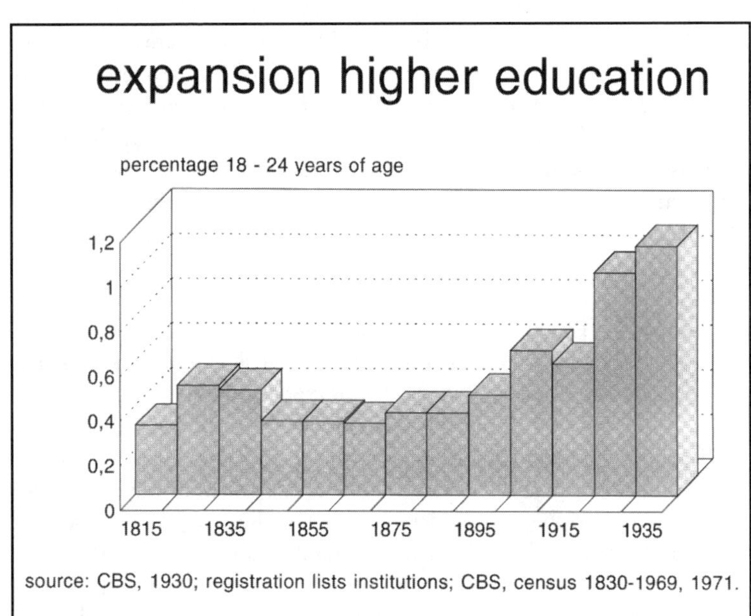

Figure 20.3 Number of Students in Higher Education

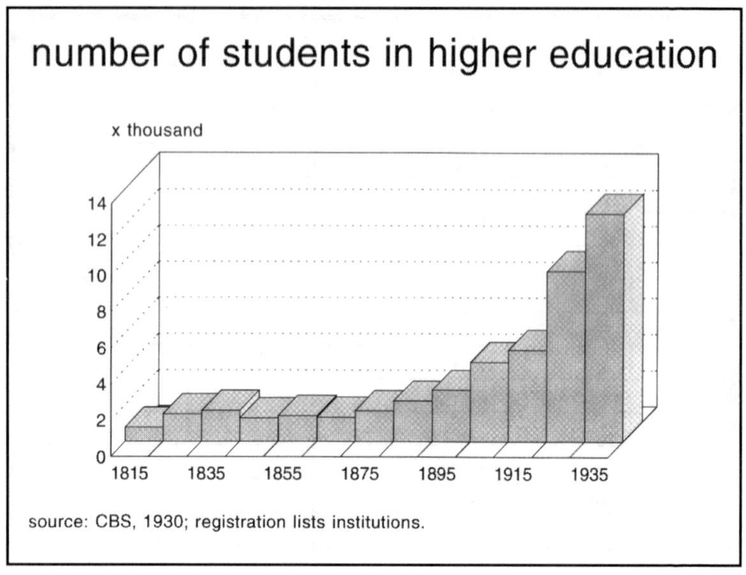

The decrease, both relative and absolute, in 1845 was caused by a change in access to the universities. In 1845 matriculation was introduced, because of complaints about the low level of the entrance examination and the inadequate education level of the students. Many students did not pass this examination. At the same time scholarships were abolished due to economic considerations, these measures led to the decrease in enrolments. In 1853 the situation was as it had been before 1845, and the regulations were abolished. Strangely enough this had no effect on relative enrolments, although the absolute number did increase. (CBS 1930, Groen 1987, Wingelaar 1989).

Hypotheses 1 and 2 predicted an increase in expansion at the start of diversification. The foundation of the former Dutch High School in 1863, mentioned above, can be seen as the first change which resulted from the modernising of the system (hypothesis 2). It affected the expansion in two ways, in the first place it meant an enlargement of career possibilities in the field of secondary education. This made the faculties of natural sciences, and language and philosophy more attractive. Secondly, the broadening of access to the universities by admitting those pupils increased the number of students. Table 20.1, and figures 20.2 and 20.3 show that from 1865 onwards there was an increase in the number of students (both relative and absolute). After 1885 enrolments increased more and more, due to increased opportunities to follow higher education, which have been outlined. This clearly shows that the institutional transformation had a direct effect on the enrolment.

Differences Between Institutions

Looking at the separate institutions, the overall increase in enrolments after 1865 resulted in very different patterns of enrolment by institution. Figure 20.4 shows the relative positions of the five largest institutions during the research period.

Figure 20.4 Number of Students per University

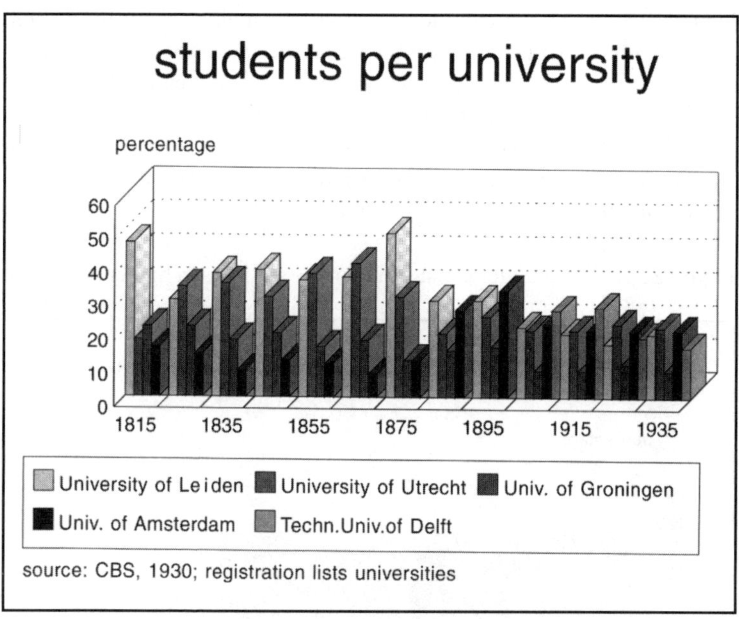

Until about 1885 Leiden almost consistently had the greatest absolute and relative number of students. This was probably due to the fact that Leiden was the premier university and because of this had more money, more professors (who earned more) better facilities and so on. In 1885 its relative share decreased drastically, due to the equalisation of the universities in 1876. In 1875 49 percent of the students were still attending the University of Leiden, by 1885 this had decreased to 29 percent. By the end of the period of research, Utrecht, Leiden and Amsterdam had reached the same level, both relatively and absolutely.

After Amsterdam had become a university, in 1877, its absolute number of students more than tripled and its relative number more than doubled, while at the same time the number of students at Leiden and Utrecht decreased relatively and absolutely. The technical academy of Delft showed remarkable growth in 1905, the year in which it was recognised officially as a higher education institution. The number of students more than tripled, and it suddenly accounted for a quarter of the students in higher education. Clearly, the institutional transformation had different effects on enrolment at the various institutions.

Female Students

Figure 20.5 gives the distribution of female and male students in the sample. In 1874 the first female student entered the University of Groningen.[11] Afterwards the number of female students slowly increased. In the next sample year, 1885, they formed 0.9 percent of the student population. By 1895 this number had increased to 1.9 percent, distributed over the four large universities. By 1905 it had grown to 8.4 percent, to reach about 15 percent in 1915, 1925 and 1935.

Figure 20.5 Percentage of male and female students in higher education

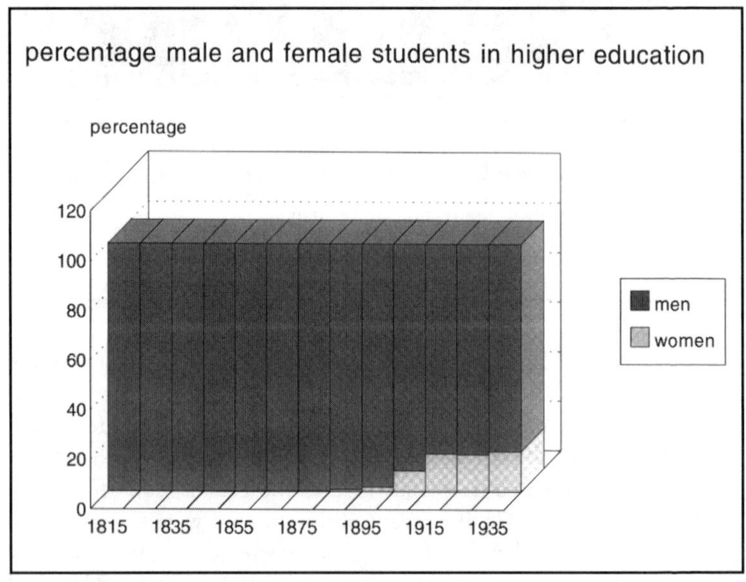

11. Aletta Jacobs, famous in the Netherlands for being the first female university student.

Nobility

Finally, I would like to say something about the students' backgrounds, based on the number of fathers who can be traced in the books on the Dutch nobility and patricians, which I mentioned earlier. Of the total sample, 23 percent were found in these books, 3.4 percent in the nobility series and 19.6 percent in the patricians series. Figure 20.6 shows the distributions by sample year. According to hypotheses 1 and 2 the expectation is that when diversification gets underway, higher education becomes more socially accessible. As can be seen in figure 20.6, after about 1875 the percentage of fathers found in both series decreases. It goes down from 31.2 to 20.3 percent. This coincides almost exactly with the expansion.

This might serve as an indication that, from that time, the higher education system not only expanded but also became more socially accessible.[12]

Table 20.6 Dutch Nobility and Patricians

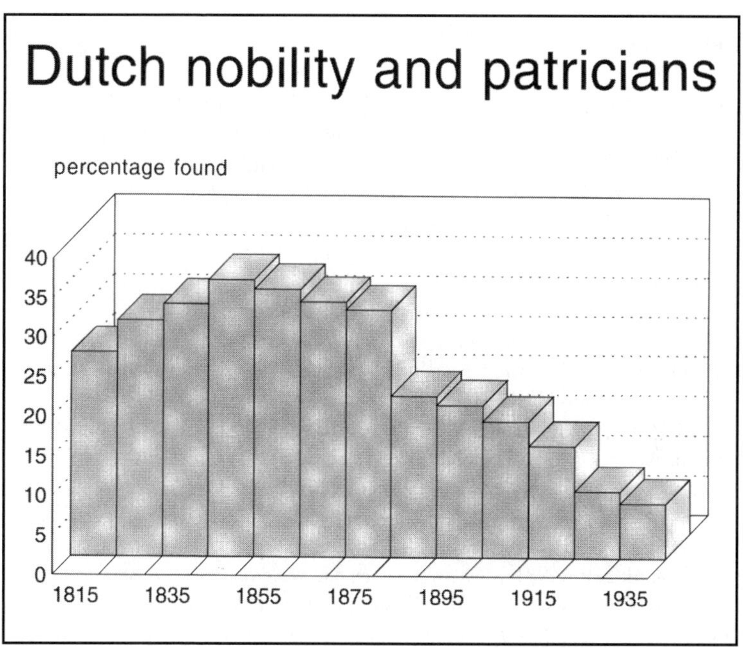

12. Research (among others Ringer 1979, 1992, Jarausch 1983, Muller et al. 1987, Kaelble 1985, van Lente et al. 1993) shows that in the second half of the last century a change took place in the social composition of the student population in favour of the middle classes. Jarausch talks about 'the emergence of the middle-class university'.

Conclusion

The aim of this chapter was to describe the expansion of enrolment in higher education and to relate it to the development of the higher education system (institutional diversification).

The diversification hypothesis seems to be supported. The data shows that from 1865 the enrolments started to increase. The pattern of expansion indicates when the social transformation may have started. So after 1865 the whole system of higher education can be expected to have started to open up socially. The results from the investigation into the number of students from noble families also point in the same direction.

References

Boekholt, P.T.F.M. and E.P. de Booy (1987), *Geschiedenis van de school in Nederland vanaf de Middeleeuwen tot de huidige tijd,* Assen/Maastricht.

Boli, J., F.O. Ramirez and J. W. Meyer (1985), 'Explaining the Origins and Expansion of Mass education', *Comparative Education Review*, 29, 1:145-70.

Bourdieu, P., (1979), *La distinction*, Paris.

Bourdieu, P., and A. Darbel (1969), *L'amour de l'art: les musées d'art européens et leur public*, Paris.

Bourdieu, P., and J.-C. Passeron (1970), *La reproduction*, Paris.

CBS, (1930), *Statistiek van het hooger onderwijs*, Den Haag.

CBS, (1971), *Bevolking van Nederland naar geslacht, leeftijd en burgerlijke staat 1830-1969*, Den Haag.

Frijhoff, W.T.F., (1981), *La société Néerlandaise et ses gradués 575-1814,* Amsterdam.

Frijhoff, W.T.F., (1992), 'The Netherlands', in R. Burton et al. (eds), *The Encyclopedia of Higher Education*, vol. I, Oxford.

Gedenkboek ter gelegenheid van het vijfde halve eeuws feest van de Universiteit van Groningen, (1864), Groningen.

Goudswaard, N.B. (1981), *Vijfenzestig jaren nijverheidsonderwijs*, Assen.

Goudswaard, N.B. (1986), *Agrarisch onderwijs in Nederland*, Culemborg.

Groen, M., (1987-1989), *Het wetenschappelijk onderwijs in Nederland van 1815 tot 1980: een onderwijskundig overzicht*, Eindhoven.

Idenburg, P.J., (1964), *Schets van het Nederlandse schoolwezen*, Groningen.

Jarausch, K.H. (1983) (ed.), *The Transformation of Higher Learning 1860-1930*, Chicago.

Kaelble, H., (1983), *Sociale Mobilität und Changengleichheit im 19. und 20. Jahrhundert*, Göttingen.

Kaelble, H., (1985), *Social Mobility in the Nineteenth and Twentieth Centuries: Europe and America in Comparative Perspective*, Leamington Spa/ Heidelberg/Dover.

Kemenade, van J.A. (1968), *De katholieken en hun onderwijs*, Meppel.

Kemenade, van J.A., (1981), 'Levenbeschouwelijke verscheidenheid', in J.A. van Kemenade (ed.), *Onderwijs: Bestel en beleid*, Groningen.

Kerr, C. (1973), *The Uses of the University*, Cambridge Mass.

Kerr, C. (1991), *The Great Transformation in Higher Education, 1960-1980*, Albany.

Kruyt, H.R. (1931), *Hoogeschool en Maatschappij*, Amsterdam.

Lente van R., K. Mandemakers, and R. Rottier (1993), *De sociale achtergronden van studenten aan de hogere technische opleidingen te Delft 1842-1940*, Rotterdam.

Meyer, J. W., F. O. Ramirez and Y. Nuhoglu Soysal (1992), 'World Expansion of Mass Education, 1870-1980', *Sociology of Education*, 65:128-49.

Muller, D., F.Ringer and B.Simon (1987), *The Rise of the Modern Educational System: Structural Changes and Social Reproduction*, Cambridge.

Oosterhoff, J.L. (1987), 'Enkele kanttekeningen bij de studie naar natuurkundige laboratoria in Nederland in de tweede helft van de negentiende eeuw', in *Batavia Academica*, V, no. 2.

Otterspeer, W. (1992), *De wiekslag van hun geest. De Leidse universiteit in de negentiende eeuw*, Den Haag/Haarlem.

Ringer, F. K. (1979), *Education and Society in Modern Europe*, London.

Ringer, F.K. (1992), *Fields of Knowledge: French Academic Culture in Comparative Perspective, 1890-1920*, Cambridge/Paris.

Rupp, J.C.C. and R. de Lange (1989), 'Social Order, Cultural Capital and Citizenship. An essay concerning educational status and educational power versus comprehensiveness of elementary schools', *The Sociological Review*, vol. 37, no. 4:668-705.

Rupp, J.C.C. (1991) , 'Citizenship, education and the nation-state. The inclusiveness of the educational systems in the United States and the Netherlands', in B. Rang and Jan C.C.Rupp (eds) *The Cultural Change of Citizenship*, Utrecht.

Rupp, J.C.C., (1992), 'Politieke sociologie van onderwijsdeelname en nationale curricula', in P. Dykstra, P. Kooy and J. Rupp (eds), *Onderwijs in de tijd. Ontwikkelingen in onderwijsdeelname en nationale curriculs*, Amsterdam.

Schama, S. (1977), *Patriots and Liberators. Revolution in the Netherlands 1780-1813*, London.

Trow, M. (1962), 'The Democratization of Higher Education in America', *European Journal of Sociology*, vol. III, 231-62.

Wachelder, J.C.M (1992), *Universiteit tussen vorming en opleiding*, Hilversum Verloren.

Wingelaar, K. (1989) , *Studeren in Utrecht in de Negentiende Eeuw*, Utrecht.

Chapter 21

THE INFLUENCE OF SCHOOLING ON THE PROFESSIONAL CAREERS OF WOMEN AND MEN BORN IN TWENTE IN THE LATE 1950s

Lisette Bros

Introduction

Since the last decade the participation of women in the labour market has increased throughout the European Community. In the Netherlands, in particular, more and more women have been entering the labour force: 35 percent in 1983 and 45 percent in 1993.[1] In the Dutch region of Twente 36 percent of women had paid jobs in 1993 compared to 31 percent in 1987.[2] Despite this increased participation the majority of Dutch women have low-status and low-income jobs (De Bruijn 1989). This might be due to the fact that most of them have part-time jobs. Another more plausible reason for women having low-status and low-income jobs might be the key value of education in their lives. Educational attainment may differ for men and women and, consequently, so may their prospects of reaching a favourable position on the labour market i.e., their intragenerational mobility.

1. See Ophuysen (1994).

2. In 1992 the net participation of women in Twente was 38 percent. In the Netherlands the net participation of women increased from 35 percent in 1987 to 41 percent in 1992 and 42 percent in 1993.

However, the structure of the labour market itself could also be one of the causes of the unequal 'labour market' opportunities for women and men. It is obvious that the labour market is differentiated into various segments. Each segment has its own internal developments i.e., provides specific possibilities for certain careers (Glebbeek 1993). In addition to the segmentation of the labour market, we have to mention the existence of different labour sectors and occupational groups which are unequally occupied by the two genders. This is known to be the essence of the sex-segregated labour market: the so-called 'male and female' labour market. In the Netherlands sex segregation has not lessened, despite the growing participation of women on the labour market (Blees-Booij 1994). Although the exclusion of both women and men from certain branches and jobs is diminishing somewhat (Faber 1994), their labour market participation and intragenerational mobility might still be mediated through that.

The aim of this chapter is to examine the interrelationship between gender differences in educational attainment and professional careers, and to formulate a new hypothesis on gender-biased careers and sex segregation on the labour market.

Research Questions

Gender differences in school careers

The first group of research questions refers to gender differences in educational attainment. Educational attainment is an indicator of the 'human capital' with which one enters the labour market. This key to the labour market may differ for men and women.

Normally, educational attainment is operationalised as educational level. It might be more convenient to say that educational attainment comprises two interrelated elements: educational level and educational sector. Educational sectors are defined either by the chosen set of examination subjects, dominated by language skills for instance, or by the type of school, for example, technical schools or domestic science schools. Although (in the Netherlands) different educational sectors can officially lead to the same educational level, they offer unequal qualifications and, as a consequence, unequal opportunities on the labour market. That is to say that the key value of education may differ for men and women because of both educational level and educational sector.

Broadly speaking, there is enough evidence that gender-specific inequality in educational attainment has disappeared in the Netherlands, if judged only by educational level (Dronkers 1991). So, the *first* question is whether this is also true for the population under investigation: a school generation, which for the most part grew up in the Dutch region of Twente. The *second* question is whether these men and women left school with identical qualifications judged by educational sector. If not, then so-called vertical inequality (by level) has been replaced by horizontal inequality (by sector). In other words, the central issue is whether the key value of education is, in all its aspects, one and the same for men and women.

Gender differences in professional careers

After analysing gender differences in the outcomes of educational careers, it is a logical step to move on to the question of gender-biased careers. The first *hypothesis* is that a person's present job position reflects that person's educational attainment. One must first ask the question: 'Do women have "lower-status and lower-income" jobs compared to men?' And if so, to what extent can this be explained by the fact of having a part-time job and by educational attainment i.e., educational level? The next question is whether and to what extent educational attainment actually is a 'key-value' for entering the labour market, and if so, is its effect different for men and women?

The relationship between educational and professional careers, which is of great interest nowadays, is usually only examined by looking at the correlation of educational level with realised (present) occupational status. Less attention has been given to developments in the professional career which might result from both educational level and educational sector. Glebbeek (1993) found that educational level keeps having a strong direct and indirect effect throughout a person's professional career. This means that it is not only a key to entering the labour market, but that it is also 'the' starting point of a professional career which may be the determining factor for one's career. So, the *second* question we are addressing here is whether educational level functions only as 'starting capital', or whether it also has an effect in the long term on successive occupational attainments i.e., intragenerational mobility. And if there are any gender differences in educational level, this must be differentially true for men and women.

Still, these results cannot provide a full explanation of supposed gender-biased careers. The effect of educational sector on developments in professional careers has been overlooked. Bakker (1987) found that this aspect is significant for a person's job opportunities.

As I stated in the introduction, the labour market is differentiated into various segments, each of them offering its own possibilities for certain careers. Thus there are different labour sectors and occupational groups, that are unequally occupied by the two genders. I intend to look into whether this holds true for the men and women of our school generation i.e., whether gender is a structuring factor in their actual participation in the various labour sectors and occupational groups in the labour market. The *third* question of our research is whether there is enough evidence to sustain the hypothesis that a sex-segregated labour market really exists.

Data And Preliminary Findings

The data set in this research comprises a school generation, a cohort, born in the Dutch region of Twente at the end of the 1950s, that entered primary school from 1964 to 1965 (for the most part in the city of Enschede) (Bros 1994). While this generation was at primary school (1964 to 1970), data was collected about their school performance, their socio-economic backgrounds, etc. Recently, new data was collected about their period at secondary school (and high school), their entry into the labour market, their professional careers up until November 1992 and about their family life. The result is a longitudinal data set of the lives of 1,123 adults: the Enschede cohort.

To answer the research questions only some of the data is relevant, starting with the pupils' 'gender' and 'socio-economic background'. Three variables were used as indicators for socio-economic background: the occupational status of the father in 1964 and the educational level of both father and mother.

The second group of data is related to school career: firstly, an IQ score (at the age of six) based on the Primary Mental Ability 5-7 test (PMA) of Thurstone and Thurstone (1954); and secondly, an indicator for educational attainment, the so-called SOI code based on the Netherlands Standard Classification of Education (CBS 1989). This code consists of five digits; the first of which relates to educational level, and the next two to educational sector. When a pupil successfully passed an exam, a code was given. This code is the outcome of his/her school career in the regular full-time education system.[3]

Finally, the data concerning income, 'part-time or full-time' job and professional careers were used. Income refers to the individual's net

3. Due to the 1968 Secondary Education Act in the Netherlands one can go through the education system by following different paths, for example junior general secondary education (MAVO) followed by senior secondary commercial education (MEAO) and by higher tradespeople's education (HMO). In all cases the SOI-code refers to the last school rounded off with a diploma.

income over the last twelve months, whether or not obtained by paid labour. The career data is based on the descriptions of their professions given by the former pupils in the questionnaire. A code, taken from the 1984 Netherlands Standard Classification of Occupations (CBS 1984) was assigned to each profession. This CBS-84 code contains four digits, of which the first refers to the labour sector, and the first and second digit together refer to the occupational group. After a verification of the codes 'over time' a person's professional career was generated as a sequence. Then, a prestige score – U-score – based on the hierarchical classification of Sixma and Ultee (1983) was determined for each profession.[4]

Not all of the data on the 1,123 cohort-pupils was used here. In view of the nature of the research questions, the population was restricted to those pupils who currently have a position on the labour market i.e., a paid job at the time when the new data was collected (November 1992). Moreover, in order to be able to accurately trace the effect of educational attainment and prevent any misunderstandings caused by unemployment for instance, only the data of those who entered the labour market directly (within six months) after leaving full-time education were included in this study. Out of the whole Enschede cohort, 88 percent made their transition from school to work within six months and 77 percent have a paid job at the present time (part-time or full-time). The two criteria taken together account for 65 percent of the cohort and result in a research population of 724 former pupils.

The selection of this population led to some important gender differences. First, the subpopulation of women (41 percent) is smaller than that of men (59 percent), due to the exclusion of women (and some men) who are occupied full-time with 'housekeeping'.[5] Therefore the women involved in our research have professional careers comparable to those of the men. This similarity is very significant to the research question. Secondly, gender was related to having a part-time or full-time job. Out of the research population 67 percent have full-time and 33 percent part-time jobs with minimally eight and maximally 36 working hours. The correlation between gender and part-time or full-time job is –0.71. Thus not everyone with a part-time job is female. Furthermore 66 percent of the research population live in Twente, of which 62 percent are male and 38 percent female.[6] If these figures are compared with the labour

4. For further, and more detailed information regarding the Enschede cohort, see Bros (1994).

5. The cohort consists of 50 percent male and 50 percent female former pupils. At present, about 30 percent of these women are occupied with housekeeping.

6. Also 67 percent of the cohort lives in Twente. There is no significant correlation between living in Twente and belonging to the research population.

participation in Twente in 1992 we find a coincidental resemblance. One reason for this is the significant link between gender and living in Twente, i.e., out of the whole population, most working men live in Twente. Finally, there is a significant correlation for the men between direct transition and having a job in November 1992.[7] The women's present labour market position is not dependent on direct transition.

Results: School Career

Gender differences in school careers: the vertical dimension

To answer the first question concerning gender differences in *educational level*, the results of former analyses, with some data from the Enschede cohort, might be sufficient. Bros and Dronkers (1994) found that working women leave school with a lower level of educational attainment than men (same IQ scores). So, there seems to be enough evidence that gender differences in educational level are still present in our generation.

After the research population had been reduced to those former pupils who not only have a job but who also made the transition from school to work within six months, gender differences in educational level were examined once more. To estimate the effects of gender, multivariate regression analysis with paired deletion was applied (see Table 21.1). The base-line model (Model A) includes gender, the three indicators for socio-economic background and educational level (the first digit of the SOI code). Table 21.1 shows that gender has no effect on educational level.[8] Then the IQ score was added to the analysis because it could provide insight into the effect of schooling (Model B). Now, 24 percent of the educational level is accounted for by three factors: the occupational status and educational level of the father, the IQ score itself and gender. So, the answer to our first question is that, in contrast with Dronkers' findings (1991), women who entered primary school in Twente still finished school on a lower educational level compared to men (same IQ scores) i.e., the vertical inequality has not disappeared. The gender effect is –0.09.

Gender differences in school careers: the horizontal dimension

The school generation left primary school in the sixth month of 1970 and then for the most part entered secondary schools. Two paths are available

7. For the cohort this corresponds with gender differences in direct transition and having a paid job.

8. These results differ for the whole cohort, where 19 percent of the educational level is explained by all the independent variables with a negative coefficient for gender (–0.11).

Table 21.1 Beta Coefficients (N = 724, missing paired)

Independent Variables	Model A	Model B	Model C	Model D	Model E	Model F	Model G
Gender	-0.07	-0.09*	0.09*	-0.16*	-0.57*	-0.06	-0.25*
Occupational status father	0.16*	0.11*	0.17*	0.07	0.06	0.07	0.04
Educational level father	0.21*	0.18*	-0.06	0.05	-0.01	0.05	0.01
Educational level mother	0.09	0.04	0.07	0.01	-0.00	0.00	-0.01
IQ-score		0.32*	0.11*	0.10*	0.03	0.10*	0.03
Educational level			0.49*	0.22*	0.18*	0.21*	0.18*
Occupational status 1				0.34*	0.00	0.35*	0.04
Occupational status present					0.24*		0.19*
Part-time or full-time job						0.14*	0.48*
Adjusted R-square	0.16	0.24	0.38	0.38	0.54	0.39	0.65

Model	Dependent variable
A:	Educational level
B:	Educational level with IQ-score
C:	First occupational status
D:	Present occupational status
E:	Income
F:	Present occupational status with part-time or full-time job
G:	Income with part-time or full-time job

in secondary education: vocational and general education. Vocational education (i.e., junior secondary vocational education) consists of various sectors like technical schools, schools of economics and domestic science schools. General education is differentiated by level (junior or senior general education and pre-university education) and by the chosen set of course options (dominated by language skills, science subjects or economics and social sciences). After leaving secondary education and having obtained all the necessary qualifications one could enter higher education. Here again a differentiation in vocational and general education exists i.e., there is senior secondary and higher vocational education for various sectors and university education with different course options or examination subjects.

Depending on the path followed through the Dutch education system and the diplomas obtained, every former pupil was given a SOI code. To answer our second question on gender differences in school careers, the second and third digit of this code were used. They refer to the horizontal dimension of education i.e., *educational sector*. Because the ‘sector’ variable is a nominal scale, it is impossible to use multivariate regression analysis. Therefore, cross tabulation was used to answer our second question.

The results show the existence of gender differences in participation in various educational sectors (see Table 21.2).

Table 21.2 Gender Differences in Educational Sectors (in %)

Sector	Male	Female	Total
General education	54	46	35
i.e.,			
- primary school & drop-out	53	47	15
- secondary school:			
* language	39	61	10
* science	78	22	4
* others[1]	63	37	7
Vocational education	63	37	65
i.e.,			
- teachers	31	69	7
- technical	99	1	21
- medical	37	63	7
- economics	70	30	9
- social service	10	90	8
- others[2]	62	38	13

Notes:

1. In these cases the chosen set of course options is either not explicit enough, or unknown.
2. The total participation in the remaining sectors is less than 7 percent.

Of former pupils who attended only general secondary education, for men science subjects are dominant in their chosen set of examination subjects, and for women language subjects are dominant. In the vocational education sector: as teachers, women mostly qualify for primary school; in the medical sector they qualify as nurses and laboratory assistants; in the field of social services they have general qualifications and specialise as domestic staff, child-care workers and geriatric helpers. The vocational qualifications obtained by men are rather different: in the technical sector they have general qualifications or mainly qualify as electrical engineers; in the field of economics they do business and commercial studies or they qualify in the retail trade. Women who qualify in the economic sector mostly do (business) administration. These gender differences are significant (Pearson Chisq $(15)=221.84$, $p < 0.05$).

Gender differences in educational attainment

The central issue is whether the key value of education is, in all its aspects, the same for the men and women that entered primary school in Twente. The analysis of both the vertical and horizontal dimension shows that this is true. Compared to men, women finished day-time education not only at a significantly lower level but also with rather different qualifications. So, vertical inequality has not disappeared, neither has it been replaced by an horizontal gender inequality.

Results: Professional Career

Gender differences in present labour market position

The second group of questions concerns the issue of gender-biased careers. The first question is whether women actually have 'low-status and low-income' jobs compared to men. Bros and Dronkers' study (1994) might have been able to answer this question. However, in this study gender differences were once again examined using multivariate regression analysis (paired deletion). The former Model B was adapted by adding educational level, first and present occupational status (Model D) and then income (Model E) (see Table 21.1). The results point in the same direction i.e., women do have low-status and low-income jobs.

The question is to what extent this can be explained by the fact of having a part-time job and by educational level. The correlation between gender and part-time or full-time job is rather high. The same is true for the correlation gender and income (-0.61). Furthermore, the analysis of gender differences in school careers shows that on average women leave school with a lower level of attainment than men. So, to get an overall picture of the effect of part-time job and of educational level on present occupational status and income separately, the variable 'part-time or full-time' was added (Model F and Model G) (see Table 21.1).[9] To answer our *first* question, only the total effect of each of the variables matters, that have been determined by using path analysis (see Table 21.3).

The effect of educational level on present occupational status is more powerful than its effect on income.[10] For the part-time job variable the results are the opposite. This means that income is best explained by the

9. The variable is coded 0 for part-time and 1 for full-time.

10. Because it might be more appropriate to differentiate according to 'working hours' in one unpublished analysis the 'part-time' variable was replaced by working hours. The total effect of working hours on present occupational status is 0.19 and on income 0.56. So, there are no striking differences.

'type' of job, and present occupational status by educational level. So, there is some evidence that our first hypothesis must be rejected. The current occupational position of women ('low-status and low-income') is not due to existing vertical inequality in educational level nor to the outcome of part-time jobs, but is a consequence of both![11]

Table 21.3 Total Effect of Educational Level and 'Part-Time or Full-Time' Job on Occupational Status and Income

Independent variables	Occupational status	Income
Educational level	0.41	0.30
Part-time or full-time	0.14	0.51

Gender differences in 'starting capital'

After leaving school if a person is lucky within some months he/she enters the labour market i.e., manages to get a job. Our second question (concerning gender-biased careers) is to what extent this can be explained by the level at which one left education. And if so, is there any long-term effect i.e., on career over time and on the current position on the labour market?

To estimate whether educational level is just a 'starting capital' or whether it has an effect in the long term, the multivariate regression with paired deletion of missing values was again applied. The baseline model (Model H) includes educational level and the data on professional careers i.e., the prestige scores for each profession in the sequence.[12] Since the issue concerns gender-biased careers, gender was added next (Model I).

Before analysing the long-term effect of educational level on careers i.e., intragenerational mobility, it might be appropriate to compare the total educational effect on the first job and on current occupational status. If there is no variation, the suggested analyses are pointless. Here, the

11. The question of whether occupational status can be explained by the variable 'part-time or full-time' remains open. If this is not is not investigated, only a total effect of 0.48 on income will be left.

12. The three indicators for socio-economic background were omitted, because they have no direct effect on the present occupational status (see Table 21.1, Model D and Model F). Also the IQ-score was left out. In an unpublished analysis the IQ-score was added because of its significance for the explanation of educational level (see Table 21.1, Model B). However, in the long term it only affects the first occupational status (0.15) and for that reason the IQ-score was not added here.

results of another earlier analysis might be sufficient. Bros and van Bergen (1994) found that in the long term, educational level is becoming less significant for the attainment of a certain occupational status. We found similar results in our population. The total effect declines from 0.49 (first occupational status) to 0.39 (present occupational status), and referring to one's present status roughly half of the effect is indirect.[13] So, there is enough evidence that educational level retains some influence and does not only function as 'starting capital'.[14] To analyse the fluctuations in the effect of educational level on successive occupational attainments, only its direct effect on every new profession in the sequence is significant.

Most of the former pupils who made their transition from school to work within six months did have a professional career in November 1992, with an average of 3.4 different jobs. As only four of them accounted for the maximum number of jobs i.e., nine, the ninth profession was left out of the analysis. The results show that educational level has the greatest influence on the first occupational status. Then, its direct effect declines slowly (until the sixth profession) being mostly superseded in importance by the successive professions (see Table 21.4a). Therefore, the answer to our *second* question is that educational level keeps having a direct (and indirect) effect throughout a professional career and counts for more than just 'starting capital'. In addition, because gender differences in educational level were found, this should be different for men and women. However, the results of the second analysis where gender was added, only differs in two cases: the third and fourth professions (see Table 21.4b).

Table 21.4A Beta Coefficients Model H (N = 724, missing paired)

Dependent Variables Independent variables	U1	U2	U3	U4	U5	U6	U7	U8
Educ. level	0.58	0.28	0.24	0.24	0.17	0.24	ns	ns
U1		0.50	0.31	0.15	ns	ns	ns	ns
U2			0.32	ns	ns	ns	-0.37	0.45
U3				0.36	0.23	ns	ns	ns
U4					0.43	ns	0.38	ns
U5						0.42	ns	0.53
U6							0.40	ns
U7								0.68
Adjusted R2	0.33	0.49	0.55	0.48	0.53	0.46	0.61	0.50

13. See Table 21.1: Model C, first occupational status and Model D, present occupational status.

14. For the total population (N=1123) 38 percent of the variation in the first occupational status is explained by a total effect of 0.49 and 38 percent of the variation in the actual status by 0.39. The indirect effect of the educational level is 0.18.

Table 21.4b Beta Coefficients Model I (N = 724, missing paired)

Dependent Variables Independent variables	U1	U2	U3	U4	U5	U6	U7	U8
Gender	0.10	ns	ns	-0.11	ns	ns	0.19	ns
Educ. level	0.58	0.28	0.25	0.23	0.17	0.24	ns	ns
U1		0.50	0.29	0.17	ns	ns	ns	ns
U2			0.32	ns	ns	ns	-0.35	0.42
U3				0.37	0.25	ns	ns	ns
U4					0.41	ns	0.41	ns
U5						0.42	ns	0.57
U6							0.38	ns
U7								0.56
Adjusted R2	0.34	0.49	0.56	0.49	0.53	0.46	0.65	0.54

As these results are so remarkable, and assuming that gender is important in the development of a professional career,[15] the analysis based on Model H was repeated for men and women separately. As there are few women with more than seven jobs, professions number 7 to 9 were left out of the analysis (see Table 21.5). The results show that for men educational level retains its influence on their successive professions. For women its direct effect disappears after the third profession.

Table 21.5 Beta Coefficients Model H: for Male (N = 430) and Female (N = 294) separately (missing paired)

Dependent Variables Independent variables	U1		U2		U3		U4		U5		U6	
	M	F	M	F	M	F	M	F	M	F	M	F
Educ. level	0.60	055	0.24	0.34	0.30	0.15	0.26	ns	0.22	ns	0.30	ns
U1			0.53	0.45	0.30	0.28	ns	ns	ns	0.30	ns	ns
U2					0.27	0.43	ns	ns	ns	ns	ns	ns
U3							0.34	0.40	0.33	ns	ns	ns
U4									0.42	0.38	ns	ns
U5										0.56	ns	
Adjusted R2	0.36	0.30	0.49	0.48	0.56	0.54	0.49	0.48	0.57	0.50	0.55	0.25

As it can be misleading to establish different effects for men and women just by eye, interaction variables between gender and educational level were added to Model H. The results of this (unpublished) analysis support the assumed gender differences in the long-term effect of education. Referring to the first occupational status the interaction

15. Bros and Van Bergen (1994) found a significant gender effect (–0.14) on the development of professional careers.

variable is significantly positive for women. For profession number 4 the interaction variable is once again significant, but negative for women. This means that although women leave school at a lower level than men, they are not disadvantaged by it and manage to get a good position when they first enter the labour market. In the long term, the opposite can be observed i.e., women leave school with less favourable diplomas and this affects their professional careers. Their diplomas are no longer significant. So, maybe educational level is a determinant only for women's careers.

Gender differences in segments

The third question refers to the problem of the sex-segregated labour market. The labour market is differentiated into various segments, each of them offering its own career possibilities. In addition, it has generally been assumed that there are gender-biased labour sectors and occupational groups. The question at issue is whether this assumption is true and whether gender is a structuring factor in the present labour market position of the men and women of our school generation.

To establish whether sex segregation exists, a definition needs to be made of labour sectors and occupational groups which can be classified as gender biased. The method used by Faber (1994) was followed, 1987 was chosen as the base year and 1992 was chosen as the reference year. In 1987 in the Netherlands the net labour market participation of women was 35 percent and in 1992 it was 41 percent. Labour sectors and occupational groups were classified as 'female' if more than 70 percent of its participants were women and 'male' if women accounted for less than 12 percent. Otherwise labour sectors and occupational groups are not gender-biased i.e., they are 'proportional'.[16]

As our question refers to the present position on the labour market, gender differences in the labour sector were analysed by using the first CBS-84 digit of the present profession. For occupational groups, both the first and second digit were taken. As the 'sector' variable is a nominal scale, the question was answered by cross tabulation.

The results show the existence of gender differences in the participation in various labour sectors (see Table 21.6).

Although gender differences are significant (Pearson Chisq (6) = 107.59, $p < .05$), according to our definition only two sectors are gender-biased i.e., the agricultural sector and the industrial sector.

16. The next formula was applied: 'female' > 41 % + [% 1992 – % 1987] and 'male' < 41% -[% 1992 – % 1987].

Table 21.6 Gender Differences in Labour Sectors (in %)

Sector	Male	Female	Total
1 Scientists and other specialists	49	51	35
2 Policymakers and executives	77	23	6
3 Administrators	45	55	18
4 Commercial functions	71	29	7
5 Services	44	56	14
6 Agricuture, etc.	91	9	2
7 Industrial workers, craftsmen, etc.	93	7	18

The analysis of occupational groups offers some more information on sectors 2 and 4.[17] According to our definition the sector 'policy makers and executives' is dominated by male policy makers, and the 'commercial' sector by male directors and supervisors. When women have jobs in the commercial sector they are usually shop assistants. There are also clear gender differences in the 'service' sector i.e., men are mostly directors in catering industry or hotel owners and women are caretakers or domestic helpers.

So, to answer our third question, gender does indeed prove to be a structuring factor in the present labour market position of our school generation. Sex segregation has penetrated even further than expected. It exists in two labour sectors and involves 20 percent of the professions of our population i.e., 31 percent of the subpopulation men. More specifically it is perceptible in 45 occupational groups[18] representing 44 percent of our population. Of these groups, 38 are 'male' groups and represent 33 percent of our population i.e., 55 percent of the subpopulation men who entered primary school in Twente, whereas seven are 'female' groups representing 12 percent of our population i.e., 28 percent of the subpopulation women.

Conclusions

In the introduction I stated that the majority of Dutch women have low-status and low-income jobs i.e., their careers seem to be less prestigious compared to those of men. The question is to what extent these supposed gender differences in professional careers are caused by gender differences in educational attainment. Normally it is seen as a result of women having part-time jobs.

17. Because the results take up too much room, a table has been left out.

18. In the CBS classification 86 occupational groups were distinguished.

The first aim of this chapter is to examine the interrelations between gender differences in educational attainment and professional careers. Necessarily the first analysis refers to gender differences in educational attainment for our research population: a school generation, a cohort, born in the Dutch region of Twente at the end of the 1950s, that entered primary school in 1964 to 1965 (for the most part in the city of Enschede). The results show that compared to men, women leave education at a significantly lower educational level (same IQ) and with rather different qualifications (vertical and horizontal dimension of educational attainment). Next is analysed whether the present position of women on the labour market is different from that of men i.e., if our women have 'low-status and low-income' jobs. The results show that this is true. However, this is not due to women having part-time jobs as is generally assumed, nor (as I supposed) is it solely the outcome of the existing vertical inequality in educational level. It is a consequence of both!

As the relationship between educational and professional careers is most often examined only by looking at the interaction of educational level with the realised (present) occupational status, the analysis was elaborated with the career data. To estimate whether educational level functions only as 'starting capital' or whether it has an effect in the long term i.e., on one's successive professions in time, again the multivariate regression was applied. The results show that educational level keeps having a direct (and indirect) effect and counts for more than the so-called 'starting capital'. However, in the long term its effect is different for men and women, although women are not disadvantaged in managing to get a first favourable labour market position.

Still, these results do not provide a full explanation with regard to the gender differences in professional careers. Also the structure of the labour market itself could be one of the causes of the unequal 'labour market' opportunities for women and men i.e., gender might be a structuring factor in one's present position on the labour market. To investigate if there is a sex-segregated labour market, a definition was made to classify labour sectors and occupational groups as gender-biased. The results of this classification show that the women and men of our research population participate in significantly different labour sectors and occupational groups. The question of how to explain the 'male and female' labour market that was revealed by the study remains.

The second aim of this chapter was to formulate new questions concerning gender-biased careers and sex segregation on the labour market, which might be an effect of gender differences in educational attainment i.e., the educational sector. The *hypothesis* is that a person's present position in a sex-segregated labour market can be explained more by educational sector than by educational level. The long-term effect of educational sector on successive occupational attainments is penetrating and is different for men and women. In other words, our new question is 'to what extent can sex-segregation in the labour market and gender differences in intragenerational mobility be explained by the educational sector?'

Another earlier analysis which contained some data of the Enschede cohort showed that there are enough grounds to formulate this as a research question. Dronkers (1994) found that the combined effect of educational level and educational sector is weaker with respect to present occupational status than the first job. So, the question is whether gender-biased careers can be more accurately explained by educational sector alone (horizontal dimension of educational attainment) than by women having a lower educational level and part-time jobs. It is perhaps because of their 'gender' that women can only get into the less favourable labour market positions.

References

Bakker, B.F.M. (1987), 'De invloed van het onderwijs op de kans op betaald werk voor verschillende categorieën werkzoekenden uit de Arbeidskrachtentelling 1985'. In: *Supplement bij de Sociaal-Economische Maandstatistiek*, no. 7, 14-24.

Blees-Booij, A. (1994), *Culturele en economische beroepsstatus van mannen en vrouwen. Een tweedimensionale ordening,* Amsterdam.

Bros, L. (1994), *Reconstructie van het Enschede cohort, een speurtocht naar de oud-leerlingen. Interimrapport,* Amsterdam.

Bros, L. and J. Dronkers (1994), 'Jencks in Twente: over de sleutelmacht van het onderwijs en de arbeidsmarktpositie van vrouwen', in *Amsterdam Sociologisch Tijdschrift,* vol. 3, no. 21, 67-88.

Bros, L. and K. van Bergen (1994), 'Enschedese Loopbaanpatronen', Paper presented at the ORD, Utrecht.

Bruijn, J. de (1989), *Haar Werk. Vrouwenarbeid en arbeidssociologie in historisch en emancipatorisch perspectief,* Amsterdam.

Brouns, M. (1993), *De homo economicus als winkeldochter. Theorieën over arbeid, macht en sekse,* Amsterdam.

Centraal Bureau voor de Statistiek (CBS), (1984), Beroepenclassificatie 1984, Voorburg.

Centraal Bureau voor de Statistiek (1989), Standaard Onderwijsindeling SOI-1978, editie 1989, Voorburg.

Dronkers, J. (1991), 'Verbeterden de loopbanen in het voortgezet onderwijs van meisjes door de Mammoetwet of door veranderingen in het gezin?', in *Pedagogische Studiën*, 68, 125-38.

Dronkers, J. (1994), *Het gecombineerde effect van onderwijsniveau en afstudeerrichting op verschillende aspecten van de beroepsloopbaan bij een 35-jarige generatie Enschedese leerlingen*, Amsterdam (Eindrapport SVO-96303).

Faber, F. (1994), 'De veranderingen in de seksesamenstelling van de beroepen in Nederland tussen 1971 en 1989', Paper presented at the Sociaal Wetenschappelijke Studiedagen, Amsterdam.

Glebbeek, A.C. (1993), *Perspectieven op loopbanen*, Assen.

Ophuysen, T. (1994), *Vrouwen en Europa. Over werk, beleid en invloed in de EG*, Leiden.

Sixma, H. and W. Ultee (1983), 'Een beroepsprestigeschaal voor Nederland in de jaren tachtig', in *Mens en Maatschappij*, 4, 58, 360-82.

Thurstone T.G. and L.L. Thurstone (1954), *Examiner manual for the SRA Primary Mental Abilities for ages 5 to 7*, 4th edn, Chicago.

Chapter 22

UNIVERSITY ENTRANCE QUALIFICATIONS OBTAINED AFTER LEAVING SCHOOL

Germany's 'Second Path to Matriculation'

Barbara Drinck

Introduction

Presenting Germany's 'Second Path to Matriculation' points out the dilemma of how difficult it is to provide at least a graphic, structural allocation within the overall school system (Schreiber 1992). The division of education into primary, secondary and tertiary sectors, meaningful for comparative observation of various European school systems, is of little help with regard to the Second Path; on the contrary, it is only confusing. Traditional schematic presentations place the Second Path in the tertiary sector (Mohr 1991). The focus lies, in fact, on the age-group, not the educational level, of the participants. While this takes account of the fact that it is only possible to attend certain educational institutions after one's compulsory schooling, the contents of the curriculum are in no way comparable with those of institutions in the tertiary sector.
The following chart is intended to present an approximation of both implications: the age of the pupils and the comparability of the teaching contents at ordinary secondary-school levels.

A two-dimensional diagram cannot adequately portray the German educational system. Thus Figure 22.1 of my schema includes Second Path niches which are presented in more concrete form in Figure 22.2. School-leaving qualifications which pupils failed to obtain at grammar, secondary-technical or even secondary-modern schools can be taken directly after a pupil has left school, or even later, via the Second Path to Matriculation, at the same level as the corresponding grades at the corresponding institute of secondary education. The result is a three-dimensional structure: pupils on the 'post-qualification plateau' obtain the entitlement to enter one of the vertically arranged levels of further education.

Figure 22.1 The First Path to Matriculation

UNIVERSITY OR POLYTECHNIC							
	2nd Path	Gymnasium	2nd Path	Gymnasium		2nd Path	Gymnasium
	Vocational School / Firms	Realschule	Vocational Sch. / Firms			Vocational Sch./ Firms	
	10 th Grade						
SPECIAL EDUCATION	HAUPTSCHULE (Secondary Modern)		REALSCHULE (Secondary Technical)		GYMNASIUM (Grammar School)	COMPREHENSIVE SCHOOL	
	ORIENTATION STAGE (dependent on or independent of type of school)						
SPECIAL EDUCATION	PRIMARY SCHOOL						
KINDERGARTEN (voluntary)							

Historical Outline of the Present Significance of the Second Path to Matriculation

The first school courses in adult education were offered during the course of industrialisation and at the onset of modern times. Association Schools such as those attached to trade associations or museums and Sunday Schools offered teaching and further education in their programmes in order to increase the competence of their fellow citizens.

In those days there was an enormous need for education in the innovations brought about by science and technology. Developments in the humanities and the political scenario were reason enough to want to attend lectures and seminars. These were principally aimed at the working classes which, encouraged by liberal groups of the bourgeoisie, were to increase the level of their education. 'The Bourgeoisie also expected a general improvement in education for the people to alter the consciousness of the "lower" classes of the population and, as a result, to promote independent efforts by the workers to alter their mores, lifestyles and social condition … '(Jüttemann 1991:22).

Figure 22.2 The Second Path to Matriculation

				From age
UNIVERSITY OR POLYTECHNIC				
EVENING GRAMMAR SCHOOL / TECHNICAL HIGH SCHOOL 'KOLLEG' (EXTENSION COLLEGE) (from age 19)				19
EVENING 'REALSCHULE' / Evening classes (from age 17)		SPECIALISED (TECHNICAL) SCHOOL		18
				17
EVENING 'HAUPTSCHULE' (from age 16)	EVENING 'REALSCHULE' / Evening classes (from age 17)	VOCATIONAL EXTENSION SCHOOL (from age 16)	NON-PUPILS AND EXAM FOR GIFTED INDIVIDUALS	16

Only after the First World War were there discussions, but no action, on courses of education related to school-leaving qualifications and the award of certificates. The desire of workers to obtain a matriculation certificate via educational courses at some later date met with considerable resistance from the bourgeoisie (Ibid.:61). Humboldt's neo-Humanist ideal of education – at that time the prevalent concept of schooling – limited formal education to the training of the young mind. It was inconceivable that a mature individual might possibly be suited to sit for Matric!

When Kerschensteiner opened his further education school for young workers and apprentices he confronted Humboldt's ideal with a new alternative which was hardly acceptable to many pedagogues at that period. It was now possible to put the two previously incompatible fields of general education and vocational training on an equal footing. Not just formal education but work and vocation were given priority; jobs and life experiences were to be integrated into the educative process (Kandolf et al. 1985).

Eduard Spranger, too, opposed the bourgeois opinion that vocational training and general education were basically incompatible, because the introduction of the three-element school system at that time consisting of Volksschule (elementary school), Realschule (secondary-technical school) and Higher Schools, together with the advent of obligatory vocational schooling had necessitated extensive internal reforms within the educational sector (Blankertz 1962, cited in Lenzen et al. 1975). The problem of working-class youth, in particular, was one of Spranger's deep concerns. He thus put the case for an extension of adult education within the extra-scholastic system of the Volksschule.

In 1918 the first adult further education institutions leading to Matriculation qualifications were opened in Stuttgart, Berlin and Hamburg. In 1927 Peter Silbermann founded the first German evening grammar school in Berlin.

During the National Socialist period of government the importance of the institutions of the Second Path to Matriculation waned. Repression, particularly of the financial variety, forced the schools to close their doors once more. Only after the Second World War was the Second Path to Matriculation as we know it today consistently extended for adults as part of the restructuring of democratic education. Not only were the traditional evening grammar schools to be re-opened, adults were also to be offered daytime institutions – so-called 'Kollegs' (lecture courses) aimed at the award of university entrance qualifications. These institutions were provided specifically for those interested individuals who had already concluded an apprenticeship or course of vocational training and who wished to obtain a university entrance qualification in addition by attending a Kolleg. The Kolleg in North-Rhine/Westphalia is an exception, as participants can obtain a professional qualification at the same time as their matriculation.

In the 1950s and 1960s the associations of the economy pressed hard for the broadening of the Second Path to Matriculation, for, as uncertainty spread through the educational sector in the wake, in particular, of Georg Picht's (1964) book *Germany's Educational Catastrophe*, it seemed to Germans that such an educational catastrophe was, indeed, fast approaching. In the 1960s reforms took place within the educational system (Raschert 1980), and Ralf Dahrendorf (1966) called for the 'right of all citizens to education'.

Equality of opportunity and the permeability of educational institutions in favour of individual corrections of educational policy at all levels of the educational system were established as the great guidelines. In addition, the number of pupils obtaining grammar-school leaving certificate qualifications was to be raised and brought into a balanced relationship with the calculated number of academics to ensure that the necessary demand for academically qualified personnel could be met.

The trend, even in the 1960s, was for academic evening classes to be attended not only by working people but, increasingly, by drop-outs from grammar schools who wished to correct some previous academic failure as a follow-up measure. This form of resocialisation was not one of the original intentions of the Second Path. It was to be an alternative to, not a regulatory mechanism for the First Path to Matriculation.

At that time the task of the Second Path was being taken over to a greater and greater extent by the Volkshochschulen (adult education centres) and was increasingly restricting itself to the more elementary school-leaving certificates, such as the secondary-modern school certificate.

There now arose a confusion in definitions (Jütting and Scherer 1986:7): though the term 'Second Path to Matriculation' was, on the one hand, supposed to comprise exclusively the categories evening grammar school and Kolleg, i.e., those institutions leading to a matriculation certificate, the Further Education Act passed in 1974 by North-Rhine/Westphalia lumped together everything connected with the acquisition of elementary, intermediate or higher school-leaving certificates by adults outside the normal school system under the term 'Second Path to Matriculation'.

The original concept of the Second Path to Matriculation as picking up a grammar-school type matriculation qualification at a later stage was, in the first decades after the Second World War, mainly associated with the idea of certain target groups: POWs returning home, refugees and late developers. They were to be offered, in abbreviated form, a programme of school education that would enable them to catch up on that which had been denied them up to then by the confusions of war and lack of support. Alongside the evening grammar schools, evening secondary-technical and evening secondary-modern schools were soon introduced. The aim of the Second Path was now no longer primarily the acquisition of a matriculation certificate: it was to be the ultimate education aid to the needy under certain modalities. The extension of the Kollegs and leaving-certificate courses at adult education centres must also be seen in connection with this reorientation of adult education towards 'leaving-certificate related further education' or 'catching up on secondary-school certificates'. The spotlight is now at the acquisition of school-leaving qualifications of any and every kind, incorporating all existing institutions – from evening schools, private schools or adult education centres – whatever their organisational embodiment in their respective sectors of the educational system may be.

In every state of the Federal Republic of Germany an unbroken network of provisions for the belated acquisition of school-leaving qualifications has thus grown up. Over the past fifteen years the main direction of development has been the broad 'opening downwards' – the acquisition of a secondary-modern school leaving certificate – in order to improve social security and the entry into the world of work for young people who have not been able to acquire a situation as a trainee. At present the clientele is thus completely different from that of even thirty years ago. On the one hand are the highly motivated interested parties who – particularly in the new states of the Federal Republic of Germany – want to improve their qualifications, whether by obtaining a matriculation certificate or by learning a modern language such as English. On the other hand – particularly in the old states of the Federal Republic – the school-level courses contain interested parties each of whom has his or her own problems and basically requires individual counselling and care. There are foreigners with a poor knowledge of German, people of German stock recently arrived from Eastern Europe and the Asian republics of the former Soviet Union, and also asylum seekers with inadequate living accommodation and linguistic problems, who are not helped by their all too disastrous biographical backgrounds; school-leavers from the Special Education sector who are used to patient and pedagogically refined teaching guidance and who, at least during the first critical period at the beginning of the course have, to a great extent, to make do without the teacher's subjective evaluation; the jobless sent back to school by job centres because there are no trainee places or jobs for them; and young people who could not be kept on at normal schools because of massive problems with teachers or fellow pupils. Within the framework of these courses, adult education centres frequently collaborate with social workers who have the function of accompanying their charges through the courses. Such socio-pedagogical support would have been unthinkable attributes of the Second Path to Matriculation as originally understood, involving, as it did, only motivated, responsible individuals. Discontinuity of educational biography, on the other hand, is the general feature of today's courses aimed at the acquisition of the secondary-modern (Hauptschule) school-leaving certificate. This condemns the original concepts of adult-oriented teaching to failure. Many teachers now consider a further qualification in Special Education or supervision by a qualified person to be indispensable.

Institutions of the Second Path to Matriculation

Nowadays there are a number of institutions involved in the Second Path to Matriculation. The Abendgymnasium (evening grammar school) already mentioned is the original and traditional form. It took over thirty years, from its foundation in 1927 by Silbermann in Berlin, to establish itself throughout the Federal Republic of Germany, where, in 1964, there were thirty-three such institutions. Now virtually every community maintains its own evening grammar school.

Silbermann considered the Abendgymnasium to be a school for 'catching up' on qualifications, and rejected gainful employment as a hindrance to attendance at school. Nowadays, by contrast, employment and schooling are considered to be compatible. The educative force of professional employment is, indeed, expressly recognised and integrated into the pedagogical considerations. The important precondition for acceptance valid since 1946 and adopted in the agreement of the Federal Conference of Ministers of Education, that applicants should generally have completed a course of on-the-job vocational training, should be seen against this background. The Abendgymnasium – like the Kolleg is divided up into a preliminary course phase, a subsequent one-year introductory phase and a concluding two-year course phase involving basic and advanced courses. Some Abendgymnasien offer intermediate examinations allowing the secondary-technical school-leaving certificate, for instance, to be picked up 'on the way' to the grammar-school matriculation qualification.

Fachoberschulen (specialised high schools) offer employees evening courses leading, after two-year attendance, to a qualification to study at a Fachhochschule (polytechnic).

After its foundation in North-Rhine/Westphalia in 1962, the Abendrealschule (evening secondary-technical school) never managed to achieve the standing held by the Volkshochschule (adult education centres) in the field of intermediate school-leaving qualifications. Not only have several states in the Federal Republic of Germany failed to set up Abendrealschulen, there is, in addition, disagreement on the demands to be made on examination candidates, which means that the examinations are not recognised throughout the Federal Republic. Due to its somewhat subordinated position in the Second Path system, this type of school tends to attract pupils with problems.

'Picking up school-leaving qualifications at a later stage' is nowadays considered an obligatory service offered by all communities. Courses leading to Hauptschule and Realschule leaving certificates belong to the standard repertoire of all medium to large Volkshochschule establishments. By offering these courses they fulfil functions of a Second Path institution. Additionally they perform direct help with real-life problems, for they offer many people a 'last chance' to escape from the cul-de-sac of school 'failure'.

As far as the levels of responsibility of further education for allowing pupils to take school-leaving examinations are concerned, legal responsibility is vested in the state Ministries of Education and Culture, while the organisational responsibility rests with the directors of the Volkshochschulen, mostly in co-ordination with the community concerned. The organisational plane comprises, in particular, the offer of daytime and evening courses, and the recruitment of teachers. The educational legislation of the states regarding school-leaving certificates imposes important conditions on the Volkshochschulen and, in some cases, sets strict delineations; particularly, for instance, where centralised examination procedures are provided for and in which the Volkshochschulen can only play a preparatory part, as is the case in Baden-Württemberg or Rhineland-Palatinate.

The course aims and contents are oriented towards the guidelines and curricula of Hauptschule and Realschule respectively. The methodical and didactical course of the teaching, however, is arranged in accordance with experience gained from adult education. These regulations create, on the one hand, a connection between the Second Path and normal secondary schools (orientation of contents towards what is taught at normal schools) while, on the other, clearly separating the two institutions (teaching methods taken from adult education). Apart from these so-called framework conditions no further more extensive regulations have been passed, so that there is still a lot of scope for creative teaching.

The concluding courses at Volkshochschulen are offered as daytime, afternoon or evening sessions. Most take place in the evenings, one third as a combination of day and evening classes.

The possibility of obtaining various school-leaving qualifications through external examinations supervised by local educational authorities is offered by every state in the Federal Republic of Germany. Chances of repeating this examination are limited, so good preparation is essential, creating an educational market for this examination, too. In addition to private preparatory schools, the Volkshochschule once again offers courses aimed at preparing candidates for this 'external examination'.

Since the 1930s, particularly gifted employees have been able to obtain general matriculation qualifications via this examination, which also incorporates their professional knowledge and experience. Usually the following prerequisites must be fulfilled: age between twenty-five and forty, intensive preparation for the examination should be demonstrated, candidates should have completed a full-time course of on-the-job training and must have been employed or have cared for a home and children for at least five years.

The examination board of this 'examination for the gifted' consists of a representative from a university, a representative from an adult-education institution and a grammar-school teacher. Access to non-pupil examinations for Hauptschule and Realschule leaving certificates is available to those interested parties who have attended school for the compulsory period and who, often in connection with obligatory attendance at a so-called 'substitute school', which may be a Volkshochschule, or after a self-study course, apply to the examinations held by the school administration or education authorities. These individuals should, generally, be over eighteen years of age.

The Berufsaufbauschule (vocational secondary school) was originally the centre piece of an intermediate school-leaving qualification within the Second Path. It was founded in the mid 1950s with the aim of preparing participants to take over more responsible tasks in professional life and to assure them access to schools of engineering. The Berufsaufbauschule was to be an evening school attended after work, but when the Fachoberschulen (specialised high schools) were created in 1968, the former soon lost their attraction, as the latter offer a higher qualification leaving certificate and guarantee a study place at a Fachhochschule (polytechnic), something not possible for those who have attended the Berufsaufbauschule.

The Kolleg, conceived as part of a vocation-related 'Second Path', had the task of guiding to Matriculation level (Abitur) gifted secondary-modern pupils who had done a course of on-the-job training and successfully concluded a course of study at the Berufsaufbauschule.

The decisively innovative feature – deliberately in contrast to grammar-school education – was, alongside the more adult teaching approach, job-relatedness as an expressly didactical principle. Here the possibility of resolving the pedagogically and socio-politically contested separation of vocational and general education seemed to have drawn tangibly nigh, at least for one segment of the German educational system. Even so, the traditional forms of grammar-school teaching were rapidly adopted. A scientific-propaedeutic orientation increasingly ousted teaching based on job-related contents.

The Telekolleg, correspondence courses based on television lectures, consist of a combination of television broadcasts, printed accompanying material and direct teaching at compulsory Kolleg days held every third Saturday. The direct tuition plays an important role, as regular participation is a precondition of enrolment for the examination. The teaching is done at local institutions of adult education. The usual form of leaving examination is held at all schools simultaneously and on the same date. In rare cases it can be offered in separate parts within a building-block system. There are two types of Telekolleg: Telekolleg I qualifies those who pass to the Realschule certificate, while Telekolleg II leads to the award of a certificate to study at a Fachhochschule (polytechnic).

Conclusions

The attractions of the Second Way to Matriculation have altered since its possibilities were expanded after the Second World War. Today its institutions are utilised more for resocialisation purposes than as an opportunity for professional emancipation intended to be crowned by a higher qualification within a job already held. This phenomenon of regulating failures in other sectors of education is particularly plain in the case of elementary school-leaving qualifications such as that awarded by the Hauptschule: it is not always the children of socially disadvantaged groups of society who enrol in courses leading to the Hauptschule leaving certificate. On the contrary, one encounters more and more young people from well-situated families. Due to chaotic school careers, these young people or adults had been forced to drop out of courses offered at normal schools only to start a second attempt, by courtesy of the Second Path to Matriculation, after a break of several months or even years at the bottom, in some cases, of the social pyramid. In conclusion I should like to quote Baldo Blinkert's statement that the Second Path to Matriculation has taken over an important social function

> … through which one can also explain why this institution is not stagnating but continues to grow in importance: … in our society [the Second Path to Matriculation] functions as a 'safety valve' and is an institution which enables individuals to exit from a role context considered unsatisfactory in a legitimate and socially recognised way. It permits … a new start within the existing structure of position and role. Obviously such a safety valve is necessary to every imperfectly organised society, and the significance of such institutions increases proportionately to the extent to which contradictions in the social structure lead to an increase in generalised motivation crises and to a rise in preparations for retreat. (Quoted in Drinck 1994)

One may not, however, idealise this safety valve, for the drop-out rate among participants in school courses is so high that in economic terms it would make such courses uneconomical for the institutions which run them. From the social-policy point of view however, it is precisely the Hauptschule leaving-certificate courses which are extraordinarily important and – as with other courses – these will continue to be subsidised by communes and states alike. If one quizzes participants about their lack of staying power, they rarely quote intellectual overstretching but frequently a lack of accompanying socio-pedagogical or even therapeutic measures as the reason for their failure (Lenzen 1983:204). This makes it plain that the Second Path to Matriculation must, today, be more than just an offer of further academic qualifications.

It must not be forgotten that alongside this subjective motivation there stands the enormous pressure of selection: educational certificates are becoming increasingly important. Despite inflationary quotas of passes in many qualified courses of training, the market value of state-recognised leaving certificates is constantly on the increase, forcing individuals to compete for socially recognised posts. It is thus perhaps less the desire to start up a new role which motivates interested participants than, rather, a need to maintain a position that can only be secured by obtaining further qualifications via the Second Path to Matriculation.

References

Dahrendorf, R.(1966), *Bildung ist Bürgerrecht. Plädoyer für eine aktive Bildungspolitik,* Hamburg.

Drinck, B. (1994), *Schulabbrecher. Ursachen – Folgen – Hilfen. Studien zur Effizienz von Kursen zum Nachholen von Schulabschlüssen an Einrichtungen der Erwachsenenbildung,* Bad Honnef.

Jüttemann, S. (1991), *Die gegenwärtige Bedeutung des Zweiten Bildungswegs vor dem Hintergrund seiner Geschichte,* Weinheim.

Jütting, D.H. and Scherer, A. (1986), *Der Zweite Bildungsweg in der Literatur: Metapher und Mythos,* Soest.

Kandolf, S., Kersten, R. and Oelmann, G. (1985), *Weiterbildung II. Zweiter Bildungsweg – Abschlüsse der Sekundarstufe I nach dem Weiterbildungsgesetz. Landesinstitut für Schule und Weiterbildung,* Soest.

Kühnhold, G. (1985), *Der nachgeholte Schulabschluß. Beiträge zur Situation des Zweiten Bildungswegs,* Bad Honnef.

Lenzen, D.et al. (eds) (1975), *Curriculumentwicklung für die Kollegschule: Der obligatorische Lernbereich,* Frankfurt a. M.

Lenzen, D.et al. (eds) (1983), *Enzyklopädie Erziehungswissenschaft*, vol.9, 2, Stuttgart.

Mohr, B. (1991), *Bildung und Wissenschaft in Deutschland West*, Köln.

Oelmann, G. (1985), *Der Zweite Bildungsweg in Nordrhein-Westfalen. Struktur und Geschichte*, Paderborn.

Picht, G. (1964), *Die deutsche Bildungskatastrophe*, München.

Raschert, J. (1980), 'Bildungspolitik im kooperativen Föderalismus. Die Entwicklung der länderübergreifenden Planung und Koordination des Bildungswesens in der Bundesrepublik Deutschland', in Max-Planck-Institut für Bildungsforschung, Projektgruppe Bildungsberichte (eds), *Bildung in der Bundesrepublik Deutschland. Daten und Analysen*, vol. 1, Reinbek.

Schreiber, R. (1992), *Aus- und Weiterbildungshandbuch für Schule und Beruf*, Ludwigshafen.

NOTES ON CONTRIBUTORS

Pieter L. J. Boerman

Research themes:

Organisational structure and effectiveness of colleges for vocational education

Lisette Bros

Research themes:

Social inequality of educational attainment, the role of education for professional careers and how education structures class and gender destinations.

Publications:

Bros, L. (1994), *Reconstructie van het Enschede-cohort, een speurtocht naar de oudleerlingen. Interimrapport.* Amsterdam.

Bros, L. and Dronkers, J. (1994), 'Jencks in Twente: over de sleutelmacht van het onderwijs en de arbeidsmarktpositie van vrouwen', in *Amsterdam Sociologisch Tijdschrift*, 3, 21, 67-88.

Bros, L. and Bergen, K. van (1994), 'Enschedese Loopbaanpatronen', paper presented at Education Research Days, Utrecht, May.

Karen Dohle

Research themes:

Empirical research in education, determinants of school selection , processes of socialisation in children of late Polish emigrants *(Spätaussiedler)*.

Barbara Drinck

Research themes:

The Japanese educational system, outsiders and drop outs in school, qualitative research in socialisation.

Publications:

Drinck, B. (1988), *Reformen als Fortschritt? Über gegenwärtige Reformpläne für das japanische Erziehungs- und Bildungssystem*, Bonn.

Drinck, B. (1994), *Schulabbrecher. Ursachen – Folgen – Hilfen. Studien zur Effizienz von Kursen zum Nachholen von Hauptschulabschlüssen.* Bad Honnef.

Yvonne Ehrenspeck

Research themes:

Anthropology of education, aesthetic education, science of science in educational research.

Publications:

Ehrenspeck, Y. (1993). '"What´s the Difference?" Anmerkungen zu Paul de Mans Rousseaulektüre', in *Emile. Zeitschrift für Erziehungskultur*, 19, 75-95.

Ehrenspeck, Y. (1995). '"Den Mythos ins Humane umfunktionieren" Frühe Rehabilitierung des Mythos angesichts des Faschismus bei Thomas Mann', in *Neue Sammlung*, 35, 3, 129-42.

Axel Gehrmann

Research themes:

The German educational system.

Transformation of school systems in Eastern Europe.

Publications:

Gehmann, A. (1966), *Schule in der Transformation. Eine empirisch-vergleichende Untersuchung an vier Gesamtschulen im Berliner Bezirk Treptow* (1991-1993), Frankfurt am Main.

Adrian T.G. van Gennep

Research themes:

Mental handicaps

Publications:

Gennep, A. van (1994), *De zorg om het bestaan*, Amsterdam/Meppel.

Gennep, A. van (1989), *De kwaliteit van het bestaan van de zwaksten in de samenleving*, Meppel.

Gennep, A. van et al. (1983), Inleiding tot de orthopedagogiek,

Frieda Heyting

Research themes:

Educational theory and constructivist epistemology; education and high-modern society, dynamic systems approaches to educational theory

Publications:

Heyting, F. (1987), *Autonomie en socialiteit in de opvoeding,* Amersfoort.

Heyting, F. (1995). 'Tendences toward Pluralization in Society and the Pedagogic Control of Risk', in Benner, D. and Lenzen, D., *Education for the New Europe*, Providence/Oxford.

Heyting, G.F. and Tenorth, H.E. (eds) (1994), *Pädagogik und Pluralismus. Deutsche und niederländische Erfahrungen im Umgang mit Pluralität in Erziehung und Erziehungswissenschaft*, Weinheim.

Gerd R. Hoff

Research themes:

International comparison of intercultural education, school pedagogy, media-pedagogy

Publications:

Hoff, G.R. (1995), 'Multicultural Education in Germany', in Banks, J.A. (ed.), *Handbook of Research on Multicultural Education*, New York, 821-38.

Hoff, G.R. (1992), 'Culture in Transition...', in K.A.Moodley (ed.), *Beyond Multicultural Education. International Perspectives*, Calgary, Alberta, 67-77.

Barkowski, H. andHoff G.R. (eds) (1991), *Berlin Interkulturell – Ergebnisse einer Konferenz zu Migration und Pädagogik*, Berlin.

Meta L. Krüger

Research themes:

School leadership and school management

Publications:

Krüger, M.L. (1994), 'School leadership and gender; comparative research on differences and effects', in J.T. Voorbach (ed.), *Teacher Education* 10, research and developments on teacher education in the Netherlands. De Lier, 135-43.

Krüger, M.L. et al. (1994), 'Peer Assisted Leadership: implementation of a professional development program for principals in several European countries', in K. Hamalainen and A. van Wieringen, (eds), *Reforming Educational Management in Europe*, De Lier, 259-80.

Krüger, M.L. (1994), *Sekseverschillen in schoolleiderschap*, Samsom H.D. Tjeenk Willink, Alphen aan de Rijn.

Harm Kuper

Research themes:

Development of corporate-culture, pedagogical organisations, learning in organisations (Organisationslernen) and further education

Publications:

Kuper, H. (1995), 'Leitbilder in einem Projekt für ökologische Berufsvorbereitung', in *Berichte aus der Arbeit des Instituts für Allgemeine und Vergleichende Erziehungswissenschaft. Abteilung Empirische Erziehungswissenschaft*, FU Berlin.

Guuske Ledoux

Research themes:

Ethnic minorities, disadvantaged children, multicultural and multiethnic schools,

Publications:

Ledoux, G., and P. Deckers, E. de Bruijn, E. Voncken (1992), *Met het oog op de toekomst. Ideeën over onderwijs en arbeid van ouders en kinderen uit de doelgroepen van het onderwijsvoorrangsbeleid,* Amsterdam.

Ledoux, G., and M. Derriks (1994), *Allochtone jongeren en voortijdig schoolverlaten. Stand van zaken notitie over de overgang onderwijs-arbeidsmarkt voor allochtone jongeren, deelgebied onderwijs.* Ten behoeve van de TWCM. Amsterdam.

Eck, E. van, G. Ledoux, and A. Veen, (1994), 'Schoolloopbanen en strijdige verwachtingen', in *Pedagogische Studiën*, 71, 1, 16-35.

Dieter Lenzen

Research themes:

Philosophy of education, historical anthropology and cultural anthropology of education

Publications:

Lenzen, D. (ed.)(1983ff.), *Enzyklopädie Erziehungswissenschaft*. 12 vols, Stuttgart.

Lenzen, D. (1985), *Mythologie der Kindheit. Die Verewigung des Kindlichen in der Erwachsenenkultur. Versteckte Bilder und vergessene Geschichten*, Reinbek.

Lenzen, D. (1991), *Vaterschaft. Vom Patriarchat zur Alimentation*, Reinbek.

Benner, D. and Lenzen, D. (1996), *Education for the New Europe*, Providence/Oxford.

Hans Merkens

Research themes:

Adolescence, socialisation in organisational cultures, education in families of migrant workers, qualitative and quantitative methods and methodology

Publications:

Merkens, H. & Schmidt, F. (eds) (1995), *Lebenslagen Schuljugendlicher und sozialer Wandel. Jugendforschung aktuell*, vol. 1. Hohengehren.

Hagan, J., Merkens, H. and Boehnke, K. (1995), 'Delinquency and disdain: Social capital and the control of right-wing extremism among East and West Berlin youth', in *American Journal of Sociology*, 100, 4, 1,028-1,052.

Merkens, H. (1994), 'Youth at risk', in *Zeitschrift für Pädagogik*, 32. Beiheft, Bildung und Erziehung in Europa, Weinheim, 93-116.

Ernst Mulder

Research themes:

History of social science, history of the relationship between social science and biology

Publications:

Mulder, E. (1989), *Beginsel en beroep. Pedagogiek aan de universiteit in Nederland, 1900-1940*, Amsterdam.

Mulder, E. (1992), 'Kohnstamm en het idee van kinderlijke ontwikkeling', in *Pedagogische Tijdschrift*, 17, 388-95.

Mulder, E. (1993), 'Matig intellect. De introductie van intelligentiemetingen in Nederland', in *Pedagogisch Tijdschrift*, 18, 123-30.

Elly Singer

Research themes:

Early childhood education and child care, child abuse

Publications:

Singer, E. (1992), *Child Care and the Psychology of Development,* London/New York.

Singer, E. (1993), 'Shared care for children, a new pedagogical concept challenges developmental psychology', in *Theory and Psychology*, 3, 429-49.

Singer, E. and Miltenburg, R. (1994), 'Quality in child care centres: how to promote it?' in *Early Child Development and Care,* 102, 1-16.

Heleen A. van der Stege

Research themes:

Parents' cognition, notably parents' visions of the impact of talent, education and environment on their childrens´ development – dyslexia notably research into sub-types such as 'guessers' and 'spellers'.

Publications:

Stege, H.A. van der (1992), 'Waarom kinderen zijn zoals ze zijn: ideeën van ouders', in *Kind & Adolescent*, 13, 4, 185-88.

Rispens, J., Stege, H.A. van der and Bode, H. (1994), 'The clinical relevance of dyslexia sub-type research', in Bos, K.P. van den, Siegel, L.S., Bakker, D.J., and Share, D.L. (eds), *Current directions in dyslexia research*, Lisse.

Stege, H. van der (1995), 'Attributions of parents with young children', in Hox, J.J., Meulen, B. F. van der, Janssens, J.M.A.M. ter, and Tavecchio, L.W.C. (eds), *Advances in family research*, Amsterdam.

Felicitas Thiel

Research themes:

The educational system and its environment, educational focus on social crisis, social movements and education.

Publications:

Thiel, F. (1996), *Ökologie als Thema. Überlegungen zur Pädagogisierung gesellschaftlicher Krisen,* Weinheim.

Wolfgang Tietze

Research themes:

Early childhood education, international comparative research, pedagogical qualities of surroundings of early childhood care.

Publications:

Tietze, W. (1987), 'A Structural Model for the Evaluation of Preschool Effects', in *Early Childhood Quarterly*, 2, 133ff.

Tietze, W. and Paterak, H. (1993), 'Hilfen für die Betreuung und Erziehung von Kindern im Vorschulalter in den Ländern der Europäischen Gemeinschaft', in W. Tietze and H.-G. Roßbach (eds), *Erfahrungsfelder in der frühen Kindheit*. Freiburg.

Tietze, W. and Roßbach, H.-G. (1991), 'Die Betreuung von Kindern im Vorschulalter', in *Zeitschrift für Pädagogik*, 4.

Hermann Veith

Research themes:

Theory of socialisation

Publications:

Veith, H. (1995), *Theorien der Sozialisation. Zur Rekonstruktion des modernen sozialisationstheoretischen Denkens*, Frankfurt a.M./New York.

Veith, H. (1995), 'Überlegungen zur Theorie und Geschichte der Sozialisationstheorie', in *Zeitschrift für Sozialisationsforschung und Erziehungssoziologie*, Weinheim.

Kees van der Wolf

Research themes:

School quality, colourful schools, teacher's tacit knowledge

Publications:

Letiche, H.K., J.C. van der Wolf, and F.X. Plooy (eds) (1991), *The Practioner's Power of Choice in Staff-Development and Inservice-Training*, Lisse.

Wolf, J.C. van der (1992), 'Colorful Schools: Effects of the Ethnic Situation in the Classroom', in Bashi, J. and Z. Sass, *School Effectiveness & Improvement: Proceedings of the Third International Congress for School Effectiveness*. Jerusalem.

Wolf, J.C. van der (1995), 'Mag het wat meer orthopedagogiek zijn? zorgen over diagnostiek volgens het hypothesentoetsend model', *Nederlands Tijdschrift voor opvoeding*, Vorming en Onderwijs, 11, 2, 73-85.

Bibi van Wolput

Research themes:

History of higher education and social inequality.

Christoph Wulf

Research themes:

Basics of education, philosophy of education, historical anthropology, cultural anthropology of education, intercultural learning, peace and global studies

Publications:

Gebauer G. and Wulf, C. (1995), *Mimesis, Art, Culture, Society*.

Wulf, C. (1995), *Introduction à la Science d'Education*. Paris.

Wulf, C. (ed.) (1995), *Education in Europe. An Intercultural Task*, Münster/New York.

INDEX

C

D

E

I

J

K

L

T

V

W

Y

Z

International Political Currents

A Friedrich-Ebert Stiftung Series

General Editor: Dieter Dettke, Washington Office of the Friedrich Ebert Stiftung

Volume 1

TOWARD A GLOBAL CIVIL SOCIETY

Edited by Michael Walzer

The demise of Communism has not only affected Eastern Europe, but also the countries of the West where a far-reaching examination of political and economic systems has begun. This collection of essays by internationally renowned scholars of political theory from Europe and the United States explores both the concept and the reality of civil society and its institutions.

Michael Walzer is a permanent faculty member of the School of Social Science, Institute for Advances Study, Princeton.

344 pages • ISBN 1-57181-138-9
LC: 94-33656

Volume 2

UNIVERSITIES IN THE TWENTY-FIRST CENTURY

Edited by **Steven Muller,** *Chairman of the Twenty-first Century Foundation*

On the eve of the twenty-first century, the United States and Germany face common but also separate challenges that will be met in part by significant activity on the university level. This volume offers views and expert opinions from leading American and German educators and university administrators on the future role of this vital educational and cultural institution in both societies.

From the Contents: Concepts for the University of the Twenty-first Century – Planning, Financing, and Accountability – Teaching and Reform – Globalization of the New University.

Contributors: P. Fischer-Appelt – D. Stokes – M. Ash – S. Wittig – G. Konow – M. Daxner – B. Clark – J. Rosebrock – M. Nugent – H. Weiler – L. Krickau-Richter – B. Burn – B. Kehm.

192 pages • ISBN 1-57181-026-9 • hardback
LC: 95-31519

EDUCATION FOR THE NEW EUROPE

Edited by **Dietrich Benner,** *Professor of Education, Institute of Education, Humboldt University, Berlin,* and **Dieter Lenzen,** *Professor of Education at the Institute of General and Comparative Education, Free University of Berlin, President of the German Society for Education.*

Important contributions to the development of new perspectives for a future European educational system.

From the Contents: D. Lenzen, Education and Training for Europe? – A. Kárpáti, Hungarian Adolescents of the 1990s: Ideals, Beliefs, Expectations – H. Merkens, Youth at Risk: Attitudes and Value Concepts among Youths in Europe at a Time of Social Change – G. Geißler, School Reform Between Dictatorships: Pedagogics and Politics during the Early Years in the Soviet Occupation Zone of Germany – G. Ossenbach-Sauter, Democratisation and Europeanisation: Challenges to the Spanish Educational System since 1970 – P. Mortimore, School Effectiveness: Its Challenge for the Future – T. Rauschenbach, The New Generational Contract: From Private Education to Social Services – F. Heyting, Tendencies Toward Pluralisation in Society and the Pedagogical Control of Risk

192 pages • ISBN 1-57181-074-9 • hardback
LC: 95-31517

GERMAN UNIVERSITIES: PAST AND FUTURE
Crisis or Renewal?

Edited by Mitchell G. Ash

In the late 1980s, commentators generally agreed that West German universities were in a state of crisis. Now that universities in East Germany have been restructured largely in the image of the West German system, the question is whether true reform of the whole German university system can and will finally begin. Answering this question will make an important statement about the vitality of cultural institutions in the new Germany. This volume examines the historical background and future prospects of German universities. The contributors include historians of German universities as well as current university leaders and higher-education policy-makers from Germany and the United States.

Mitchell G. Ash has taught at Harvard University and the universities of Berlin and Mainz. He is currently Professor of History at the University of Iowa.

288 pages, bibliog., index • ISBN 1-57181-070-6 • hardback
LC: 96-52552